Children, Health, and Learning

Children, Health, and Learning

A Guide to the Issues

Mary E. Walsh and Jennifer A. Murphy

Contemporary Youth Issues
Richard M. Lerner, Series Editor

Westport, Connecticut
London

Library of Congress Cataloging-in-Publication Data

Walsh, Mary E. (Mary Elizabeth), 1941–
    Children, health, and learning : a guide to the issues / Mary E. Walsh and
Jennifer A. Murphy.
        p. cm. — (Contemporary youth issues)
    Includes bibliographical references and index.
    ISBN 0–275–97979–2 (alk. paper)
    1. School health services—United States. 2. School children—Health and
hygiene—United States. 3. Health education—United States. I. Murphy,
Jennifer A. II. Title. III. Series.
LB3409.U5W35   2003
371.7'1—dc21   2003042851

British Library Cataloguing in Publication Data is available.

Library of Congress Catalog Card Number: 2003042851
ISBN: 0–275–97979–2

First published in 2003

Praeger Publishers, 88 Post Road West, Westport, CT 06881
An imprint of Greenwood Publishing Group, Inc.
www.praeger.com

Printed in the United States of America

The paper used in this book complies with the
Permanent Paper Standard issued by the National
Information Standards Organization (Z39.48–1984).

10   9   8   7   6   5   4   3   2   1

Contents

Series Foreword

Contemporary Youth Issues is a series of volumes that provides new and important educational materials for the youth and adults involved in middle schools, high schools, and public libraries. Volumes in the series offer accessible information about the nature of the issues facing contemporary youth (children in the first two decades of life), parents, and youth-serving professionals—for example, teachers, practitioners, and governmental and nongovernmental organization personnel.

Both the challenges to healthy development confronting contemporary youth and the assets or strengths of adolescents and of the communities that contribute to their positive development are represented. Each book in the series reviews current knowledge about these challenges and assets, directs youth and adults to current community resources available to address challenges or enhance assets, and discusses key issues of policy and program design pertinent to improving the lives of the diverse youth of the United States and the world.

THE CONCEPT OF THE SERIES

Childhood and adolescence are developmental periods during which most of a person's biological, cognitive, psychological, and social characteristics are changing from what is present at birth to what is considered adultlike. For children and adolescents, and for the parents, friends, and teachers who support and nurture them, the first two decades of life are a time of dramatic challenge requiring adjustment to changes in the self, in the family, and in the peer group. In contemporary Western society, youth experience institutional changes as well. Infants and young children leave the home for preschool and then elementary school. Among young adolescents, there is a change in school setting, typically involving a transition from elementary school to either junior high school or middle school; and in late adolescence, there is a transition from high school to the worlds of work, university, or childrearing.

Given the changes and challenges of the first two decades—especially now when issues of youth population growth; insufficient economic, energy, educational, and employment resources; inequalities of opportunity; and violence and war affect hundreds of millions of young people daily—childhood and adolescence are periods replete with the possibilities of developmental problems. Indeed, because of the strong connection (correlation) that exists among the several problems of youth, and as a consequence of the high rates of these problems, the combined challenge to healthy child and adolescent development exists today at historically unprecedented levels.

As well, however, childhood and adolescence are periods wherein there is a great potential for positive and healthy behavior and development. Children and adolescents may possess considerable physical, psychological, and interpersonal abilities. These strengths may be coupled with the assets provided by friends supporting healthy choices, by parents providing authoritative guidance, and by caregivers, teachers, and communities creating opportunities for positive contributions and leadership. When the individual and ecological strengths, or assets, of youth align, developmental thriving can result. Instead of possessing a set of problem behaviors (associated with unsafe sex, substance use, crime, violence, educational failure, poor health, and poverty), the possession of developmental assets can result in youth who are marked by competence, confidence, character, connection, and caring/compassion.

Accordingly, this series is aimed at issues pertinent to both the challenges to and the opportunities for healthy development among contemporary youth and presents both the problems and positive potential of youth. In each volume in this series young people and the adults charged with promoting their healthy development are informed about:

1. The key concepts and substantive issues pertinent to each issue of concern in a given volume in the series;

2. The important events in the development of the issue, of knowledge about it, and of policies and programs pertinent to it;

3. The biographical backgrounds of key people who have worked and/or are working to address the issue;

4. Contemporary data pertinent to the incidence, impact, or developmental course of the issue;

5. The key organizations, associations, and national and international governmental and nongovernmental organizations addressing the issue;

6. Key, annotated print and nonprint resources pertinent to the issue; and

Each book in the series also includes an index.

Across the volumes in the series, the scholarship that is presented focuses on the advances of the last several decades in the medical, biological, and social scientific study of childhood and adolescence, and in the corresponding advances made by youth-serving professionals and practitioners in the design, delivery, and evaluation of programs that are effective not only in preventing youth problems but, in turn, in promoting the positive development of young people. In short, each volume in the series integratively presents the best "basic" and "applied" information currently available about the physical, psychological, behavioral, social, and cultural dimensions of a contemporary issue relevant to the adolescent period.

All volumes inform youth and their adult caregivers about the richness, challenges, and positive potentials of this dynamic developmental period. The volumes illustrate the diversity of child and adolescent life found across different physical, behavioral, racial, ethnic, religious, national, and cultural characteristics; emphasize the numerous (diverse) life paths that may result in positive, healthy development; present the key social relationships (e.g., involving peer groups, siblings, parents, extended family members, teachers, or mentors) and institutional contexts (e.g., schools, community organizations, faith institutions, and the workplace) that influence the development of today's youth; and discuss and evaluate the policies and programs useful for alleviating problems, for preventing problems, and for promoting positive and healthy development among contemporary youth.

1

Overview: Children, Health, and Learning

> Once it was common to define a school's mission in narrow terms focused on educational goals and methods alone. But as more and more teachers and school administrators have come to appreciate, there is an inextricable link between students' health and their ability to learn.
>
> Marx, Wooley, and Northrup 1998

Teachers, parents, and researchers no longer believe that a child's success in school depends exclusively on the knowledge and academic skills that the student brings to the classroom (West, Germino-Hausken, and Collins 1993). It is now widely recognized that learning is not an isolated process but is profoundly embedded in the complex biological, psychological, and social aspects of a child's functioning. Students who are safe, healthy, and emotionally stable are more likely to be academically successful. The multiple health-related domains—a student's physical health and motor coordination, emotional well-being, ability to cooperate with other children, curiosity, and eagerness to learn—are viewed as being critically important for academic success (Kagan 1990; Kagan, Moore, and Bredekamp 1995). The acknowledgment of the role of health in learning has prompted many professional organizations to urge society to ensure that all learners receive the nutrition, health care, and general physical and emotional support they need to participate actively in and benefit from their environment—in particular, from schooling (Marx, Wooley, and Northrop 1998).

Despite this deep connection between health and learning, formal schooling has often been slow to engage in educational practices that recognize the importance of students' health. In the nineteenth century, Elizabeth and Emily Blackwell, two of the first British-American women physicians, noted that, "Our school education ignores, in a thousand ways, the rules of healthy development" (Blackwell and Blackwell 1860). In the twentieth century, educators' gradual recognition of the role of health in learning was reinforced by the research in the natural and social sciences that confirmed the many ways in which health impacts learning. Furthermore, emerging theories of human development as well as numerous empirical studies by psychologists, educators, and medical researchers have pointed to the critical impact of health on learning.

The goal of this chapter is to explore the relationship between health and learning from the perspectives of theory, research, and practice and to review current and historic efforts to provide health services to schoolchildren and youth. After reviewing the current health status of our nation's schoolchildren and youth, the chapter will briefly outline how contemporary theories of human development explain the relationship between health and learning, and present some of the extensive research findings about the impact of health on learning. Finally, the chapter will review how health and other support services in schools have evolved over the last century, and offer some examples of various interventions that have been implemented in schools across the nation to promote health development.

Before examining more specific links between health and learning, it is important to consider the definitions of each of these domains. Health, in this context, is understood broadly as encompassing physical vigor, mental and emotional stability, social competence, and safe and supportive environments. Thus, health, as a term, is not confined to the absence of disease; rather, it is understood more broadly as physical, mental, and social well-being (Marx, Wooley, and Northrup 1998; McKenzie and Richmond 1998). This broader understanding of the word health leads to a more comprehensive conceptualization of the link between health and learning.

Learning, in the present context, is understood as the process through which children's knowledge and understanding of various domains of experience are attained or mastered (Bandura 1986). In other words, learning, in a general sense, refers to both the mastery of developmental tasks and the achievement of benchmarks as delineated by social norms. In educational settings, children's learning is typically measured by academic success as indicated by grades and particularly, by performance on standardized tests. Recent education reform efforts in this country have put today's schoolchildren and youth under increasing pressure to perform academically (Portz 2000). The demand for skilled workers and productive citizens has contributed to the vaulting of academic achievement to the top of our nation's political agenda (Learning First Alliance 2001). Education is the focus of a substantial portion of the nation's budget. However, in the face of political pressure to raise test scores, society is beginning to recognize that learning is not a simple process, but rather it is affected by a number of variables, including motivation, developmental status, and most especially by the health of the learner. In examining the critical link between health and learning we will first review the health issues confronting today's schoolchildren and youth.

CURRENT HEALTH STATUS OF SCHOOLCHILDREN

In recent years, the significant health needs of today's schoolchildren and youth have become increasingly apparent to educators, health workers, and social service providers (Dryfoos 1990). The new morbidities—poor nutrition, unsafe sex, drug and alcohol abuse, familial and community violence, teenage pregnancy and parenting, lack of job skills, inadequate access to health care, and homelessness—are threatening the healthy development of children and youth (Dryfoos 1990; Lerner 1995). Children and families in the United States are facing substantial challenges to their survival and development. Census data from the last decade indicate that, in the United States, more children live in poverty than in any other industrialized country in the world (The Annie E. Casey Foundation 2000). The Annie E. Casey Foundation (1999) reports that the percentage of children and youth living in poor neighborhoods where there are large numbers of welfare recipients, unemployed individuals, and single-parent families increased from 3 percent in 1970 to 17 percent in 1990. These conditions provide a context in which an increasing number of youth become involved in risky behavior. The 2001 Youth Behavior Survey (Centers for Disease Control and Prevention 2002) indicated that the following percentages of 14 to 17 year olds in the United States engaged in diverse problem behaviors:

Sexual activity: 33.4 percent had engaged in sexual intercourse during the prior three months, and 14.2 percent had had four or more sexual partners in their lifetime.

Substance abuse: 29.9 percent had had five or more drinks on one or more occasion during the prior 30 days, 28.5 percent had smoked cigarettes at least once during the prior 30 days, and 42.4 percent had smoked marijuana at least once in their lifetime.

Suicide: during the prior 12 months, 8.8 percent reported attempting suicide, and 19.0 percent had seriously considered suicide.

Violence: during the prior 12 months, 33.2 percent had been involved in a physical fight, and during the prior 30 days, 5.7 percent had carried a gun.

A leading advocate for improved youth services, Dryfoos (1990), estimated that 25 percent of 10 to 17 year olds engage in multiple high-risk behaviors and that another 25 percent place themselves at moderate risk by engaging in some problem behaviors. Although the remaining 50 percent have no or low-risk behavior involvement, they require strong and consistent support to avoid becoming involved.

How does society make a difference in improving the health status of children and youth? Over the years, this question has been tackled by numerous professions and disciplines. At the core of this question is the notion that in order to promote positive developmental outcomes we need to understand the basic processes underlying healthy development. In the next section, we examine what developmental psychologists believe children and youth need in order to be healthy and to succeed in school. These beliefs are embedded in theories of human development. These theories both inform and have been informed by the numerous research studies that have investigated how children develop. This discussion of theory will lay the groundwork for our subsequent discussion on effective empirical research and clinical practice.

THEORIES OF HUMAN DEVELOPMENT

Over the years, a number of theories about how children develop into adults have helped to guide the work of professionals whose role it is to promote positive and healthy outcomes for children. These developmental theories, while differing from one another in some ways, agree on some major fundamental principles about how human beings move from infancy through adulthood. One of the most prominent of these theories is known as "developmental-contextualism" (Lerner 1984, 1986, 1995). This theory draws on earlier theories of human development that were articulated by psychologists such as Werner (1948), Piaget (1952), and Bronfenbrenner (1979). Developmental-contextualism proposes that development is a complex process in which the many parts of the person (e.g., cognitive, emotional, biological, social processes) continuously interact with one another to produce a complex whole person. For our purposes in this book, we will discuss four of the commonly agreed upon principles that undergird Lerner's and other psychologists' understanding of how humans develop. Development occurs (1) in relationship to context; (2) at bio-psycho-social levels; (3) across the lifespan; and (4) in a pattern involving both risk and resilience.

It is important to note that these principles represent a change in the way psychologists have looked at development over the years. In contrast to earlier notions, development is no longer considered to be an isolated process occurring within the person, but reflects an interaction between the person and his/her environment, with each continually impacting and changing the other. Moreover, development is recognized as occurring not simply in a single domain, but simultaneously across multiple domains and levels—cognitive, emotional, biological, psychological, and social—that are continuously interacting with and changing one another. The heavy emphasis of earlier theories on the time period of childhood has evolved into a lifespan developmental perspective. Finally, in contrast to their earlier focus on developmental deficits, developmental psychologists now recognize the critical role of strengths in human development. We will review and illustrate each of these principles of development.

Context

The first of these principles reflects our growing understanding that children's development does not occur in a vacuum, but rather it is embedded in the various contexts in which children exist. These contexts include both the immediate interpersonal or physical situation the child is in as well as the larger environment in which the child exists—that is, the particular family, school, neighborhood, culture, and society. These contexts continuously affect and change the way children are developing. Safe school environments, for example, support and enhance the cognitive development of schoolchildren resulting in better learning outcomes. Furthermore, the interaction between context and development is a two-way street. Children and youth, in turn, also shape various aspects of the diverse contexts in which they live. For example, students whose developmental progress results in academic success often contribute positively to their school environments thus leading to safer schools (Roeser and Eccles 2000).

The mutual impact of context and development is particularly apparent when we consider the increasing diversity of our nation's schools. In large urban schools, for example, dozens of languages may be spoken by the students' families. It is generally agreed that immigrant children and families are profoundly impacted by their new surroundings. Although immigrant families undergo a process of acculturation, there is an increasing understanding that this is a bilateral process and that immigrant groups contribute substantial aspects of their own culture to the dominant culture (Atkinson and Thompson 1992; Suarez-Orozco and Suarez-Orozco 2001). The mutual interaction of these various cultures and ethnic groups with the dominant culture reflected in the schools results in changes in school climates. This mutual impact also requires specific interventions that are not only respectful and responsive to the diverse needs of these families, but that also promote positive racial, cultural, and ethnic identities among the students (Helms 1990; Vargas and Koss-Chioino 1992). Taking into account the multiple contexts that simultaneously impact children is a critical issue for schools, which represent one of the many institutions that have been developed by the dominant culture and organized around its value system (Sue, Arredondo, and McDavis 1992).

In summary, theories about how children develop make clear that contexts that promote children's health and safety simultaneously provide conditions that support children's academic achievement. Conversely, contexts that impede children's physical, emotional, and social development are likely to contribute to academic failure.

Bio-Psycho-Social Levels

A second principle of human development on which psychologists and others generally agree is that children's development occurs simultaneously at many levels—biological, psychological, and social. These various levels of development are continually interacting with and changing one another. We know that the biological level, for example children's physical health, has an impact on their emotional and social development. A child whose health needs are chronically unmet is less likely to be successful in school or on the playground. Similarly, children whose emotional needs for love and attention are unmet are more likely to have health and learning problems. Difficulties in any one of these areas frequently contribute to difficulties in another, sometimes resulting in so-called vicious cycles for the child. For example, poor health can lead to inconsistent school attendance, which can bring about poor school performance, which can result in negative behavior, which can contribute to negative peer interactions, which can lead to anxiety and depression, which can impact the immune system, which can result in increased illness. In a parallel fashion, success in any of these areas helps to promote success in other areas. Recognizing that malnourishment constitutes a significant barrier to learning, the Federal School Lunch Program, implemented in 1946, was developed.

This principle of development helps to explain why interventions that focus on only one level of development can often be limited in their effectiveness. For example, new methods of teaching reading will have limited success if students are malnourished and ill. Similarly, children who regularly experience family or neighborhood violence are less likely to attend classroom activities. Later in this chapter we will describe some school-based interventions that simultaneously address multiple levels of development.

Lifespan Development

A third principle of human development involves the time period in life in which development is thought to occur. In prior decades, developmental psychologists placed a substantial emphasis on childhood. Often times, it appeared from the theory and research that development was confined to childhood and stopped at age 18. In recent years, however, it has become much more evident from the research as well as clinical practice that development continues over the course of the entire lifespan (Baltes, Staudinger, and Lindenberger 1999; Lerner 1984, 1998; Lerner, Walsh, and Howard 1998). Adults continue to change—physically, emotionally, cognitively, and socially—for as long as they live. As a consequence, the developmental status of adults varies substantially from one adult to another. Adults, of the same age, can be at different developmental places. If they are developmentally mature, they are more likely to be positive influences on the children for whom they care (Lykken 2001). The developmental status of teachers, for example, has a significant impact on the academic achievement of children. Teachers who experience good health, positive personal and work relationships, and job satisfaction are more likely to engender academic success in their students (Henson and Eller 1999). As another example, parents who can meet children's personal needs for safety and positive relationships are in a better position to encourage and support the academic achievement of their children.

Our understanding of development as occurring across the lifespan suggests that earlier developmental outcomes significantly impact later ones. It is now widely recognized that positive learning and social experiences in young children are more likely to contribute to their academic success as adolescents and young adults. So-called healthy starts for children—physically, emotionally, and socially—are considered crucial for later success in school. The widely acclaimed Head Start Program for preschool children was developed on the basis of this developmental principle. Head Start not only provides a positive boost to young children so that they will grow into healthy adults, it also provides supports and training to their parents and other adults in the community.

Risk and Resilience

The final principle of human development to be presented here suggests that the direction of development can change at any point in the life of a person. Children who are developing in healthy ways can experience certain risks that might turn the course of development in a more negative direction. At the same time, children who are initially developing in negative directions can be supported to develop in more positive ways. In light of the possibility of altering the course of development, psychologists have come to recognize the critical role of strengths. The promotion of strengths can serve to buffer the effects of other negative influences on development, that is, help children to be resilient in the face of adversity. Resilience is a concept that explains how children, families, and communities are able to cope and to thrive despite environmental challenges (McLoyd 1990, 1998). Resilience can be the result of individual factors such as personality or intelligence (Masten and Coatsworth 1998) or environmental factors, such as social support or the quality of family life (Black and Krishnakumar 1998; Spencer 1990; Stack 1975). Interventions that promote strengths as well as address deficits are more likely to lead to academic success. The impact of health on learning is mediated by interventions that incorporate strengths and diminish risks.

The key roles that risk and resilience play in development suggest that professionals working with children cannot focus on only one of these domains to the exclusion of the other. They must take both strengths and deficits into account. In the past, psychologists and other service providers have tended to adopt a more deficit-oriented approach. More recently, programs have been developed to address the promotion of strengths of children and youth. For example, the Search Institute of Minneapolis has developed a list of 40 assets that characterizes children, families, and communities that can be used to support healthy development. Twenty of the assets, called external assets, focus on the positive experiences that children receive from the people and institutions in their lives. The four categories of these assets include support, empowerment, boundaries and expectations, and constructive uses of time. In addition, there are 20 internal assets that refer to internal qualities that the community must nurture in order to promote healthy development. The four categories of the internal assets include commitment to learning, positive values, social competencies, and positive identity (Benson et al. 1998).

In summary, these theoretical principles of human development, particularly as they are described within the perspective of "developmental-contextualism" (Lerner 1986), outline a basic explanation of how humans develop. Most critically, they help to account for the ways in which health and learning interact. These theoretical principles of development have been supported by the large body of empirical research in child development that has occurred over the past 50 years. A significant portion of that research provides evidence of the strong relationship between health and learning. In the following section we will review the findings of the specific studies linking health and learning.

RESEARCH LINKING HEALTH AND LEARNING

Over the past several decades there has been a substantial increase in the amount of research conducted on various aspects of child development. A large body of this research has examined factors that affect children's learning. Two types of research readily document the impact of health on learning: (1) studies demonstrating that poor health leads to negative academic outcomes, and (2) studies demonstrating that interventions aimed at improving children's health have a positive impact on learning. Both areas of research reinforce and illustrate the critical connection between health and learning. Let us look at each of these types of studies in turn.

Impact of Poor Health Status on Learning

Poor Physical Health and Learning

Several studies have demonstrated that strong links have been found between school performance and poor physical health. Health problems identified in these studies include, but are not limited to, lead poisoning, asthma, diabetes, cancer, epilepsy, low birthweight, and other chronic illnesses. Some researchers, depending on their definition of chronic illness, estimate that as many as 6 to 15 percent of children and adolescents in schools are struggling with some form of chronic illness (Thies and McAllister 2001). This number can be as high as 30 percent in rural areas (Thies and McAllister 2001). For many of these children, struggles with physical health have profound implications for academic achievement. For example, researchers have determined that children who had a low birthweight and who suffered various perinatal illnesses experience less favorable academic outcomes and more frequent school absences (McGauhey et al. 1991; Taylor, Klein, and Hack 2000). In another example, several studies have shown that lead contamination—found in such various sources as house paint and yard soil—is associated with cognitive deficits and lower school achievement (Needleman et al. 1990). Additionally, children with some types of epilepsy have difficulty succeeding academically. For example, Austin and colleagues (1999) have found that children with more severe seizures had mean scores on academic achievement tests that were below national norms.

Another critical dimension of physical health for children is the surrounding environment, particularly the school building itself. The incidence of environmentally related illnesses, such as tuberculosis, asthma, allergies, respiratory disease, depression, and violent anger is increasing (Books 1998) and the effects of these illnesses is often overlooked in discussing factors that affect academic outcomes.

One critical dimension of the physical environment for children is the school building itself. Almost one out of every two public school buildings in this nation contains an environmental hazard, such as asbestos, peeling lead-based paint, radon gas, lead-contaminated water, or biologically contaminated heating and ventilating systems (Kowalski 1995). These dangerous environmental conditions have the potential to contribute to children and teachers' ill-health.

Family Dysfunction and Learning

One important dimension of the well-being of children is the level of functioning of their families. Several studies have pointed to the relationship between family dysfunction (including marital instability, frequent relocations, family violence, and homelessness) and low academic achievement (Masten, Best, and Garmezy 1991; Wang and Gordon 1994). Family dysfunction can often threaten children's personal safety, which is a fundamental aspect of children's health and well-being. One major threat to safety—child maltreatment—is becoming increasingly prevalent in children's lives and contributes substantially to the lack of well-being and overall health of children. One-fourth of 10 to 16 year olds report being assaulted or abused in the previous year (Finkelhor and Dziuba-Leatherman 1994). Both physical and sexual abuse, as well as neglect, have been implicated in a range of negative developmental and academic outcomes for school-aged children, including below average intelligence quotients (IQ), learning problems, and a range of social-emotional problems—from aggression and hostility to apathy and withdrawal (Sexton 1999). Maltreated children demonstrate less academic engagement, more social-skills deficits, and lower ego resiliency than non-maltreated children. Additionally, maltreated children manifest multiple forms of academic risk and show more externalizing and internalizing behavior problems (Shonk and Cicchetti 2001).

Leiter and Johnson (1997) conducted a study that demonstrates a significant relationship between child maltreatment and declines in a diverse set of school outcomes, including falling grades, increasing absenteeism, worsening elementary school behavior, retention in a grade, and involvement in special education programs. Academic difficulties have not only been demonstrated in children who are victims of family violence but also in children who witness family violence. Exposure to family violence has been linked with a rise in absenteeism, an increase in behavior problems, and an overall detrimental impact on the child's school experience (Brener 1999). Other aspects of family dysfunction have been shown to impact learning outcomes. For example, some studies have shown that the absence of the biological father contributes to unhealthy outcomes and limited academic achievement for youth. Lykken (2001) demonstrated that boys raised in homes without the biological father are more likely to be involved in juvenile crimes.

Family dysfunction can also lead to compromised living conditions for children. For example, homelessness appears to have a particularly profound influence on academic achievement. On any given night, more than 100,000 children are homeless (U.S. Department of Education and U.S. Department of Health and Human Services 1993). The disruptions caused by homelessness have been found to have a profoundly negative effect on the cognitive development and educational progress of children. Frequent moves create inconsistencies in their schooling. In a study of homeless families in New York City, Rafferty and Rollins (1989) found that most children had transferred schools upon becoming homeless, with 33 percent having transferred between two and six times. Trouble with paperwork or other access-related issues, lack of transportation or clothing, and chronic health problems are only some of the myriad factors that cause homeless children to miss a significant amount of schooling (Walsh 1992). It has been reported that 43 percent of school-aged homeless children are not attending school at all, and that 30 percent of those who are in school fall at least one grade behind their peers (Hall and Maza 1990). Homeless children are more likely to have been retained, to be receiving special education services, and to be behind their classmates academically (Bassuk and Rubin 1987).

In the last decade, federal and local policies have been directed at relieving the impact of homelessness on children's education. For example, children who move to or from a shelter (and out of their school district) can continue to be transported to and from their prior school for a specified period of time. These policies appear to be having a positive effect. For example, one recent study examining the effects of homelessness on children found little or no difference between homeless children and their peers on rates of absenteeism and other school-related problems when transportation programs are used (Bassuk, Buckner, and Weinreb 2001).

Community-Based Risks and Learning

Community-based risks can contribute to poor health and limited academic outcomes for children. A recent series of longitudinal studies found a direct relationship between the number of community-based risks experienced by children and the likelihood of poor academic performance (Furstenberg et al. 1999). Research has also demonstrated that students are less likely to succeed when communities are economically deprived, disorganized, and lack opportunities for employment or youth involvement (Hawkins, Catalano, and Miller 1992). These neighborhoods have effects on childhood IQ and school-leaving, even after the differences in the socioeconomic characteristics of families were taken into account. For example, the socioeconomic mix of children's neighborhoods is related to completed years of schooling. Research has demonstrated that youth who grow up in affluent communities or communities with a higher percentage of affluent families complete more years of school and have lower school drop-out rates than youth from similar families who grow up in poor neighborhoods or neighborhoods with fewer affluent families (Brooks-Gunn et al. 1993).

Recent research has also demonstrated a link between exposure to community violence and academic functioning. Community violence generally refers to both direct victimization and witnessing potentially lethal acts of violence in a neighborhood. Although many researchers have acknowledged the negative effect of direct victimization on academic performance (e.g., Skurulsky 2001), it is not until recently that researchers have begun to acknowledge that witnessing community violence has a negative impact on student's learning capability as well. For example, Overstreet and Braun (1999) found that exposure to community violence was negatively correlated with academic functioning. Additionally, in a later study, Shavers (2000) found that exposure to community violence significantly influenced reported behavioral patterns and academic performance among students.

Unsupervised Out-of-School Time and Learning

Children's out-of-school time has become an increasing concern in recent years (Bryant 1989; Carpenter, Huston, and Spera 1989; Larson and Richards 1989; Medrich et al. 1982; Miller 1995; Pettit et al. 1997). It is estimated that the parents of nearly 30 million school-age children maintain jobs outside the home, and somewhere between 7 and 15 million children return from school to an empty house on any given day (Afterschool Alliance 2000). Moreover, the National Institute on Out-of-School-Time (2001) reports that approximately 8 million children in the United States age 5 to 14 spend time without adult supervision. Cain and Hofferth (1989) report that the percentage of children who are unsupervised increases steadily with age. Unsupervised afterschool time leaves children vulnerable to a range of risk factors. For example, these unsupervised children are more likely than their supervised peers to spend afterschool time in passive activities, averaging 23 hours of television viewing each week (Afterschool Alliance, 2000). Statistics indicate that risky behavior such as sexual activity, alcohol and drug use, and juvenile crime increase significantly from 3:00 to 6:00 P.M. (Fox and Newman 1997). Further, violent juvenile crime triples, and children are at a greater risk of being victims of violent crime in the afterschool hours (National Institute on Out-of-School-Time 2001). These risk factors contribute significantly to children's academic difficulties. For example, even when the family's social class and the child's prior adjustment are taken into account, both first and third graders who spent more time unsupervised were less socially competent and received lower academic grades in sixth grade than children who spent less time on their own (Pettit et al. 1997). The Boston After-School Time Study found that children from low-income households displayed more behavior problems such as aggression, defiance, and hyperactivity when they were unsupervised for longer periods of time (Marshall et al. 1997). Finally, despite the obvious need for afterschool programming, the U.S. General Accounting Office estimates that, in the year 2002, the current number of out-of-school time programs for school-age children will meet as little as 25 percent of the demand in urban areas (National Institute on Out-of-School Time 2001).

Negative School Climate and Learning

A negative interpersonal climate in the school also contributes to a lack of well-being in children and, ultimately, to poor school performance. School climate is broadly defined as the set of characteristics of schools and classrooms that define their interpersonal atmosphere (e.g., teachers' attitudes, school values, classroom climate, school safety) (Marx, Wooley, and Northrup 1998). Schools function as organizations and have climates and cultures that can affect students in ways that go beyond their unique classroom experiences (Fine 1991; Maehr 1991; Rutter 1980). Factors that constitute a school's climate are significant sources of variation in students' achievement (Brookover et al. 1979; Rutter 1983). For example, competitive environments in middle and high schools have been associated with higher rates of delinquency, emotional distress, and diminished motivation among adolescents (Fiqueria-McDonough 1986; Roeser, Eccles, and Strobel 1998a). When young people feel unsafe or victimized at school because of the behaviors of other students, they are more likely to suffer socially, emotionally, and academically (Scales and Leffert 1999). When schools present a negative climate and do not help students and their families to feel involved, students are less likely to succeed (Hawkins, Catalano, and Miller 1992).

School climate encompasses the personal safety of staff and students. Violence, which has become an increasing concern in our nation's schools, poses many sorts of threats to the well-being of both students and staff. Research in this area indicates that a culture of violence has arisen in some schools, negatively affecting students, teachers and administrators (U.S. Public Health Service 2001). Students fearing violence in school may choose to cope by staying home or bringing a weapon to school. In 1995, a survey of U.S. high school students revealed that 4.5 percent of students had missed at least one day of school in the preceding month because they felt unsafe either being at school or on their way to and from school (Kann et al. 1996). During the same 30-day period, 1 out of 10 students and 1 out of 7 males had carried a weapon to school on one or more days. Moreover, 1 out of 12 students interviewed reported being threatened or injured with a weapon on school property, and one-third of the students had property stolen or deliberately damaged on school grounds (Kann et al. 1996). One in three Latinos, one in five African Americans, and one in eight whites reported that gangs operated in their schools in 1989 (Rendon and Hope 1996). Lower attendance rates and the presence of physical violence in the schools are known contributors to poor academic outcomes.

Additionally, research has demonstrated that peer groups combined with the school climate assert a powerful impact on children and adolescents in schools. One study of adolescent boys found that some schools have dominant peer groups that value academic achievement and shun violence, while other schools have dominant groups that endorse the use of violence (Felson et al. 1994). This research study showed that the risk of becoming involved in violence in school varied according to the peer culture in the school, despite, the adolescent's own view of violence.

Inadequate Nutrition and Learning

Inadequate nutrition has been identified in the research as an important factor in poor academic outcomes. Even moderate undernutrition or hunger can reduce children's cognitive development and school performance (American Dietetic Association 1990; Center on Hunger, Poverty, and Nutrition Policy 1993; National Health and Education Consortium 1993). Children's brain function, and consequently school performance, is also diminished by short-term or periodic hunger or malnutrition caused by missing or skipping meals (Pollitt 1995). Several studies have indicated that omission of breakfast or consumption of an inadequate breakfast is a factor contributing to poor school performance (Nicklas, O'Neil, and Berenson 1998).

Cognitive defects can result from complex interactions between malnutrition and environmental insults that result from living in poverty (Black 2000). Results from a recent series of surveys from nine states and the District of Columbia by the Community Childhood Hunger Identification Project provide an estimate that 4 million

American children experience prolonged periodic food insufficiency and hunger each year. The same studies show that an additional 10 million children are at risk for hunger. The negative impact of inadequate nutrition on learning is an important concern for U.S. schools when one considers the extent of hunger in this country. Children from families that report multiple experiences of food insufficiency and hunger are more likely to show behavioral, emotional, and academic problems on a standardized measure of psychosocial dysfunction (Kleinman et al. 1998). Even children who experience food insufficiency and hunger on an intermittent basis manifest poor behavioral and academic difficulties (Murphy et al. 1998).

Mental Health Difficulties and Learning

One of the most significant factors impacting children's academic achievement is the status of their mental and emotional health. In the U.S. civilian population, 8.2 percent or 4.1 million children have a reported mental and/or emotional disorder (Center for Mental Health Services 2000). These youth have severe emotional or behavioral problems that significantly interfere with their daily functioning. Despite the significant percentage of children with reported emotional difficulties, these statistics are estimated to represent less than one-third of the true number of children under the age of 18 with serious emotional disturbance. Those children who are not reported—an estimated two-thirds of those who suffer from mental illness—often do not receive mental health services (U.S. Public Health Service 2000). The Surgeon General's 1999 report on *Mental Health* states that one in five children and adolescents experience the signs and symptoms of an emotional or behavioral disorder during the course of a year and that about 5 percent of all children experience extreme functional impairment as the result of a disorder. This report also estimates that 6 to 9 million children with serious emotional disturbances are not receiving the help they need—especially those children from low-income families (U.S. Department of Health and Human Services 1999).

Mental health difficulties in children are usually manifested as either internalizing (withdrawing) behavior or externalizing (acting-out) behavior. Children with internalized problems have difficulties in academic functioning. They often fail to engage in tasks (e.g., homework) that will help them to be successful (e.g., Roeser and Eccles 2000). Symptoms of depression, an internalizing disorder, are associated with lower teacher-rated grades and standardized test scores, lack of persistence in the face of academic difficulties, and a lack of classroom participation among both children and adolescents (Becker and Luther 2002; Blechman et al. 1986; Dweck and Wortman 1982; Kellam et al. 1994; Kovacs 1992; Nolen-Hoeksema, Girgus, and Seligman 1986).

Children with externalized distress in the form of conduct problems and/or attention problems, also evidence poor school performance (Roeser and Eccles 2000). Externalizing difficulties in children are associated with poorer teacher-rated grades and standardized test scores, more time off-task in the classroom, and more behavioral problems within and outside class at school (Astor 1998; Barkley 1998; Dishion, French, and Patterson 1995; Hinshaw 1992; Ollendick et al. 1992; Parker and Asher 1987; Roeser, Eccles, and Strobel 1998b). Aggressive children are also more likely to experience social difficulties at school, such as rejection by peers and disfavor on the part of teachers (Parker and Asher 1987; Walsh and Barrett, in press; Wentzel and Asher 1995). There is strong evidence of long-term academic difficulties—such as poor achievement, poor attendance, and school dropout—among children who manifest high levels of externalized distress earlier in development (Becker and Luther 2002; Cairns, Cairns, and Neckerman 1989).

Research has also demonstrated that learning difficulties and psychosocial issues can be mutually reinforcing over time. Roeser and Eccles (2000) outline two distinct pathways explaining why academic and psychosocial difficulties co-occur in some children and why these problems exacerbate one another. In one pathway, poor school performance can lead to psychosocial difficulties. Children who do poorly in school, and attribute the poor performance to their own personal incompetence, generate within themselves feelings of shame, self-doubt, low self-esteem, and alienation. These feelings often result in internalizing disorders. Similarly, children who do poorly in school, and attribute the poor performance to others, generate feelings of anger, alienation, and hostility resulting in externalizing disorders. In the second pathway, emotional distress influences cognitive processes leading to academic difficulties. Children who are struggling with anxiety or depression can experience difficulties with attention, concentration, memory, energy level, and motivation resulting in lowered academic performance.

Poverty and Learning

Chief among the conditions leading to poor health is poverty. Several studies demonstrate that poor nutrition, episodic or chronic health issues, socioemotional problems, limited physical activity, and unsafe and violence-ridden surroundings are often related to more widespread family and community poverty. In the last decade, childhood poverty has reached epidemic proportions in the United States (McLloyd 1998). As of 1999, 17 percent of American children lived in families with cash incomes below the poverty threshold and more than 4 million of these children are under the age of six (National Center for Children in Poverty 2002). The official poverty line is about $16,800 for a family of four. More than 15 million children (more than 5 million under the age of six) live in low-income households that are only a little above this line (National Center for Children in Poverty 2002). Poverty rates are highest among Native American, African American, and Hispanic children; among children living in single-parent, female-headed households; and among central-city residents (National Center for Children in Poverty 2002).

It has long been known that children who live in poverty are more likely to experience educational difficulties that place them at risk for school failure. Research demonstrates that poor children, as well as children living near the poverty-level, on average, perform significantly less well than non-poor and middle-class children on many indicators of academic achievement, including achievement test scores, grade retentions, course failures, placement in special education, high school graduation rates, high school drop-out rates, and completed years of schooling (Conger, Conger, and Elder 1997; Entwisle and Alexander 1990; Haveman and Wolfe 1995; Hill and Duncan 1987; Patterson, Kupersmidt, and Vaden 1990; White 1982). Furthermore, analyses suggest that among traditional indicators of socioeconomic status (SES), family income is the highest single correlate of academic achievement (White 1982). Additionally, research indicates that teachers tend to perceive poor and low-SES students less positively and to have lower achievement expectations for them than for non-poor children, largely on the basis of noncognitive considerations (e.g., speech patterns and dress) (White 1982).

In sum, the academic achievement of our young people is inextricably linked to their family, community, and school environments as well as to their physical and mental health statuses. Although the complexity and multiplicity of factors that contributes to children's academic achievement may seem overwhelming, it also provides us with numerous entry points for interventions. In the next section, we will examine how interventions that improve health status can produce positive outcomes regarding academic performance.

The Positive Effect on Learning of Interventions to Improve Health and Well-Being

The impact of health on learning is evident not only in the research that looks at the consequences of poor health conditions, but also in the studies that examine the effects of positive interventions on academic outcomes. In recent years, research has clearly demonstrated how interventions that improve children's health also contribute in a positive manner to their academic performance.

Nutrition Interventions

Interventions directed at helping children and adolescents change their dietary behaviors may have immediate social and health benefits, including improved cognitive abilities and emotional functioning (Baranowski et al. 2000; McGraw et al. 2000). Strong evidence suggests that higher rates of participation in the school breakfast programs are associated in the short-term with improved student functioning on a broad range of psychosocial and academic measures (Murphy et al. 1998). School-based interdisciplinary interventions directed toward diet and physical activity have been shown to reduce television viewing and promote healthy eating (Gortmaker et al. 1999). It is the position of the American Dietetic Association (2000) that the school and community have a shared responsibility to provide all students with access to high-quality foods and nutrition services. Collaboration between key school and community-based constituents results in effective and useful plans for local school nutrition programs.

The role of the community environment in shaping dietary behaviors has received increasing attention in recent years. Although schools are a key part of the community environment, interventions that promote healthy eating among students through changes in the school environment have received relatively little attention. Research has demonstrated that various aspects of the school environment have the potential to affect healthy eating, including recess periods, intramural sports and physical education programs, physical education facilities, foods and beverages available outside of the school meals program, and psychosocial support for physical activity and healthy eating (Wechsler et al. 2000).

Increased Family Involvement

Family involvement in a child's education has consistently emerged in the research as an important factor in promoting both academic and emotional well-being (Comer 1988; Eccles and Harold 1993; Epstein 1992). Most families want to be involved in their children's education in ways that not only enhance the school's activities but that also contribute positively to their own health knowledge and behaviors (Birch 1996). When parents are involved in their children's education, children do better in school (Henderson 1987). When schools have good relationships with parents, parents are more likely to become engaged with school health programs and other related efforts (National Coalition for Parent Involvement in Education 1995). In addition, when parents are comfortable with the school and have regular communication with school personnel, they are more likely to understand and support school health programs (Marx and Northup 1995). Family involvement can increase students' adoption of health enhancing behaviors (Perry et al. 1989).

The home environment provides many resources that support children's development among families that have limited economic means and/or are facing such severe hardships as chronic illness, divorce, or early parental death. Studies demonstrate that factors protecting against adversity include a positive parent-child relationship, family cohesion, warmth, assigned chores, responsibilities for the family's well-being, an absence of discord, and other secure childhood attachments. Other family attributes associated with school attendance and achievement among students include monitoring of television viewing, reading to young children on a daily basis, expressing high expectations for academic success, and helping with homework (Wang, Haertel, and Walberg 1997). Active engagement of families (e.g., participating in school management teams, being involved in parent-developed workshops, providing tutoring, assisting teachers in classroom or afterschool activities) is associated with improved student achievement, increased school attendance, and decreased student drop-out, delinquency, and pregnancy rates. Furthermore, educational intervention programs designed to involve family members are significantly more effective than those targeted exclusively to students (Epstein, Salinas, and Simon 1996; Walberg 1984).

Epstein (1995) describes six types of involvement for parents to build a supportive relationship with the student, his or her family, and the school. The first type is parenting, and schools are encouraged to assist families in developing a home environment that will support the child and his or needs as a student. The next type, communicating, involves direct, effective, and open communication so that parents receive clear messages about school programs and their child's progress. Volunteering helps the parents to become involved in the classroom and school. Learning at home is described as a way to help parents support their children with homework assignments. Decision making is a type of involvement that helps parents to become involved in the decisions that affect the schools and school reform and improvements. The last type of involvement that is described is collaborating with the community, which draws in resources from the community to strengthen the family bond with the schools as well as to support family practices for student learning and development (Epstein 1995, 2001).

Family functioning may also include factors of resilience within the family constellation. For example, in African American families, strong kinship bonds, the elasticity and adaptability of households and family roles, high achievement orientation, the central role of spirituality and religion, racial biculturalism, positive self-esteem, and development of ethnic awareness often buffer youth against environmental stressors (Littlejohn-Blake and Darling 1993).

Authors of several studies have provided evidence supporting a positive relationship between various aspects of family involvement in children's learning and school outcomes (Shirley 1997). Unfortunately, home-school connections are relatively infrequent during the elementary school years and become almost nonexistent during the middle and high school years (e.g., Carnegie Council on Adolescent Development 1995; Eccles and Harold 1993).

Out-of-School Time Programs and Learning

Children's afterschool hours have been identified as an important part of their day (Bryant 1989; Carpenter, Huston, and Spera 1989; Larson and Richards 1989; Medrich et al. 1982; Miller 1995; Pettit et al. 1997). Afterschool programs have the potential to keep children safe and out of trouble and can help to improve the academic performance of children (Chung 2000). Quality afterschool programs keep children out of trouble and prevent crime, juvenile delinquency, school vandalism, and violent victimization (Pederson et al. 1998). Adolescents who are carefully monitored (i.e., parents know where their children are, what they are doing, and whom they are with) are less likely to engage in risky behavior and are more likely to perform well in school (Steinberg et al. 1992).

There is considerable evidence that participation in out-of-school activities is related to children's adjustment. Compared with peers who are not in afterschool programs, children who attend high-quality programs have better peer relations, emotional adjustment, conflict resolution skills, grades, and conduct in school (National Institute on Out-of-School-Time 2001). One study of a small program that offered an hour of afterschool tutoring to second- and third-grade children four days a week documented improvements in the reading and spelling scores of children who participated (Morris, Shaw, and Perney 1990). The Ecological Study of After-School Care demonstrated that third graders who spent more time than their peers in enrichment activities received better grades in conduct and were reported by their teachers to have better work habits, better relationships with peers, and better emotional adjustment (Posner and Vandell 1999). Finally, studies have demonstrated that students who spend one to four hours per week in extracurricular activities are 49 percent less likely to use drugs and 37 percent less likely to become teen parents than students who do not participate in extracurricular activities (National Institute on Out-of-School Time 2001).

Mentoring programs have also had documented success intervening in the lives of children. The involvement of an adult mentor in a young person's life for just one year decreased first-time drug use by 46 percent, cut school absenteeism by 52 percent, and reduced violent behavior by 33 percent. Mentored youth were also more likely to perform well in school, get along better with family and friends, be less likely to assault someone, and be much less likely to start using alcohol (Quinn 1999). Further, school-based mentoring programs have been demonstrated to have a positive effect on children's attitude toward school and school performance (Curtis and Hansen-Schwoebel 1999).

Improving School Climate

Influences such as teacher actions and expectations, effective instructional methods and curriculum, schoolwide policies, and school climate play key roles in raising student learning, motivation, and attitudes toward school (Marx, Wooley, and Northrup 1998). When students perceive their secondary schools as places where teachers hold high expectations for all students regardless of their ability level, and where effort, improvement, and task mastery are emphasized as the signs of success, adolescents act out less, experience less emotional distress, and are motivated to learn more (Roeser, Midgley, and Urdan 1996; Rutter 1980; Urdan and Roeser 1993).

Selected dimensions of classroom climate are consistently associated with enhanced student cognitive and affective outcomes, including cooperation among teachers and students; shared interests, values, and goals; an academic orientation; well-organized lessons with clear learning objectives; and student satisfaction. Changes in school life, organization, and culture have been shown to improve student learning and motivation (Newmann and Wehlage 1995). Communities with well-developed and integrated networks of social organizations demonstrate how community-based actions can help children and youth who live in high-risk circumstances overcome adversity and facilitate the development of resilience leading to school success (Ludwig, Duncan, and Hirschfield 2001). Social support by caring adults in the community helps sustain support for academic tasks and increases community-based opportunities for students to develop new interests and skills (Rigsby, Reynolds, and Wang 1995).

When children feel valued, they are more likely to develop important skills, avoid risk-taking behavior, and remain in school (Epstein 1995). Students feel competent and do well in school when (1) their communities have accessible resources and supportive networks and involve students in community services; (2) their families seek preventative care, value and encourage education, spend time with their children, and have clear expectations; (3) schools involve families and students and encourage the development of positive behaviors; and (4) schools, families, and communities deliver clear, consistent messages (Hawkins, Catalano, and Miller 1992).

Additionally, youth who are committed to school and who have embraced the goals and values of the school are less likely to engage in violence (Jessor et al. 1995). Schools can give youth who face a multitude of risk factors a place in which to excel socially and academically. Schools with peer groups that value academic achievement may lower students' risk of becoming involved in violence (Felson et al. 1994).

Improved Physical Health

Improved health status enhances school attendance and learning (Centers for Disease Control and Prevention 1995). Several researchers studying the effectiveness of school-based health education programs have found that these programs contribute to the significant improvement of students' health knowledge, skills, and practices (Connell, Turner, and Mason 1985; Walter, Vaughan, and Wynder 1994). School health education not only can positively change students' health behaviors and attitudes (Dusenbury and Falco 1995; Gold 1994; Kirby et al. 1994) but is also an effective public health measure (Rothman et al.

1993). These curricula have been demonstrated to reduce risk behaviors (such as tobacco, alcohol, and drug use) among youth (Dusenbury and Lake 1996). However, school-based curricula alone seem to have limited success in changing adolescent behaviors (Dryfoos 1990). Apparently, these school-based programs do not sustain behavioral change over several years unless they are embedded in combinations of different community-based strategies. The wide range of services offered by many school-based health clinics ultimately can have more successful outcomes for youth (Dryfoos 1994).

School-based health centers provide access to preventive health services while educating youth about activities to promote their well-being. Additionally, school-based health care centers have the potential to increase student attendance at school and reduce the suspension and drop-out rates (Dryfoos 1994) and have the potential to provide early intervention services to high-risk adolescents (Walter et al. 1996). Screenings provided by these health clinics can help identify problems, such as vision and hearing deficits, that can interfere with learning (Young 1986). The emergence of centers within schools that provide actual screening, diagnosis, and treatment for physical and psychosocial disorders is very promising.

Access to Mental Health Interventions

Counseling, psychological, and social service interventions in schools provide programs and services that address mental health conditions that interfere with student learning as well as focus on enhancing healthy psychosocial development for all students (Conoley and Conoley 1991; Freeman and Pennekamp 1988; Gibson and Mitchell 1990; Holtzman 1992). Mental health interventions that address specific emotional and/or behavioral concerns have been found to have a positive impact on the academic functioning of students. For example, Kennedy and Doepke (1999) found that the anxiety level of students decreased significantly and the academic performance increased significantly when the student participated in relaxation training and cognitive-behavioral treatment interventions. Additionally, Pelham and Gnagy (1999) found that behavioral treatments were effective in improving the behavior and academic achievement of children with Attention Deficit/Hyperactivity Disorder (currently the most common mental health disorder of childhood).

In addition to addressing specific mental health concerns, interventions can be designed to address the psychosocial development of all children. Research demonstrates that emotional well-being is positively associated with academic success and, in turn, positive beliefs about success (e.g., effort and hard work) contribute to children's sense that they are competent and school is valuable. These positive beliefs lead to feelings of pride, self-esteem, and enjoyment of learning (Covington 1992; Deci and Ryan 1985; Weiner 1986).

Children's positive experiences in school contribute to their healthy development and have the capacity to increase competencies associated with learning and achievement motivation, emotional functioning, social relationships, and, in some instances, can address difficulties in these aspects of functioning (Roeser and Eccles 2000). Research on risk and protective factors that influence academic achievement point to processes that protect against adversity and support healthy development and learning.

Interventions to Improve Social Climate and Youth Development

Urban youth particularly place security as the first requirement for a desirable youth program (McLaughlin 2000). DuBois and colleagues (1994) found an association between high levels of school support and student outcomes (better grades and lower alcohol use) only for youth with multiple disadvantages, such as living in poverty and experiencing family breakup. This relationship was not found for youth without disadvantages. In a 16-year longitudinal study of school adaptation and social development, Cairns and Cairns (1994) found that engagement in extracurricular activities reduced health-compromising behaviors, particularly for students at the greatest risk for dropping out.

In addition to advocating improved methods of teaching, the evaluation literature suggests that extracurricular programs can enhance healthy development, for example, by encouraging a strong commitment and connection to school. This connection typically occurs indirectly through program staff's expectations for youth achievement, as well as directly through homework assistance or staff contact with participants, teachers, and school personnel (Roth et al. 1998). Additionally, successful programs offer youth the opportunity to develop academic skills through active participation in structured activities that create challenges and provide fulfilling experiences (McLaughlin 2000).

Healthy home and community environments also contribute to the academic success of children. In a review of numerous studies conducted in 1993, Wang, Haertel, and Walberg pointed to the range of contextual influences that can serve as protective factors to mitigate against negative life circumstances while facilitating development and educational resilience. According to their analysis, the factors exerting the most influence on school learning include psychological variables (i.e., cognition, motivation, and affect), instructional (i.e., instructional techniques, classroom management strategies, and teacher-student social interactions), and home environment.

In short, the research studies demonstrate that interventions that improve health, mental health, or social climate have positive effects on academic outcomes. The combined research findings suggest that family, community, and school contexts play key roles in fostering healthy development and educational achievement. While considerable attention has been focused on preventions and interventions in the context of both family and community, schools have only recently come to be viewed as sites where traditional prevention and intervention activities can be deepened, expanded, and ultimately integrated with efforts across families and communities.

THE HISTORY OF SCHOOLS AS A CONTEXT FOR SUPPORTING HEALTHY DEVELOPMENT

The research and theory pointing to the links between health and learning suggest that schools have a key role to play in helping to ensure that students are healthy. The appropriateness of the school context for prevention and intervention efforts is further supported by the position of schools in the community. In the next section, we review the history of student supports in schools as well as the reasons that schools are currently considered an ideal context for providing interventions on behalf of schoolchildren and their families. A more detailed chronology of the history of student support services is provided in chapter two of this volume.

Over the past 100 years, schools in varying ways and to varying degrees, have sought to provide opportunities for students to have some degree of access to medical care, proper nutrition, physical activity, and mental health counseling. In the early part of this century, schools struggled to lessen, or at least manage, the impact of negative health-related conditions on student learning by providing some essential services, such as medical or dental examinations, school lunches, and recreational activities (Tyack 1992). However, in later decades, government policies and community-based agencies began to play a larger role in responding to some of these needs particularly through entitlement programs for health care (e.g., Medicaid) and nutrition (e.g., food stamps, Women, Infants, and Children [WIC]). Gradually, school doctors became less visible in schools and treated children in local clinics and medical practices. Local community health centers and private health care providers assumed a larger role in addressing the ongoing physical needs of schoolchildren (e.g., health, dental, and nutritional). Consequently, school-based health care professionals, in particular, school nurses, were able to focus on acute and preventive services (e.g., screening for childhood medical problems such as scoliosis, vision, learning deficits, and immunizations).

As schools became less essential in addressing the long-term medical needs of children, they increasingly directed their service efforts to children's social and psychological needs. These efforts, along with the specialized needs of some children, gave rise to the school-related practices that were developed by a number of professions, such as school counseling, school psychology, school adjustment counseling, and school social work (Baker 2000; Brabeck et al. 1997; Gibelman and Schervish 1995; Short and Talley 1997).

However, in the past 20 years, as federal and local budgets tightened, schools have struggled to meet the health needs of children as all school-based health services have become more limited in scope and availability. These services were further limited in the last 10 years with the advent of educational reform—a national effort to improve academic outcomes. Educational reform efforts targeted school's fiscal resources almost exclusively to teaching and learning activities, leaving only a slim portion of the budget for services that ensure healthy students. This laser-like focus on academic achievement led to a decrease in the number and availability of the already limited health-related services for school-aged children and adolescents (Walsh et al. 2002)

Recently, however, there has been a recognition of the importance of support services. The nation's inability to substantially narrow the achievement gap is a glaring example of the need for more services. Recognition of a large number of new morbidities in the young population has led a number of social service providers and policymakers to recognize the potential for schools to provide a natural setting for support services and resources to be effectively delivered to children and youth for a number of reasons.

Policymakers at both national and local levels are increasingly aware that "if schools do not deal with children's health by design, they deal with it by default" (McKenzie and Richmond 1998; Marx, Wooley, and

Northrup 1998). This realization has lead to a rediscovery of sorts of the potential for linking schools and health with the goal of creating positive learning environments for children.

Schools are increasingly being recognized as excellent settings in which to deliver specific prevention and intervention programs (Kolbe, Collins, and Cortese 1997). Schools are usually the only institution in the community that have contact with every family that has children between the ages of 5 and 18. Additionally, schools are often the place in which any barriers that may impede children's learning often emerge and are identified. Schools are often located in the center of the community and are easily accessible not just to children but also to families and other community members. They are efficient and cost-effective sites for programs and interventions designed to promote developmental competence. These services, delivered during the school day, can create a one-stop setting for all child-serving agencies and can maximize the services' impact on learning. The centrality of schools in the lives of children make them the ideal center for a comprehensive community-based system of care. Schools also provide accessible portals of entry, which are nonstigmatizing, and a naturalistic setting in which to observe behavior and integrate interventions into a child's environment (Pumariega and Vance 1999).

However, school-based programs have often been difficult to implement and sustain (Dryfoos 1994; U.S. Department of Education 1995). Schools have not always been able to support these programs on a long-term basis. Educational reform efforts, with their intense focus on instruction, leave little energy and funding for programs that address barriers to learning. Short-term external funding typically supports the initial stages of various nonacademic programs. However, these programs do not have an opportunity to become institutionalized before the external funds have dried up. To enhance the effectiveness and longevity of such interventions, they must be quickly integrated more fully into the educational process.

At the same time that schools are being recognized as critical sites for prevention and intervention programs to enhance development, society is also acknowledging that schools cannot do it alone (Riley 1998). Teachers cannot also be social workers, nurses, lawyers, or psychologists. The community has a vital role to play offering a wide range of services and resources to children and families. While schools can provide a limited range of services and resources to students, they need assistance to address the wide range of issues that prevent some students from achieving at high levels. Community agencies and institutions offer many services that will support and enhance the development of children. In addition to supplementing services offered by schools—such as mental health, health care, and afterschool programs—community agencies are likely to offer services and resources that are typically not available in the school (e.g., legal assistance for youth and families, more intensive medical care, and government-based social services). Collaborative arrangements between schools and community agencies and resources can help to deliver needed support to schoolchildren and their families.

Well-designed systems of prevention and intervention programs will address long-term costs including personal suffering, unemployment, and poverty, as well as social costs such as lost productivity and increased burdens on the criminal justice, social welfare, and health care systems (Carnegie Council on Adolescent Development 1995; Cowen 1991). These collaborative arrangements, which have existed on an ad hoc, individual basis, are now beginning to be designed in a more systemic manner.

In the face of calls for altered approaches that address the multiple challenges confronting school-aged children, it is important to review the current state of school programs that promote healthy development. These existing programs will constitute the foundation for a transformation to new approaches in comprehensive school health. The following section will examine various aspects of student health services, sometimes referred to as "student support," in school districts around the country. We will draw attention particularly to the range of practices evident across these school districts and note the ways in which they are moving toward the newer effective practices in comprehensive school health.

IMPORTANT DIMENSIONS OF A SCHOOL HEALTH PROGRAM

Currently, in school districts nationwide, there is significant variability in student health practices both across and within districts. There is not a uniform or standard manner in which schools and school districts deliver health services to students. The differences in health programs across schools and school districts revolve around a number of issues. These issues include the use of a conceptual framework to ground the program, the breadth of the program's goals, the degree of connection to the community, the emphasis on prevention/intervention services, the extent of service fragmentation/coordination, the degree of collaboration across professions, and the evaluation of the program. As we consider these differences, we will describe current practices as well as point to some of the newer practices in contemporary school health programs.

Conceptual Framework

In many school districts, school health programs are premised on a traditional definition of health, usually a narrow definition of health encompassing only health education and/or mental health services. Many, if not most, school health programs are not organized on the basis of a particular conceptual framework or model. Rather they are organized around a traditional definition of health. By contrast, "effective practice" school health programs are typically grounded in a rationale or conceptual framework that provides an organizing principle as well as a set of goals to guide the development and implementation of the health program. While a number of conceptual models have been proposed in the literature, the most widely used conceptual framework for comprehensive school health is the "coordinated school health" model. In 1995, the Centers for Disease Control and Prevention (CDC), the federal agency that addresses public health issues in the United States, offered a new way to think about school supports for healthy development. To convey their belief that student health should be an integrated effort within school systems, the CDC, in particular Allensworth and Kolbe (1987), first used the term "comprehensive school health." As the concept became further defined, particularly by Marx, Wooley, and Northrup (1998), it was referred to as "coordinated" school health. The CDC identified eight major components they considered critical to a coordinated or comprehensive program of school health. A description of these components follows.

Health education. Classroom instruction that addresses the physical, mental, emotional, and social dimensions of health; develops health knowledge, attitudes, and skills; and is tailored to each age level. Designed to motivate and assist students to maintain and improve their health, prevent disease, and reduce health-related risk behaviors.

Physical education. Planned, sequential instruction that promotes lifelong physical activity. Designed to develop basic movement skills, sports skills, and physical fitness as well as to enhance mental, social, and emotional abilities.

Health services. Preventive services, education, emergency care, referral, and management of acute and chronic health conditions. Designed to promote the health of students, identify and prevent health problems and injuries, and ensure care for students.

Nutrition services. Integrates nutritious, affordable, and appealing meals; nutrition education; and an environment that promotes healthy eating behaviors for all children. Designed to maximize each child's education and health potential for a lifetime.

Counseling, psychological, and social services. Activities that focus on cognitive, emotional, behavioral, and social needs of individuals, groups, and families. Designed to prevent and address problems, facilitate positive learning and healthy behavior, and enhance healthy development.

Healthy school environment. The physical, emotional, and social climate of the school. Designed to provide a safe physical plant, as well as a healthy and supportive environment that fosters learning.

Health promotion for staff. Assessment, education, and fitness activities for school faculty and staff. Designed to maintain and improve the health and well-being of school staff, who serve as role models for students.

Parent/community involvement. Partnerships among schools, families, community groups, and individuals. Designed to share and maximize resources and expertise in addressing the healthy development of children, youth, and their families.

These eight components can serve as a conceptual framework for school districts that are reorganizing or redesigning student health services. They are consistent with recent national reports on healthy development, including *Education Goals 2000* and *Healthy People 2010*.

Goals of Student Support Services

All school health programs are directed in some way toward improving the academic achievement of students. Some districts limit the goals of their student support program so that they exclusively attend to the academic needs of students. Consequently, they are more likely to offer services that are directly related to learning, (e.g., special education or programs that address the classroom behavior of students who act in ways that prevent them or their classmates from learning). In these districts, the supports that might be offered to such students typically fall into the realm of specialized teaching strategies or behavior management (e.g., classroom-based behavior management programs, parent consultation to request their help in changing the student's behavior, or mental health counseling to address the causes and/or consequences of the inappropriate behavior). Districts that attend solely to improving academic achievement provide only very basic and essential services on the assumption that more extensive services are the responsibility of the family or community. These school districts consider a concern for the broader aspects of development—physical, social, emotional, among others—as diverting school staff from their central educative mission. These schools and/or school districts believe that most nonacademic needs are better met in nonacademic settings, (e.g., hospitals, clinics, or mental health centers).

However, school districts are beginning to subscribe to a broader set of goals for their student health services. They view their responsibility not only as improving academic achievement but also as enhancing the wider life chances of students. In the face of serious challenges to teaching and learning, many schools now realize that they have no choice but to address a wide range of nonacademic needs precisely because these needs constitute a serious impediment to the primary educational mission of the school (Adelman 1996). From this perspective, the goal of school health services is to contribute to the well-being of the student.

These school districts are becoming more cognizant of a broader purpose, that is, to educate tomorrow's citizens, not just today's children (Harkavy 1999). There is an increasing awareness that children who can read but are unable to make positive moral choices have not been truly educated. The school's recognition of their role in supporting the development of the whole child emerges from society's growing concern about the ability of tomorrow's citizens to continue building and maintaining a democracy. When the bonds that bind family and community have eroded, the process of value instruction, or educating children about positive behavior, is jeopardized (McLaughlin, Irby, and Laughman 1994).

From the perspective of these districts, learning to solve problems of living goes hand in hand with learning to solve equations. Many schools are now recognizing that educating children and youth for democracy requires schools to attend to more than just cognitive mastery. School districts that subscribe to the broader goal of producing educated citizens are more likely to have more comprehensive student health programs that address a wider array of student needs, including health, social service, youth development, and out-of-school-time programs. Some also extend offerings to families, (e.g., ESL (English as a Second Language) and/or literacy classes).

Community-School Partnerships

The degree to which student health programs in schools are connected to community agencies and resources also varies widely from one school district to another. Some schools provide services using only school-based professionals. While they occasionally, or even frequently, refer students or their families to community agencies, they typically have few formal or informal connections to these agencies and little if any interaction with the providers who work in the agencies.

As schools move toward newer and more effective practices in student health, they are beginning to forge strong links with the community. To support these connections, school-community partnerships have been implemented using many different models. These models can usually be categorized as either a school-linked partnership or a school-based partnership. School-linked models of student health are defined as programs that have developed and implemented formal, collaborative arrangements with a number of community agencies, including local hospitals, community mental health centers, and community recreation centers. Their regular contact typically follows a child from referral through follow-up. Using formal agreements and memoranda, school student support staff work collaboratively with community agency personnel to design and deliver effective prevention and intervention programs to students and their families.

School-based models of prevention and intervention allow for deeper and more complex relationships with community agencies and resources. Schools implementing this model are known as "community schools," "community learning centers," or "full/extended services schools," and they function from the perspective of the school-in-relationship-to-the-community. They offer programs for students and community members before school, after school, and during evening hours. They offer a wide range of services both within the school building and through formal arrangements with community agencies.

Emphasis on Prevention and/or Intervention

Currently, in many school districts, the emphasis of school health programs is on providing intervention services for students in crisis or facing other ongoing problems. This heavy concentration on intervention has led to little time and few resources for efforts directed at the prevention of later psychosocial or health problems. The focus of many school health programs has primarily been on the remediation or rehabilitation of students with problems. This uneven devotion of time and resources to intervention programs parallels the relative emphasis in the broader fields of health and mental health.

By contrast, a small number of school districts are initiating a more preventive approach in an effort to enhance the development of strengths as well as to remediate deficits. A focus on helping children cope in spite of difficulties in their lives typically leads to the implementation of individual or large group psychoeducational programs directed at all the children in the school. These programs focus on various aspects of prevention, such as violence and substance abuse prevention, and on the development of social competence. Prevention programs are gradually becoming adopted in school districts around the country.

A focus on prevention has even led some school districts to reorganize the range of services and supports they offer to students (e.g., special education, pupil support, mental health, etc.). Many school districts committed to effective practices are beginning to unify their various services and, at the same time, offer a greater variety of services that support the growth and development of all children rather than addressing problems in only a few. These unified services are being categorized along a continuum of levels ranging from prevention to intervention. Adelman (2001) and others have identified a continuum of services ranging from less intensive to more intensive. At the least intensive level, prevention programs serve all children and are directed at reducing the number of severe and/or chronic problems that develop over time. At the next level of intensity, schools have systems in place for intervening as early after onset as possible with a limited number of children who need intervention. Finally, at the most intensive level, school districts need interventions in place to meet the needs of the small number of children who are presented with pervasive and chronic problems. Schools need this integrated and overlapping continuum of services to meet the differing needs of all students. Although this organizational perspective has been applied by Adelman (2001) to describe diversity in mental health services, it can be easily expanded to create an organizational framework for all the domains of comprehensive health. We will now examine this continuum of services in more detail.

Prevention

At the least intensive level of services, all children in the school setting are exposed to programs that decrease the likelihood of problems in later years. These systemic interventions for primary prevention are designed and implemented in ways that augment and link with what families and communities are already doing well. This ensures that interventions are in place that may eliminate and/or minimize factors that can contribute to psychosocial and health problems. Examples of these programs include general health education, drug and alcohol education, support for transitions, conflict resolution, parent involvement, public health and safety programs, prenatal care, immunizations, recreation and enrichment, and child abuse education.

Early-after-Onset Intervention

At the next level of intensity, programs are directed to a subset of children whose difficulties are identified early. Increasingly, school staff are able to identify problems and barriers that are interfering with development and learning. Often, school staff are the first to identify such issues. Once a problem has been identified, school staff can work with parents to identify resources and strategies to support the child before the difficulty worsens. Examples of intervening early after onset include pregnancy prevention, violence prevention, drop-out prevention, learning/behavior accommodations, work programs, early identification to treat health problems, monitoring health problems, short-term counseling, family support, shelter, food, clothing, and job programs.

Intensive Intervention

For a small number of children with serious problems, schools have long offered specialized learning environments to help them succeed. All schools currently provide special education services, but many schools also are expanding their interventions. For instance, schools are increasingly providing short-term and crisis intervention as well as developing well-coordinated referral systems with links to community resources. Examples of programs that schools might offer or provide referrals to are special education for children with learning disabilities, emotional disturbance, and other health impairments; emergency/crisis treatment; family preservation programs; long-term therapy; and hospitalization.

Comprehensive Programs

Many professions serving schoolchildren have begun to move in the direction of comprehensive health programs in contrast to discrete health-related activities. Comprehensive approaches to care ensure that the full range of a child's needs—educational, medical, psychological, social, recreational, and legal—are met. For example, guidance counselors made this shift as far back as the 1970s when the concept of "guidance for development" emerged. Guidance counselors were encouraged to shift the focus of their work from day-to-day, crisis-oriented interventions to guidance activities conducted on a regular, planned, and systemic basis to assist students in achieving competencies (Gysbers and Henderson 2000). The primary thrust of this movement was the integration of guidance within the educational process. Although the immediate and crisis needs of students continued to be addressed, a major focus of the new guidance programs was to provide all students with experiences to help them grow and develop. Guidance programs, at this time, were thus expanded to include a comprehensive range of services, such as assessment, information, consultation, counseling, referral, placement, follow-up, and follow-through (Gysbers and Henderson 2000). A comprehensive guidance program also required the involvement of all school staff. School counselors were now expected not only to provide direct service but also to work in consultative and collaborative relations with other members of the guidance team as well as school staff, parents, and community members.

Coordination of Services

School districts differ in the degree to which student health services are interconnected with one another. Within some school districts, student support is understood as a set of various programs and activities falling within certain domains (e.g., mental health issues, health-related issues, and violence prevention). These activities and programs are not perceived to have any necessary relationship to one another and are not seen as falling under any larger umbrella. In short, student health is viewed as a collection of discrete programs and activities that address a wide range of nonacademic issues.

Among other school districts, however, there is now a growing understanding that piecemeal, competitive, or uncoordinated efforts to address the intertwined social, educational, psychological, and health needs of young people are counterproductive (McKenzie and Richmond 1998; Marx, Wooley, and Northrup 1998). These school districts have begun to recognize that the issues confronting children and youth are typically complex and cannot be addressed by a single service. For example, substance abuse interventions often involve various aspects of child development, such as health, mental health, and legal services. School health services that are coordinated and integrated have been shown to be more effective than the single-service approach, leading to better outcomes for students and families. Slowly, districts are becoming committed to a coherent model of student support that is comprehensive and built on an understanding of the child as a whole. Within such a model, all programs and activities are conceptually and operationally linked. These districts avoid the fragmentation of services evident in districts without a coherent model.

When services are delivered in a coordinated manner, students and families can avoid falling through the proverbial cracks. As an effective practice, coordination of services can occur at many levels. For example, various school- and community-based professionals may collaborate in developing an intervention for individual students. Similarly, prevention programs for all students can be designed to incorporate a number of services. Effective violence prevention, for instance, often requires educational, psychological, social, and health domains. Coordinated services are also more efficient and cost-effective because they avoid the unnecessary duplication of services and can reduce the number of providers involved with a particular family. In addition, the positive outcomes that are likely to result from a coordinated approach will reduce the need for additional services in the future.

Coordinated systems of care do not leave the child and family to determine the needs and seek various services on their own but, rather, help families to identify the needs, access the appropriate services, and integrate the recommendations and treatments suggested. Partnerships across schools and community agencies make the delivery of comprehensive, coordinated services more feasible. Reliance on a combination of both school and community resources ensures that a full range of needs—social, psychological, medical, and legal—are addressed. Spanning school and community boundaries allows for coordinated access to and delivery of services. Services can be either delivered at the school site or delivered at a community-based site.

Interprofessional Collaboration

Provision of comprehensive, coordinated student services requires new approaches by service providers. In the past, most human service, health, and other professionals have worked in a relatively isolated manner, and they typically have not collaborated with professionals from other fields. Physicians, for example, usually did not communicate with school counselors; teachers were not readily in touch with the community social workers. The resulting care was sometimes fragmented with students and families left to coordinate their own care and often falling between the cracks as they searched out the various services and resources.

It has been well established that children and families are better served by systems of care that are comprehensive and coordinated (Dryfoos 1994; Lerner 1995; Marx, Wooley, and Northup 1998; Schorr 1997). The complex issues facing today's children and families can rarely be effectively divided into neat discipline-shaped boxes. Conversely, in school districts where services are coordinated, staff from a wide range of professions collaborate regularly and effectively. While focused professional expertise is clearly warranted and valuable, the lack of collaboration across the professions has resulted in uncoordinated, fragmented, and disjointed service delivery (Brabeck et al. 1997; Lerner 1995; Schorr 1988; Walsh, Brabeck, and Howard 1999).

In contrast to this traditional isolated manner of providing services, collaborative delivery requires that providers from various professions—such as social work, nursing, counseling, and teaching—actively work with one another to ensure that the full range of the child's needs are addressed. Collaboration across professions is now explicitly advocated by every major professional organization, including the American Academy of Pediatrics, the American Association for Counseling and Development, the American School Counselor Association, the National Association of School Psychologists, the National Association of Social Workers, the American Bar Association, the American Psychological Association, and the National Association of School Nurses. Interprofessional collaboration is an effective practice that is critical to adequately addressing the issues confronting children and families in today's society (Brabeck et al. 1997; Walsh, Brabeck, and Howard 1999; Walsh and Park-Taylor 2003).

Assurance of Quality and Effectiveness of Interventions

However, in recent years, with the advent of national curriculum standards, schools have become more results oriented. They recognize that effective practices in prevention and intervention presume evidence of effectiveness in the form of sound empirical research. Research is now readily available to document the empirical effectiveness of a wide range of prevention and intervention programs that address barriers to learning. This research can assist school districts in selecting effective programs. Many federal agencies that provide funding to school districts require schools to utilize research-based curricula programs (Greenberg, Domitrovich, and Bumbarger 2001).

Effective practices in the delivery of student health services provide procedures to ensure that the service is delivered in accordance with the guidelines utilized in the research. These procedures also provide a basis for determining whether the services meet the standards of good practice for that particular field. Services delivered in a school health clinic, for example, should meet the standard of care required for all school-based clinical services. These standards are generally established by the appropriate governing professional organization. Regular monitoring of the services will allow providers to change and improve the services where necessary.

It is usually very helpful to have relevant stakeholders (e.g., youth, families, teachers, counselors, and social service providers) participate in monitoring quality. Quality assurance procedures review the policies, infrastructure, mechanisms, procedures, and personnel of the service delivery system. These procedures recommend improvements with respect to how well the various professionals who deliver services to students (e.g., counselors, nurses, and social workers) adhere to the ethical codes and standards of practice—that is, the system of principles and rules that guide professional behavior. Quality assurance procedures can also recommend improvements with respect to the settings in which the services are provided. Inappropriate settings (e.g., those that do not provide privacy) can result in negative outcomes for students. Finally, quality assurance procedures focus on the degree to which various interventions are known to make a positive difference.

Upon reviewing the various dimensions of current practices in student health or student support programs from across the country, there is extensive evidence of variability from district to district—and even from school to school. These programs use different conceptual frameworks, have different goals, place different emphases on prevention and intervention, and coordinate services to varying degrees. However, regardless of where school districts across the country currently find themselves, increasing numbers are moving in the direction of more comprehensive and coordinated services. We will now review the range of ways that health services for children and youth are delivered in and through the school district.

DELIVERY OF SERVICES

School health programs not only vary along the dimensions described above, but they also differ in the organization and structure of their service delivery. A wide variety of service delivery systems for school health programs are evident in school districts across the country. Adelman (2001) delineates five major delivery systems that are being used by schools to provide mental health services. These categories of service delivery mechanisms can be extended to describe the organization of health-related services more generally. Each of these mechanisms varies in three important ways: (1) how the system operates, (2) the focus of the school health program, and (3) the level of comprehension and coordination of the services. These service delivery mechanisms can be generally grouped into five different types: (1) school-financed student support services; (2) school-district health unit; (3) formal connections with community support and youth development services; (4) classroom-based curriculum and special pull-out interventions; and (5) comprehensive, multifaceted, and coordinated approaches. In the following sections each of these five approaches is described in more detail.

School-Financed Student Support Services

This approach primarily entails school districts employing student support professionals, such as psychologists, counselors, social workers, nurses, and family support personnel. These service professionals, employed by the school district and working primarily in the school, focus on delivering or arranging for direct services (including services targeted for special education students) as well as on developing and implementing targeted programs (e.g., substance abuse or violence prevention). This type of school health program usually is a combination of school-based services and districtwide services.

Examples of this type of service delivery mechanism can be found in school districts across the nation. Most school districts distribute their student support personnel on a part-time basis to multiple schools. For example, a school counselor might be responsible for the students in three schools within a given district. Some schools rearrange their funding streams, using Title I funds or other special project grants to allow for the hiring of additional staff. Under this type of organizational structure, support services staff maintain fairly traditional roles and functions within the boundaries of their discipline of training. Often, the result of this type of service delivery system is a significant amount of fragmentation of services.

In contrast, some school districts have attempted to alter the way in which student support service staff are allocated to schools. For example, the Denver Public Schools have designed a new way to allocate support staff to the school in which the schools have a substantial amount of say regarding their needs and the most effective combination of support staff (e.g., nurses, social workers, psychologists, etc.). This process involves detailing skills that could be carried out by any staff member. Then, on an individual basis, schools can decide on the best combination of support staff based on the needs of their school community rather than being confined to the guidelines set by the district.

School-District Health Unit

Some school districts have chosen to develop districtwide school health units designed to offer a range of health services to children and families attending school within the district. These health units typically include clinic facilities, as well as service programs and consultation to schools. Other school districts have started financing their own school-based health clinics, offering a range of health and mental health services within a school building. The organization of health services in most schools districts tends to be by profession (e.g., school psychology, nursing, and counseling). In a few instances, districts have set up multi-disciplinary units that operate from centralized locations and provide intensive interventions for students and families to address a range of psychosocial concerns.

The Memphis City School District has developed a unit to integrate mental health services within its schools. The staff are mostly school psychologists and social workers organized into teams. The unit provides a variety of clinical and consultation mental health services in support of school programs. There are three satellite mental health center housing staff who rotate through each school in the district on a regular basis. Their primary functions are to offer psychological evaluations, counseling/therapy, abused/neglected children's services, alcohol and drug abuse services, school-based prevention efforts, homemaker services, staff development, parent study groups, a speaker's bureau, and compliance/reporting/record keeping.

Formal Connections with Community Support and Youth Development Services

This type of school health program focuses on developing connections with community agencies. This school-community collaboration can take a variety of forms. Some programs co-locate community agency personnel and services at schools—sometimes in the context of school-based health clinics partly financed by community health organizations. Other programs link schools with agencies to enhance access and service coordination for students and families at the agency, at a nearby satellite clinic, or in a school-based or -linked family resource center. Still other health programs have created formal partnerships between a school district and community agencies to establish or expand school-based or -linked facilities that include the provision of health services. Finally, some schools have created contracts with community providers to provide needed student services. These delivery systems attempt to increase the number and variety of services available to students and to enhance coordination among services for students and their families.

Baltimore offers one example of a school system that has approached the delivery of student health services in this manner. The Baltimore School-Based Health Centers work with the Baltimore Mental Health Systems, an independent local mental health agency, to integrate mental health care into school-based health centers that are under the state's managed care plan. In some of the centers, the mental health component is part of a full-service school-based health center, in others, the mental health provider comes into the schools on a periodic basis to provide services.

Classroom-Based Curriculum and Special Pull-Out Interventions

Most schools include some classroom-based curricula that focus on enhancing health, social, and emotional functioning in their school programming. Specific instructional activities may be designed to promote healthy development and/or prevent physical or psychosocial problems, such as behavioral and emotional problems, school violence, teen pregnancy, and drug abuse. Additionally, special education classrooms are expected to have a constant focus on mental health and health concerns.

In some schools, this type of instruction is integrated as part of the regular classroom content and processes. In others, a specific curriculum or special intervention is implemented by personnel specially trained to carry out the processes. Some schools include this curriculum as part of a larger, more multifaceted set of interventions designed to enhance positive development and prevent problems.

One example of a classroom-based curricula approach is "Promoting Alternative Thinking Strategies" (PATHS). The PATHS curriculum was designed by Greenberg and Kusche (1998) and addresses self-control, feelings and relationships, and interpersonal problem solving in the classroom. Through structured lessons and reinforcement, children are taught problem solving skills and techniques. Children are encouraged to use these skills as problems arise throughout their day. The curriculum also focuses on emotional and interpersonal understanding. Children learn to recognize and monitor emotions in themselves and others.

Comprehensive, Multifaceted, and Coordinated Approaches

A few school districts have begun the process of reconceptualizing their piecemeal and fragmented approaches to addressing barriers that interfere with students having an equal opportunity to succeed at school. These districts are starting to restructure their student health programs to include community resources and to integrate these services into the academic world of the student with the goal of the child's overall healthy development. The intent is to develop a full continuum of programs and services encompassing efforts to promote positive development, prevent problems, respond as early after onset as is feasible, and offer treatment regimens. Health concerns are a major focus of the continuum of interventions. Efforts to move toward comprehensive, multifaceted approaches are likely to be enhanced by initiatives that aim to integrate schools more fully into systems of care and the growing movement to create community schools.

An example of this approach is the "Connect 5" initiative implemented in one geographical segment (known as Allston-Brighton/Mission Hill) of the Boston Public Schools—a segment known as "Cluster 5," which services approximately 5,500 schoolchildren. This initiative, a community-school-university partnership consisting of the Boston Public Schools (in Cluster 5), the local Young Men's Christian Association (YMCA), and Boston College, is working toward coordinating and integrating the delivery of student support services to elementary school-children —a vast number of whom face significant barriers to learning. The goals of the partnership are twofold. The first is to offer school students in the Allston-Brighton/Mission Hill communities access to a full range of student services and resources through an assessment of student needs, coordination of community-based service delivery, school-based support of students and teachers, design and implementation of professional development programming, and ongoing and longitudinal evaluation of the initiative and its individual components. The second goal is to build a strong infrastructure to manage and support the partnership among the participating elementary schools, community agencies, and university, and to ensure that project objectives are carefully defined, progress is systematically measured and evaluated, and accountability to funders and one another is achieved.

The structure of the Allston-Brighton/Mission Hill "Connect 5" project includes three interactive components: School-based Instructional Support Teams, a Cluster-wide Student and Family Instructional Support Center, and a Resource Coordinating Council. The School-based Instructional Support Team includes a coordinator, teachers, and other on-site and community-based professionals working in the schools, such as a nurse, educational psychologist, mental health clinician, and/or social worker. The Team provides instructional and behavioral consultation to classroom teachers and works to identify and meet the individual direct service needs of students and their families. The School-based Coordinator serves as the school's liaison to the centrally-based Student and Family Instructional Support Center. The Student and Family Instructional Support Center serves as the base for the Coordinators of the Center and the Health Educators, who work across the schools, and the Parent-Family Outreach Worker who works with schools to assist families in addressing issues that interfere with children's progress in school. This centrally located Center allows for the most efficient deployment of resources within the community. Finally, the Resource Coordinating Council advises and supports the Center Coordinator regarding existing and needed programs and services in the neighborhood that address barriers to learning and development. The Council also provides leadership and advocacy in the coordination, integration, and strengthening of student support services and in establishing links with community, city, state, and federal agencies.

The five types of service delivery systems described in this section broadly encompass the majority of service programs currently connected with schools in this country. These programs vary greatly from school to school and district to district. At the same time, newly developed methods of promoting student health are being designed and implemented. In the following section, we outline some of the most promising examples of programs in coordinated and comprehensive school health.

EXEMPLAR PROGRAMS IN COORDINATED, COMPREHENSIVE SCHOOL HEALTH

Over the years, researchers, service delivery professionals, teachers, and policymakers have been searching for answers to the complex problem of delivering a broad range of health services to children in a way that maximizes their chances for a successful future. As schools have moved to the center of this conversation, a variety of different programs have been developed and implemented across the country utilizing one or another conceptual model, various levels of service, and multiple service delivery systems. These programs have been developed at a variety of different levels ranging from statewide prevention and intervention efforts to individual classrooms that are implementing curricula. In the following section, we generally describe and provide examples of each of these types of implementation.

State-Based Designs

A number of school health programs are being implemented and designed on the state-based level. These programs have attempted to develop a coordinated, comprehensive system of service delivery across the state. These programs often range from prevention efforts to crisis intervention services and encompass health, mental health, education, legal, and afterschool enrichment programs.

The Comprehensive Student Support System (CSSS) is one example of a state-based school health program. Developed in the state of Hawaii, this program attempts to pull together resources from the classroom, school, neighborhood, and community to provide comprehensive social, emotional, and physical supports to students and their families (School Mental Health Project/Center for Mental Health in Schools 2001). The Hawaii State Superintendent of Education described the CSSS, which was implemented by the Hawaii School System, as a program designed on the premise that if schools succeed in providing support services in an efficient manner, the result will be a reduction in the number of students who require intensive services in the future.

CSSS has three overarching goals. The first goal is to provide students with a comprehensive, integrated, and customized system of support—delivered effectively and expediently—that promotes academic success and encourages healthy development. The second goal is to join families and the educational community in a collaborative effort to build a supportive and respectful learning environment. The third goal is to use financial resources from public and private sources to help build caring communities in the schools.

The CSSS program is designed on a five level continuum that encompasses a broad range of support services. The five levels include (1) basic support for all students, (2) informal additional support through collaboration, (3) individualized school- and community-based programs, (4) specialized services from the department of education and/or other agencies, and (5) intensive and multiple agency services (School Mental Health Project/Center for Mental Health in Schools 2001). By providing preventive services to all students, fewer students require the more intensive services offered at the higher levels. The system also provides a classification system for requests for student assistance. A core committee uses the levels system to designate the appropriate intervention to meet the needs of that student.

The first level of the continuum takes place in the classroom with differentiated classroom practices offered to students as a primary basis of support. Teachers link students to school and community resources, which serve as additional preventive supports. CSSS also works to link families to resources in the community, which helps unite the community and ensures that services are delivered effectively. Interventions in the school stress a caring approach that works to engage and re-engage the student after a disciplinary problem and to respond to such a problem with a collaborative approach that involves the teachers, support staff, parents, and community resources if applicable.

Realizing that the people who implement the program are critical to its success, the CSSS and the Hawaii School System have emphasized the thorough training of CSSS members. In August of 1999, the role of Student Services Coordinator was developed to help build and maintain student support systems in the schools. The State of Hawaii is currently working with the University of Hawaii and will soon be working with the Center for Mental Health in Schools at University of California, Los Angeles (UCLA) to develop training programs for the Student Services Coordinators. So far, those programs have included graduate courses at the University of Hawaii taught by instructors from the state's Department of Education, professors from the university, and parents from the "Families as Allies" program in Hawaii.

The infrastructure of the CSSS is built through such organizational leaders as a resource-oriented team, who ensures that funding and resources are being used effectively and that the program is cost-efficient. A site administrative leader, who can be a vice principal or other administrator, is responsible for the day-to-day implementation of the CSSS programs and interventions and also works with the resource team. Finally, the CSSS also has a complex school renewal specialist, who works with groups or families of schools within the system to broker resources and coordinate planning and professional development within a certain family of schools. Finally, a council is formed from members of the resource-based team to coordinate programs serving multiple schools, identify common problems, provide staff training, and link schools with community agencies, particularly those who do not have the staff or resources to contact individual schools.

The Hawaii Public Schools are still developing the CSSS and are trying to find the most comprehensive approach to affect change in the school system. The schools are currently working toward ensuring that students achieve the Hawaii Content and Performance Standards and the Expected Schoolwide Learning Results. The CSSS continues to work to ensure that each school in the system has a continuum of supports in place to enhance the ability of the classroom teacher and enable learning, promote home involvement in learning, support transitions that students or families experience, expand community involvement, and address concerns early and respond to crises when they arise (School Mental Health Project/Center for Mental Health in Schools 2001).

Many states, in addition to Hawaii, have now developed models of comprehensive, coordinated support services that reach across the boundaries of school districts and local and state agencies. Another example of a statewide school health program can be found in Kentucky. As part of the Kentucky Education Reform Act (KERA) of 1990, legislators laid the groundwork to deliver comprehensive and integrated services to children in schools. The centers that deliver these services are called Family Resource and Youth Service Centers. Today there are 560 centers serving 911 schools across the state of Kentucky. The centers are located at or near school sites, and provide various services according to the needs of the community in which they are established.

The Family Resource Centers cater their services to children under the age of 12 and to their families. These centers provide access to child care, parent support and training, parent and child education, and health screening and referrals. The Youth Service Centers offer services for children over the age of 12 and provide employment counseling, job training and placement, drug and alcohol abuse counseling, and family and mental health counseling. An advisory council, made up of local school and parent representatives, provides guidance and support for the various service providers who work with participating schools. The advisory council is responsible for conducting assessments, establishing policy guidelines, reviewing budgets, and planning for the future.

In addition to the services that the Family Resource Centers and the Youth Services Centers provide, the Kentucky school programs strengthen their ability to serve students and families through close collaboration with community agencies. Such agencies include juvenile and divorce courts, the YMCA, the local health department, businesses, and a university. By bringing in the resources of the community, the Kentucky schools aim to broaden the range of available services and help that would otherwise be impossible to fund given the limited budgets of the Family Resource and the Youth Services Centers.

The Kentucky legislature has approved these programs to help ensure that teachers in the classroom are not encumbered by the duties of a social worker in addition to their teaching responsibilities. This is accomplished by integrating programs and services into the schools such as counseling, home visits, a teen crisis line, parent lifeline, school-to-work transition programs, a health clinic, and classroom and community outreach (North Central Regional Educational Laboratory 2000). The following quote explains in greater detail how these services are implemented.

> Grants are given to secondary schools for Youth Service Centers to set up a designated room with a full-time coordinator to oversee referrals to community agencies for health and social services and to provide on-site counseling related to employment, substance abuse, and mental health. The program also supports Family Resource Centers in elementary schools, offering parenting education, after-school child care, and referral for parents to infant and child care, health services, and other community organizations. (Dryfoos 2000)

An evaluation conducted with 20 randomly selected schools in Kentucky revealed that teacher ratings of classroom performance had improved. However, the same evaluation indicated that classroom achievement improved only in the elementary schools (Illback, Kalafat, and Sanders 1997). These findings suggest that there does seem to be evidence that the Youth and Family Centers may indirectly affect school achievement and progress with at-risk youth, yet the centers are more successful at the elementary school level. The Youth and Family Centers are now seeking to improve their middle and high school level services.

A third example of a state-based school health program has been developed in the state of California. Beginning in 1991, Healthy Start grants were provided by the State Department of Education to local school systems and their collaborative partners to integrate child and family services. Grants are awarded to schools and their collaborative partners to create more child and family centered services systems, at or near school sites. The initiative is built around the premise that educational success, physical health, emotional support, and family strength are inseparable goals. A special emphasis is placed on improved school performance (Dryfoos 2000). Some of the services include academic services, youth development services, family support services, fulfillment of basic needs, medical/health care, mental health care and counseling, and employment resources and services (California Department of Education 2001).

In order that the above services can be delivered effectively, Healthy Start identifies key elements that must be in place. First, the facility needs to have adequate space and to be clean and comfortable so that it is a place where children want to come and spend time. Active, collaborative leadership is required to improve the Healthy Start program and representation should include the schools, children and their families, private business, and community organizations. The utilization of community and private resources should be committed to the long-term support of children and families. Healthy Start programs should involve administrative staff, student support staff, and teachers. Additionally, these programs should incorporate continuous evaluation and dissemination of relevant community outcomes (California Department of Education 2001).

An evaluation of this program indicated that student behavior, academic performance, and the climate of the school all showed improvement in the Healthy Start Schools. A 1997 evaluation showed an increase in students' self-esteem and perception of support, and a decrease in student drug use. An improvement in elementary school classroom behavior was also evident. Students' test scores for the lowest quartile in Healthy Start Schools increased by 25 percent for reading and 50 percent for math. Healthy Start Schools were also able to reduce half of the number of unmet needs that families had in terms of being able to access goods and services. There was also an increase in addressing students' health needs, an increase in parents' awareness about child development, and a decrease in the occurrence of domestic violence (California Department of Education 2001).

The fourth example of a state-based school health program is in the state of Missouri. This program started in 1989 and was established from a "belief that children's ultimate success in school—and in life—cannot be separated from the critical out-of-school factors that affect their lives" (Missouri Department of Elementary and Secondary Education 2001). Caring Communities is a partnership among state agencies, local communities, and schools designed to help enrich the lives of children and families. Community and school leaders define the priorities and agendas of the program based on the individual community's needs, assets, and vision. The state of Missouri helps by providing financial and technical assistance, working to remove bureaucratic barriers, encouraging innovative ideas, and promoting broad participation in Caring Communities activities (Missouri Department of Elementary and Secondary Education 2001).

Caring Communities outlines six goals: (1) parents working; (2) healthy children and families; (3) children safe in their families, and families safe in their communities; (4) children prepared to enter school; (5) children and youth succeeding in school; and (6) youth ready to enter productive adulthood (Missouri Department of Elementary and Secondary Education 2001).

For Caring Communities to achieve the above goals, they identify four key policies. First, Caring Communities works toward being accountable for achieving results in the areas outlined above. Caring Communities has established benchmarks that are reported annually so the program is accountable to the public. Caring Communities also strives to bring the services as close as possible to where the children and families live and go to school. Once the services are in place, Caring Communities stays active in decision making within the community. Finally, Caring Communities also works to establish flexible funds for the community to meet its needs (Family and Community Trust 2001).

Philliber Research Associates (1994) conducted a study with 62 of the neighborhoods that received Caring Community grants. This study found that, between the years of 1996 and 1998, instances of child abuse or neglect dropped by 15 percent. This rate was compared with the 10 percent decline that was found in other communities in the state of Missouri. Increases in math and reading scores were found in the 62 schools, as well as a decline in suspensions, drop-out rates, and teen pregnancy.

Districtwide Models

Districtwide models of comprehensive, coordinated services provide an integrated array of services and resources on a smaller scale than the statewide efforts. Because the geographical boundaries of these efforts are identical to that of the school district, there is substantial opportunity and motivation to coordinate services across school and community boundaries.

Unified Student Services in Boston Public Schools

In 1999, the Boston Public Schools (BPS) combined the Special Education Department and the Student Support Services Department to form the Unified Student Services Team. This move was designed to better support the reforms that are being sought in the BPS. The primary goal of the BPS is to "improve teaching and learning to enable all students to achieve high standards of performance" (National Institute for Urban School Improvement 2001). The BPS identified ancillary goals to help realize the primary goal. The ideas and themes in the ancillary goals include providing safe and supportive schools, and working and communicating with the parents and communities toward school improvement.

The BPS found that many of the goals toward which student services were working were not always aligned with district goals. Also, teachers complained that they often were not aware of the extent of nonacademic services that a student was receiving and were also unaware whether the goals of those services matched the student's classroom goals. The Unified Student Services Team was created to address some of these problems to better meet the goals of the BPS.

The BPS identify three guiding principles for the scope of the work of the Unified Student Services Team. The first principle indicates that schools alone cannot address all the needs students bring to the classroom door. The district must consider student needs and determine what supports the system can realistically provide to enhance teaching and learning and to accelerate student achievement. The second principle suggests that models of effective practice must be identified to guide delivery of services provided by individual schools. Finally, the third principle indicates that services, which can best be provided by community-based organizations and other partners, must be aligned and connected to the schools' work (National Institute for Urban School Improvement 2001).

To implement this plan, the BPS identified four areas of strategic action: direct services, indirect services, crisis services, and prevention services. Direct services are meant to encompass those services that are provided to students in the schools by both BPS staff and outside providers. One goal was to increase the amount of services provided in the schools to reduce the number of students who had to be referred to outside placements because of inadequate services in the BPS. Indirect services address support services that the students receive outside of school. Efforts are being made for stronger partnerships with the community agencies and with the schools. Lack of communication between schools and mental health agencies and other support services in the community is also identified as a significant concern, by teachers and external agencies alike. Crisis services are meant to address crisis needs of students in schools. The BPS work with the Boston Emergency Services Team (BEST) to respond to acute crises. Also, the Department of Mental Health has awarded a grant to BPS to train teachers on how to respond in crisis situations. Finally, prevention services are designed to address health issues, particularly how they affect the student in the classroom (National Institute for Urban School Improvement 2001).

Hartford Public Schools

The Division of Student Support Services in the Hartford Public Schools (HPS) aspires to "engage the family and students in a positive, problem-solving process that facilitates the utilization of internal and external resources for the benefit and ultimate success of each student" (Hartford Public Schools 2001). Student Support Services in HPS take a case management approach to providing for the nonacademic and developmental needs of the students, while also supporting the teaching and learning that takes place in the classroom.

Student Support Services is partnered with more than 29 nonprofit organizations in the Hartford area and uses these supports to conduct activities such as summer programs. The goal of this collaboration is to increase student achievement in the classroom while at the same time serving as a support to the students and their families. The Student Services Division provides programs such as extended day and extended year programs, parental education and family resource centers, and community projects such as "Yo Hartford!" which is funded by the Department of Labor and works to provide job training and education for students (Hartford Public Schools 2001).

Aside from programs such as the ones outlined above, the Student Services Division attends to issues such as school climate and character education. The Student Services Division also includes special education in the HPS and the pupil personnel services, which provide occupational therapy, speech and language therapy, psychological services, and social work services. To bolster the work of the student services, HPS also includes programs in which parents can become involved such as the Office of Parent Involvement and the Parent Help Desk. These programs are designed to link parents with schools and community resources, provide an opportunity for parents to become involved in the schools, provide parents with support services, and provide a voice for parents in the HPS (Hartford Public Schools 2001).

Finally, HPS has outlined five initiatives to target in terms of their Student Services Division. The first, attendance, aims to reduce truancy and dropouts and to create a comprehensive system for parental notification and increased school staff vigilance when a student is truant. Guidance is the next area that has been targeted by HPS, based on a developmental approach. Through training programs and professional development, a shift in the philosophy of the guidance department is being made from working with individuals to working with all students through group activities. A guidance curriculum has been developed that stresses prevention and a systematic approach to addressing student needs (Hartford Public Schools 2001).

Multicultural programs and activities have also been targeted as an initiative for the HPS. These programs focus on bringing students from different cultures together through parades, music, and art programs as well as history lessons. HPS have also targeted health education as an initiative and have been successful in assigning a health education teacher to every school for a minimum of one day per week. The curriculum is being formatted to compact disc-read only memory (CD-ROM), thereby giving educators the opportunity to integrate the computer and the Internet into lesson plans. High school students also have a chance to get involved with the Postponing Sexual Involvement (PSI) program, which affords them the opportunity to present five classroom activities to students in fifth grade about postponing sexual involvement. The final initiative targeted by HPS is a uniform discipline code that is designed to provide a systematic response to disciplinary violations with consistent consequences from pre-kindergarten to twelfth grade (Hartford Public Schools 2001).

Los Angeles Unified School District

A few years ago, the Los Angeles Unified School District (LAUSD) originated a Strategic Plan for Restructuring of Student Health and Human Services. The objectives of this project were (1) to increase the effectiveness and efficacy in providing learning supports to students and their families and (2) to enhance partnerships among parents, schools, and community-based efforts to improve outcomes for children. At the core of this plan was the major restructuring of school-owned student services in order to develop a comprehensive, multifaceted, and integrated Learning Supports component, which addressed barriers to learning. The key components of this effort are the school-based resource team and a cluster coordinating council, which focus on identifying resources and effectively accessing them. To facilitate this restructuring plan, a group of change agents called Organizational Facilitators was developed. This group's role was to assist each school in establishing a school infrastructure and reorganizing the individual schools into clusters to facilitate resource use and integrate community and school resources.

The LAUSD also offers various support services to parents. In addition to providing valuable resources on the World Wide Web and in print, parents can also access a homework help center on the LAUSD Web site. This link provides study tips, an on-line dictionary, help with specific subject areas, and access to maps and atlases (Los Angeles Unified School District 2001).

School-Based Models

There are multiple on-the-ground models of comprehensive student support programs. Most of these programs have been located in traditional public schools that have been transformed in order to support children's learning. Alternatively referred to as "community schools" or "full/extended services schools," these schools integrate academic programs with a full range of nonacademic services for children and families.

A community or a full-service school is usually defined as a school that operates in a public school building and that is open to students, families, and the community before, during, and after school, seven days a week, all year long. It is jointly operated through a partnership between the school system and one or more community agencies. Families, youth, principals, teachers, and neighborhood residents help design and implement activities that promote high educational achievement and positive youth development. The school is oriented toward the community, encouraging student learning through community service and service learning. A before- and afterschool learning component encourages students to build on their classroom experiences, expand their horizons, contribute to their communities, and have fun. A family support unit is designed to help families with child rearing, employment, housing, immigration, and other services. Medical, dental, and mental health services are usually available. College faculty and students, business people, youth workers, neighborhoods, and family members come to support and bolster what schools are working hard to accomplish—ensuring young people's academic, interpersonal, and career success. A version of these types of schools was described in the early 1990s by Joy Dryfoos— a sociologist and policy advocate—in a book entitled *Full-Service Schools* (Dryfoos 1994). Modified versions of full-service schools that offer a more limited number of services are called extended services schools. The Coalition for Community Schools, an organization that supports and promotes the transformation of schools into community schools, has termed these types of schools as "both a set of partnerships and a place where services, supports and opportunities lead to improved student learning, stronger families and healthier communities" (Coalition for Community Schools 2000).

While each model is unique, they share a common feature insofar as their programs are offered at school buildings through partnerships of a school district and a community-based or youth-serving organization, or a university. School buildings that otherwise would stand empty mornings, evenings, on weekends, and during summers are used to deliver much needed educational enrichment and recreational services to families in low-income neighborhoods—thereby getting a greater public good from a substantial, yet underused, public investment. Schools are in familiar locations where children and young people can easily transition from school-day to afterschool activities. They are regarded as safe and, although many communities face transportation challenges, schools are still usually accessible by walking or by public transportation. There are many models of community schools. Some of the leading models are described below.

Comer Schools

In New Haven, Connecticut, in 1968, James P. Comer, a child psychiatrist at Yale University, created a School Development Program (SDP), also known as the Comer Process. SDP aims to create learning environments that support the physical, cognitive, psychological, verbal, social, and moral development of children. SDP's mission is carried out with the help of adult caretakers, who come together to support and enhance students' development and academic success. The support team includes teachers, administrators, counselors, school staff, parents, and community members.

According to Haynes and Comer, "The SDP is conceived as a school-based intervention for realizing positive growth among students and staff through organizational and climate changes" (1996). This program recognizes that many children come to school lacking the developmental support from home that is necessary to achieve in the classroom. Although these children are deficient in their development, they are still expected to perform in schools and the SDP is designed to provide developmental support to help students achieve academic success (Yale University Bush Center in Child Development and Social Policy 2002). The SDP is structured so as to integrate mental health approaches into the schools and to fundamentally change the relationships among teachers, principals, supports staff, and students (Dryfoos 2000).

Over the years, James Comer has developed a nine-part process to improve educators' understanding of child development and to foster healthier relations between schools and homes. This nine-part process includes three mechanisms (i.e., School Planning and Management Team, Student and Staff Support Team, and Parent Team), three operations (i.e., Comprehensive School Plan, Staff Development Plan, and Monitoring and Assessment), and three guiding principles (i.e., No-Fault Approach to Problem-Solving, Consensus Decision Making, and Collaboration). James Comer and his staff emphasize that, for the SDP to be effective, a full-time program facilitator is needed to work individually with all of the schools in the district (Dryfoos 2000).

Studies of Comer Schools indicate that the program contributes to positive effects in school climate, student attendance, and student achievement. Comparative studies of Comer and non-Comer schools also reveal an improvement in student self-confidence, self-concept, and achievement for Comer students. Recently, the report from the Council of Great City Schools, titled "Beating the Odds: A City-by-City Analysis of the Student Performance and Achievement Gaps on State Assessments," heralded the Charlotte-Mecklenburg district, which has used the Comer system for a decade, for raising math scores in third through eighth grades and for closing gaps in achievement between white students and students of color (Yale University Bush Center in Child Development and Social Policy 2002).

Schools of the 21st Century (21C)

Edward Zigler, a psychologist for the Bush Center for Child Development at Yale University and one of the principle founders of the nation's Head Start program, developed a concept called Schools of the 21st Century (21C). In designing this program, Dr. Zigler took into consideration the concerns and challenges families face in modern society. Of primary importance, he saw a need for affordable and quality child care; addressing this need became the cornerstone of 21C. The program provides all day, year-round child care to preschoolers, and before- and afterschool and vacation care for school-age children. Additionally, 21C offers support services, such as health education and health care, family referrals, and guidance for parents of young children from the third trimester of pregnancy to age three (Deemer, Desimone, and Finn-Stevenson 1998). The program's aim is to help children arrive at school prepared to learn and ensure that they receive the necessary support throughout the day. The first School of the 21st Century was launched in 1988; today, the program has been implemented in more than 500 schools across the country (Yale University Bush Center in Child Development and Social Policy 2002).

The Bush Center reports that children who participated in a 21C school for at least three years had higher scores in math and reading than in a non-21C school. The Bush Center also reports that the 21C schools have yielded positive results for parents, which have included increased investment in caring for their children, increased knowledge of child development, and improved attendance at work. Principals from the 21C schools indicated decreased vandalism to school property and improved relations with the community and teaching practices. These changes were attributed to the expanded and extended services offered in the school (Dryfoos 2000).

CoZi Schools

In 1997, Zigler and Comer combined their programs to create the "CoZi" schools. These schools combine the early childhood aspects of Zigler's 21C schools with Comer's SDP to better meet the needs of children and families. In combination, the models have a synergistic effect—each program complements and strengthens the other. For example, the SDP is better able to meet its goals of creating a strong school community in which parents are active participants by starting early with young children and new parents, a goal of 21C. In combination "the two programs produce a focus on school-based, collaborative decision making, parent and child outreach, universal access to quality child care, and parent involvement and literacy training. The Parents as Teachers approach to home visiting is incorporated in this approach, along with a health clinic and referral services" (Dryfoos 2000).

The goal of the CoZi schools is to reach all children and address as many developmental needs as possible. The process of learning in CoZi schools extends outside the classroom with projects and field trips in which the parents are sometimes asked to participate. Many of the students in a CoZi school spend up to 10 hours a day on campus. These extended hours are meant to provide students with developmental services and enriching activities, while at the same time keeping them supervised and off of the streets. The team that helps to implement these services, includes the principal, who does more than act as an administrator, but must initiate team-building exercises and delegate responsibility to ensure that the school runs smoothly during its extended hours of operation (Finn-Stevenson and Stern 1996).

Evaluations of the CoZi model were conducted in Norfolk Virginia at the Bowling Park Elementary School between 1996 and 1999. Students at Bowling Park Elementary were compared with children from a control school and it was found that children in preschool and kindergarten scored 9–15 points higher on picture-vocabulary tests than did children in the control school. In addition, third and fourth graders at the Bowling Park School scored significantly higher on tests of basic skills than students at the control school (Dryfoos 2000).

Research on this model has also found that teachers are associating CoZi schools with a more favorable school climate. CoZi teachers are reporting increased levels of leadership from the staff as well as involvement with the students. Research has also shown that in the CoZi model teachers report communicating with parents more often and effectively.

Additionally, CoZi parents are becoming more engaged with their children and are displaying increased levels of participation in the classroom. As we know, students are more likely to achieve improved academic performance in a favorable school climate, where staff and parents collaborate to meet educational and socioemotional goals. (The Yale University Bush Center in Child Development and Social Policy 2002).

Children's Aid Society Schools

From its beginnings in 1853, the Children's Aid Society (CAS) has been committed to helping the impoverished and disadvantaged children of New York City. Founded by Charles Loring Brace, CAS was built on the belief that homeless and orphaned children could become self-reliant adults, if provided with education, gainful work, and a healthy family environment. In 1853, CAS opened its first industrial school for poor children, offering for the first time in the United States free lunches to those in need. Additionally, CAS provided services to working women, needy families, and disabled boys and girls during a time when minimal resources were available.

In 1986, the CAS schools, sometimes referred to as "community schools," partnered with the New York City Board of Education, a local school district, and participating agencies to better address the educational needs of poor children and families. "Through community alliances, this model broadens the school's mission to bring in parents, teachers and the community as full partners" (Children's Aid Society 2001). The community schools created by the Children's Aid Society are open six days a week for 15 hours per day. They offer a range of services, including "medical and dental care; mental health; recreation; supplemental education; youth programs; family life and parent education; and weekend and summer camp services" (Children's Aid Society 2001). The CAS extends its mission to interested schools and districts through technical assistance and training on how to build a community school.

Fordham University has worked with two of the CAS sites to study psychosocial, parent involvement, and academic outcomes for students in third and sixth grades. The research findings revealed that seven years after the CAS program was established students were displaying more positive attitudes toward school and that the afterschool services were being attended. Children were receiving much needed medical and dental care and parents were involved in their children's schooling and reported feeling a greater sense of responsibility regarding their children's education (Dryfoos 2000).

Academic achievement also improved, with one of the schools reporting reading at grade level rising from 28 percent of the students in fourth grade to 42 percent when the students reached sixth grade. Likewise, math scores for the same school increased from 43 percent at grade level for fourth graders to 50 percent by the time the students were in sixth grade. Reading scores were also found to correlate positively with students' attendance at the extended day programs. The other school in the study also demonstrated improvement, with 39 percent of the students reading at grade level in sixth grade, which rose to 45 percent by the time the students were in eighth grade. Math scores in this school rose from 49 percent performing at grade level in sixth grade to 52 percent in eighth grade (Dryfoos 2000).

Gardner Extended Services School—Boston, Massachusetts

The core belief that underlies the Gardner School is that the primary tool for removing nonacademic barriers to learning experienced by many of the students and their families is a comprehensive out-of-school-time program that integrates academic instruction with opportunities for enrichment, career development, and family support services. Developed through a partnership with Boston College, the YMCA of Greater Boston, and the local community, this program is committed to providing before- and afterschool programs for children in addition to economic, health, and education services to adults. Health, dental, and mental health care are provided both on- and off-site by local community agencies while dozens of students and faculty members from Boston College provide tutoring, mentoring, counseling, and consulting. Resources for parents are also provided including a Parents' Center that holds evening classes and workshops on such topics as immigration and legal issues.

The students and families who participate in these services and resources come from the Allston-Brighton neighborhood of Boston, which is very culturally and ethnically diverse. Seventy-eight percent of the 500 students in the Gardner School are learning English as a second language. Currently, 49 percent of the students identify as Hispanic, 23 percent as African American, 17 percent as Caucasian, and 11 percent as Asian. Eighty percent of the students meet the federal guidelines to participate in the Free or Reduced Price Lunch Program.

In the 1999 Massachusetts statewide achievement examinations (MCAS), the Gardner School was the eighth most improved school in literacy in the state. Currently, the Gardner School, in conjunction with Boston College, is in the process of implementing a schoolwide evaluation, with specific focus on the areas of academics, attendance, and behavior (Walsh et al. 2000).

Beacon Schools

Beacons, a program of the New York City Department of Youth Services, is designed to address critical issues of New York City's youth and neighborhoods. The first 10 Beacons were established in the city's poorest neighborhoods to combat the effects of substance abuse, crime, and violence. Today, there are 80 Beacons operating in each local school district throughout New York City (Dryfoos 2000). These school-based community centers provide a safe haven to youth and family members seven days a week for 10 to 12 hours a day. One of the goals of Beacon Schools is to assist youth academically and socially, so they may become self-sufficient, successful parents, and active members of the community. Beacon schools also seek to improve the neighborhoods in which they are located by serving as venues for community meetings. Some of the services that are provided include assistance with homework, educational enrichment services, vocational and recreational activities, and adult programs such as General Education Development and ESL classes. These schools also offer youths opportunities to take part in drama clubs, sports, leadership development, entrepreneurial programs, and community service (Dryfoos 2000).

As part of a research effort, 7,406 participants ranging in age from younger than 12 to older than 21 responded to surveys about the Beacons. It was found that many of the participants attended the Beacons over a number of years and they experienced the schools as a safe environment that provided interesting activities and had a capable and supportive staff. Three-fourths of the respondents indicated that the Beacons were useful in preventing violence and drug abuse and in promoting schoolwork and student leadership (Dryfoos 2000).

United Way/Bridges to Success

Bridges to Success (BTS) was established by the United Way of Central Indiana in 1991. "The purpose of the national BTS project is to promote the expansion of extended services schools in communities through the leadership of local United Ways. The goals are to enhance student performance and to build the self-sufficiency of families and communities. The model uses five key standards to facilitate success: (1)

governance; (2) results and accountability; (3) opportunities; (4) services and support management; and (5) finance" (Dryfoos 2000). The United Way sites emphasize youth development and employment programs.

The United Way BTS program is based on the premise that many of our schools today cannot meet the needs of students who face nonacademic barriers to learning, such as poverty, physical abuse in the home, or emotional distress. The BTS program seeks to increase the availability of health services to students, reduce risk factors that interfere with academic success, and improve graduation and attendance rates in school. BTS hopes to achieve this goal by building strong collaborations between communities and the schools and by increasing awareness of what services are necessary for children to succeed in school (United Way of America 2002).

WEPIC Schools, University of Pennsylvania

In 1985, students at the University of Pennsylvania established the West Philadelphia Improvement Corps (WEPIC) as the result of participation in a class. The WEPIC collaborates with the University of Pennsylvania's Center for Community Partnerships to establish community schools in the West Philadelphia area.

> WEPIC's general approach calls for program-based, hands-on learning focused on community improvement. Special areas of interest include health, the environment, nutrition, conflict resolution and peer mediation, desktop publishing, apprenticeships, entrepreneurial skills, and horticulture. (Dryfoos 2000)

The university helps to establish extra classes in the local schools for which university students and faculty help to develop the curriculum. Courses offered at the university present opportunities for university students and faculty to participate in the university-community partnership. WEPIC's approach to university-community partnerships is being replicated at other colleges and universities across the country (University of Pennsylvania 2002).

There has yet to be an overall evaluation of the WEPIC program, but there is data from individual school studies. Schools that implemented the WEPIC program showed increases in attendance and promotion rate, an increase in parental involvement, and a decrease in suspensions. Also, the University City and West Philadelphia High Schools received awards of $100,000 for attendance increases after both schools were involved in WEPIC (Dryfoos 2000).

In sum, these are a variety of models of schooling that are grounded in a comprehensive, coordinated model of health. All of these models extend the school day and expand the range of services and resources available to children and families. We will turn now to specific programs of prevention and intervention, which are designed as curricula that can be implemented in any type of school.

Classroom-Based Curricula

Schools often utilize curricula that focus on enhancing social and emotional functioning. Specific didactic activities may be designed to promote healthy social and emotional development and/or prevent psychosocial problems. Special education classrooms in particular are expected to focus on mental health and health concerns. Three formats for this approach have emerged. The first consists of integrated instruction as part of the regular classroom content and processes. The second consists of specific curriculum or special intervention implemented by personnel specially trained to carry out the processes. Finally, the third curriculum approach is part of a multifaceted set of interventions designed to enhance positive development and prevent problems.

Following are some examples of these curricula approaches.

Second Step

Second Step is a violence prevention curriculum. It consists of 20 lessons per grade level from kindergarten through ninth grade. The lessons are progressive and focus on empathy, problem-solving skills, and anger management. The lessons are conducted through the use of active discussion, activities, and written tasks. The teacher uses photographs to teach the lesson, guide a discussion, and then model the appropriate behavior. The lessons also involve the children in role-playing. Research on this program was conducted using observational data. The data showed that there was a significant decrease in aggression and verbal hostility. There was also an increase in neutral and prosocial behavior. These results were found to be maintained after a six-month follow-up.

An outcome study conducted by Grossman and colleagues (1997) paired 12 schools with similar student bodies with one school in the pair participating in Second Step and one school acting as a control with no participation in Second Step. Coders who were blind to the study observed the participants prior to the intervention, two weeks following the intervention, and then six months later.

It was found that physical aggression and hostile and aggressive comments decreased from autumn to spring in the Second Step classrooms, while those same behaviors increased in the control groups. Prosocial behavior was also found to increase in the Second Step classrooms, but did not change in the control classrooms. The Second Step classrooms also maintained a higher level of prosocial behaviors six months later.

PATHS (Promoting Alternative Thinking Strategies)

The PATHS curriculum was designed by Greenberg and Kusche (1998). It consists of three units—(1) self-control, (2) feelings and relationships, and (3) interpersonal problem solving. During the self-control unit, children are taught through structured lessons and reinforcement. The lessons are taught in such a way that the children are able to generalize them throughout the day. The feelings and relationships unit introduces emotional and interpersonal understanding. Specific emotions are taught in a hierarchy—from basic to more complex. Children are taught how to recognize specific emotions in themselves and in others and to monitor the emotions within themselves. Children are also taught how to see things from another's point of view and to have empathy for others. This unit is taught using group discussions, skits, art, stories, and educational games. This unit also covers the topic of anger management and the difference between feelings and behaviors so that they may understand that, although it is okay to have certain feelings, it is not always okay to display behaviors associated with those feelings.

The interpersonal cognitive problem-solving unit follows a specific sequence for making decisions about how to solve problems. The unit progresses from (1) stop to think to (2) get ready to make a decision to (3) try something out and, finally, to (4) reflect and evaluate your decision. These three units have been designed to be delivered in a set manner over students' years of schooling to assist children in acquiring developmentally appropriate strategies for decision-making and higher-order thinking skills. The program is also designed to help children carry the lessons over into their lives outside of the curriculum, thereby helping them with their academics as well as their family lives.

Greenberg, Domitrovich, and Bumbarger (2001) describe a study that utilized three randomized controlled trials to investigate the effectiveness of the PATHS curriculum. The first trial consisted of 200 regular education first-grade children, the second trial contained 126 special needs children, and the third contained 57 deaf children. The measures included an interview of social problem solving; two tests of nonverbal cognitive abilities; achievement tests; and parent, teacher, and child ratings of behavior.

The regular education trial showed significant improvement on social problem-solving skills and emotional understanding, and participants were more likely to exhibit prosocial solutions to interpersonal conflicts. At the one-year follow-up to this study, there were significant effects found with measures of emotional understanding and on measures of interpersonal problem solving. Significant effects were also found at the two-year follow-up on teacher ratings using the externalizing behavior problems and the total adaptive functioning subscales of the Child Behavior Checklist for Ages 4–18 (CBCL/4–18) (Achenbach 1991).

The trial that used deaf children for the sample yielded significant results on problem solving, emotional understanding, social problem-solving skills, emotional recognition skills, and teacher and parent-rated social competence. These effects were maintained in the one- and two-year follow-up post-tests.

The third trial of special needs children also showed significant improvement on social problem-solving skills and emotional understanding. These children were also more likely to use prosocial solutions for interpersonal conflicts. One-year follow-up post-tests found significant increases on measures of emotional understanding and interpersonal problem-solving skills. These students also reported that they experienced a decrease in depressive symptoms. The two-year follow-up showed significant differences on the teacher ratings of children's internalizing and externalizing behavior problems as measured by the CBCL subscales.

Raising a Thinking Child/I Can Problem Solve

Raising a Thinking Child is a problem-solving program that was designed by Myrna B. Shure. It focuses on helping children make the right decisions on their own by thinking about their situation rather than by an adult telling them what to do. It is designed to be most effective with preschool children who are high risk. The materials used for this intervention are puppets and pictures. These materials are implemented in role-playing and group activities to promote and develop thinking skills. Real-life situations are used in this intervention. The intervention lasts for three months and consists of between 45 and 50 lessons. The first set of lessons focuses on introducing effective problem-solving vocabulary. The second set of lessons focuses on identifying feelings and emotions in self and others. The last set of lessons focuses on role-playing particular problem-solving situations, which have been volunteered by the participants. Research has shown that after the intervention, and at one-year follow-up, children demonstrate less impulsive behavior and there is an increase in positive problem-solving skills. A longitudinal study over five years showed the same improvements after the third and fourth years.

The Incredible Years

The Incredible Years is a training program that is designed for use in schools and at home by teachers and parents. Incredible Years is a company that produces training programs for teachers, parents, and children. The programs were designed to promote social skills and reduce conduct problems in children. The positive behaviors that are targeted include social skills, understanding of feelings, problem solving, and academic success and cooperation in the classroom. Some of the negative behaviors that are targeted include aggression, class disruption, noncompliance, and negative attributions. The materials for child training include books, puppets, cue cards, refrigerator displays, and home activities. In the child training sessions, children are taught in group sessions. They learn how to problem solve and to manage their anger. They learn how to carry on a friendly conversation. They learn how to conduct themselves appropriately in the classroom and at home. The parent training program reinforces the child training by focusing on positive discipline and effective monitoring skills for parents. Similarly, the teacher-training program focuses on effective classroom management, the promotion of positive behaviors, and the reduction of negative behaviors.

In short, there exists a wide range of curricula, many that are evidence-based, which address a variety of health-related issues in classrooms. In order to select the most appropriate school health programs for prevention and intervention, school staff are now able to access information and assistance through a number of specialized national centers. We will review a few of the better-known centers in the following section.

Centers for Specialized Issues in Schools

Over the past two decades, a number of models of comprehensive student health services have emerged. Some of the models provide overarching conceptual frameworks for comprehensive student health. Others provide technical assistance, rationales, and strategies for operationalizing student health services in local schools and school districts. Still others constitute on-the-ground models, located in schools and communities, for comprehensive student health services. Two examples of these centers, the National Technical Assistance and Research Centers and the Collaborative to Advance Social and Emotional Learning, are described here.

National Technical Assistance and Research Centers

The National Technical Assistance and Research Centers focus on various aspects of understanding and promoting student health. Typically, these organizations attempt to provide concrete rationales and strategies for implementing comprehensive student health in school-community settings. Two of these sites are located in the federally funded national Centers for Mental Health in Schools: the Center for Mental Health in Schools at UCLA and the Center for School Mental Health Assistance at the University of Maryland at Baltimore.

The Center for Mental Health in Schools at UCLA was started in 1995 with a grant from the U.S. Department of Health and Human Services by Howard Adelman, a psychologist at UCLA. The Center focuses on one component of student support, that is, psychological services. The Center also provides technical assistance to schools and school districts that are expanding or reconfiguring their mental health services in schools. In addition to this technical assistance, Adelman has articulated a conceptual framework that helps schools and school districts to organize their mental health services, and potentially, other aspects of student support. His three-component model includes a Developmental/Instructional Component, an Enabling Component, and a Management Component. According to Adelman (2001), a three-component model calls for increasing efforts to address barriers to development, learning, and teaching by addressing the fundamental and essential facets of education reform and school and community agency restructuring. He further suggests there must not only be effective instruction and well-managed schools, but that the barriers to learning must be handled in a comprehensive way. All three components are seen as essential, complementary, and overlapping.

Adelman (2001) believes that most school and community partners concentrate only on the Developmental/Instructional Component and the Management Component. In his model for improving mental health education in schools, he has added the concept of an Enabling Component. This Enabling Component allows schools to address barriers to learning by linking the health, emotional, and social supports needed by children. Development of a cohesive Enabling Component requires policy reform and operational restructuring that weave together what is available at a school, expand these available services by integrating resources from homes and communities, and enhance access to community resources by linking as many programs to the school as possible (Adelman 2001).

CASEL (Collaborative to Advance Social and Emotional Learning)

In 1994, the Collaborative to Advance Social and Emotional Learning (CASEL) was founded by Eileen Rockefeller Growald, Daniel Goleman, and Timothy Shriver. CASEL's mission was to establish social and emotional learning as an essential part of education from preschool through high school. CASEL's central office is located at the University of Illinois at Chicago (UIC), and a satellite office has recently opened in New York City. CASEL collaborates with an international network of leading researchers and practitioners in the fields of social and emotional learning, prevention, positive youth development, character education, and school reform. CASEL has been highly effective as a convening and collaborating organization among researchers, program developers, and educators as it focuses on many areas of common interest, including program design, evaluation, educator preparation, policy, and advocacy.

The goals of this collaborative are to (1) advance the science of social and emotional learning; (2) translate scientific knowledge into effective school practices; (3) disseminate information about scientifically sound educational strategies and practice; (4) enhance training so that educators effectively implement high-quality social and emotional learning programs; and (5) network and collaborate with scientists, educators, advocates, policymakers, and interested citizens to increase coordination of social and emotional efforts.

Centers for specialized issues such as school mental health or socioemotional learning, provide an intensive level of knowledge and best practices to the research and professional communities. Their focused approach to addressing the link between science and practice, and to delineating the connections between health and learning, create models that contribute to positive outcomes for children and families.

CONCLUSION

Children do not always come to school ready to learn. Children and families in the United States are facing substantial threats to their survival and healthy development. Research has made it abundantly clear that children who fear violence in their school, home or neighborhood, whose attachments to parents have been seriously disrupted, and who lack the social skills required for productive interactions are challenged both academically and socially. Connecting learning and healthy development in the lives of children necessitates focusing on the development of the whole child. Educators and policymakers are increasingly recognizing that linking health and learning cannot be accomplished by a single institution, but rather, will require collaborations that span the boundaries of schools and community-based agencies and resources. These collaborations will require renewing and rebuilding the often weak or severed connections between communities and schools.

In an effort to provide coordinated, comprehensive services to children, public schools across the country have begun to implement novel collaborative arrangements with community agencies and resources. Professionals from a variety of disciplines are working with schools and agencies in new and innovative arrangements. These arrangements span both in-school and out-of-school time, cross the boundaries of educational and health professions, focus on programmatic as well as individual interventions, and address both strengths and deficits. These school-community partnerships are seen by those outside of education as vital to addressing multiple issues confronting children. For example, the Surgeon General's Conference on Children's Mental Health, jointly sponsored by the U.S. Departments of Health and Human Services, Education, and Justice, identified one of their major outcome goals as strengthening "the resource capacity of schools to serve as a key link to a comprehensive, seamless system of school- and community-based identification, assessment and treatment services, to meet the needs of youth and their families where they are" (U.S. Public Health Service 2000).

With schools removing boundaries that historically have separated them from the community, and as community providers learn the culture, structure, and needs of schools, opportunities will increase for collaborative, comprehensive services that are delivered based on the needs of the individual and the systems in which that individual functions (Talley and Short 1996).

REFERENCES

Achenbach, T. 1991. "Child Behavior Checklist for ages 4–18." June 1999. http://www.aseba.org/support/samples/cbclsample.pdf (20 October 2003).

Adelman, H.S. 1996. "Restructuring Education Support Services and Integrating Community Resources: Beyond the Full-Service School Model." *School Psychology Review* 25(4):431–45.

———. 2001. *Mental Health in Schools: Guidelines, Models, Resources, and Policy Considerations.* Los Angeles, CA: Policy Leadership Cadre for Mental Health in Schools.

Afterschool Alliance. 2000. "Afterschool Issue Overview." *The Need.* http://www.afterschoolalliance.org/after_over.cfm (10 July 2002).

Allensworth, D., and L. Kolbe. 1987. "The Comprehensive School Health Program: Exploring an Expanded Concept." *Journal of School Health* 57(10):409–12.

American Dietetic Association. 1990. "Position: Domestic Hunger and Inadequate Access to Food." *Journal of the American Dietetic Association* 90:1437–41.

———. 2000. "Position of the American Dietetic Association: Local Support for Nutrition Integrity in Schools." *Journal of the American Dietetic Association* 100(1):39–41.

Annie E. Casey Foundation. 1999. *Kids Count Data Book.* New York: Carnegie Foundation.

———. 2000. *Kids Count Data Book.* New York: Carnegie Foundation.

Astor, R.A. 1998. "Moral Reasoning about School Violence: Informational Assumptions about Harm within School Subcontexts." *Educational Psychologist Special Issue: Schooling and Mental Health: Issues, Research, and Future Directions* 33(4):207–21.

Atkinson, D.R., and C.E. Thompson. 1992. "Racial, Ethnic, and Cultural Variables in Counseling." In *Handbook of Counseling Psychology* (2nd ed.): 349–82, eds. S.D. Brown and R.W. Lent. New York, NY: John Wiley & Sons, Inc.

Austin, J.K., T.J. Huberty, G.A. Huster, and D.W. Dunn. 1999. "Does Academic Achievement in Children with Epilepsy Change over Time?" *Developmental Medicine and Child Neurology* 41(7):473–79.

Baker, S.B. 2000. *School Counseling for the Twenty-First Century* (3rd ed.). Upper Saddle River, NJ: Merrill.

Baltes, P.B., U.M. Staudinger, and U. Lindenberger. 1999. "Lifespan psychology: Theory and Application to Intellectual Functioning." *Annual Review of Psychology* 50:471–507.

Bandura, A. 1986. *Social Foundations of Thought and Action: A Social Cognitive Theory.* Englewood Cliffs, NJ: Prentice Hall.

Baranowski, T., J. Mendlein, K. Resnicow, E. Frank, K.W. Cullen, and J. Baranowski. 2000. "Physical Activity and Nutrition in Children and Youth: An

Overview of Obesity Prevention." *Preventive Medicine: An International Journal Devoted to Practice and Theory* 31(2, Pt. 2):S1–S10.

Barkley, R.A. 1998. "Attention-Deficit Hyperactivity Disorder." *Scientific-American* 279(3):66–71.

Bassuk, E.L., J.C. Buckner, and L.F. Weinreb. 2001. "Predictors of Academic Achievement among Homeless and Low-Income Household Children." *Journal of School Psychology* 39(1):45–69.

Bassuk, E.L., and L. Rubin. 1987. "Homeless Children: A Neglected Population." *American Journal of Orthopsychiatry* 57(2):279–86.

Becker, B. E. and S. S. Luthar. 2002. "Social-Emotional Factors Affecting Achievement Outcomes Among Disadvantaged Students: Closing the Achievement Gap," *Educational Psychologist* 37(4):197–214.

Benson, P.L., N. Laffert, P.C. Scales, and D.A. Blyth. 1998. "Beyond the 'Village' Rhetoric: Creating Healthy Communities for Children and Adolescents." *Applied Developmental Science* 2(3):138–59.

Birch, D.A. 1996. *Step by Step to Involving Parents in Health Education.* Santa Cruz, CA: ETR Associates.

Black, S. 2000. "Nutrition and Learning." *American School Board Journal* 187(2):49–51.

Black, M.M., and A. Krishnakumar. 1998. "Children in Low-Income, Urban Settings: Interventions to Promote Mental Health and Well-Being." *American Psychologist* 53(6):635–46.

Blackwell, E., and E. Blackwell. 1860. "Medicine as a Profession for Women." January 2000. http://www.lemoyne.edu/library/womens/women_medicine.htm (3 July 2002).

Blechman, E.A., M.J. McEnroe, E.T. Carella, and D.P. Audette. 1986. "Childhood Competence and Depression." *Journal of Abnormal Psychology* 95(3):223–27.

Books, S. ed. 1998. *Invisible Children in the Society and its Schools: Sociocultural, Political, and Historical Studies in Education.* Mahwah, NJ: Lawrence Erlbaum Associates, Inc.

Brabeck, M., M.E. Walsh, M. Kenny, and K. Comilang. 1997. "Interprofessional Collaboration for Children and Families: Opportunities for Counseling Psychology in the 21st Century." *Counseling Psychologist* 25(4): 615–36.

Brener, M.L. 1999. "A Qualitative Examination of the Effects of Family Violence on Children's Educational Experience." Abstract in *Dissertation Abstracts International* 60(5):1509A.

Bronfenbrenner, U. 1979. *The Ecology of Human Development.* Cambridge, MA: Harvard University Press.

Brookover, W.B., C. Beady, P. Flood, J. Schweitzer, and J. Wisenbacker. 1979. *School Social Systems and Student Achievement: Schools Can Make a Difference.* New York: Praeger.

Brooks-Gunn, J., G. Duncan, P. Klebov, and N. Sealand. 1993. "Do Neighborhoods Influence Child and Adolescent Development?" *American Journal of Sociology* 99:353–95.

Bryant, B. 1989. "The Need for Support in Relation to the Need for Autonomy." In *Children's Social Networks and Social Supports,* ed. D. Belle, 332–51. New York, NY: John Wiley & Sons, Inc.

Cain, V.S. and S.L. Hofferth. 1989. "Parental Choice of Self-Care for School-Age Children." *Journal of Marriage and the Family* 51(1):65–77.

Cairns, R.B., and B.D. Cairns. 1994. *Lifelines and Risks: Pathways of Youth in our Time.* New York, NY: Cambridge University Press.

Cairns, R.B., B.D. Cairns, and H.J. Neckerman. 1989. "Early School Dropout: Configurations and Determinants." *Child Development* 60(6):1437–52.

California Department of Education. 2001. "Healthy Start and After School Partnerships Office." *Healthy Start.* July. http://www.cde.ca.gov/healthystart (17 April 2002).

Carnegie Council on Adolescent Development. 1995. *Great Transitions: Preparing Adolescents for a New Century (Concluding Report of the Carnegie Council on Adolescent Development).* New York: Carnegie Corporation of New York.

Carpenter, C.J., A. Huston, and L. Spera. 1989. "Children's Use of Time in Their Everyday Activities during Middle Childhood." In *The Ecological Context of Children's Play,* eds. M. Block and A. Pellegrini, 165–90. Norwood, NJ: Ablex.

Center for Mental Health Services. 2000. "Mental Health Statistics." *Mental Health, United States, 2000: Chapter 19.* http://www.mentalhealth.org/publications/ allpubs/SMA01–3537/chapter19.asp (2 July 2002).

Center on Hunger, Poverty, and Nutrition Policy. 1993. *Statement on the Link between Nutrition and Cognitive Development in Children.* Medford, MA: Tufts University School of Nutrition.

Centers for Disease Control and Prevention. 1995. "CDC Surveillance Summaries." *Morbidity and Mortality Weekly Report* 44(SS-1):1–56.

———. 2002. "Surveillance Summaries." *Morbidity and Mortality Weekly Report* 51(SS-4):1–32.

Children's Aid Society. 2001. "Children's Aid Society Home." *Building a Community School.* http://www.childrensaidsociety.org (17 April 2002).

Chung, A. 2000. *Working for Children and Families: Safe and Smart After-School Programs.* Washington, DC: Government Printing Office.

Coalition for Community Schools. 2000. "Partnerships for Excellence." June. http://www.communityschools.org (17 April 2002).

Comer, J.P. 1988. "Educating Poor Minority Children." *Scientific American* 259(5):42–48.

Conger, R.D., K.J. Conger, and G. Elder. 1997. "Family Economic Hardship and Adolescent Academic Performance: Mediating and Moderating Processes." In *Consequences of Growing Up Poor,* eds. G. Duncan and J. Brooks-Gunn, 288–310. New York: Russell Sage Foundation.

Connell, D.B., R.R. Turner, and E.F. Mason. 1985. "Summary of Findings of the School Health Education Evaluation: Health Promotion Effectiveness, Implementation, and Cost." *Journal of School Health* 55(8):316–21.

Conoley, J.C., and C.W. Conoley. 1991. "Collaboration for Child Adjustment: Issues for School- and Clinic-Based Psychologists." *Journal of Consulting and Clinical Psychology* 59(6):821–29.

Covington, M.V. 1992. *Making the Grade: A Self-Worth Perspective on Motivation and School Reform.* New York: Cambridge University Press.

Cowen, E.L. 1991. "In Pursuit of Wellness." *American Psychologist* 46: 404–8.

Curtis, T., and K. Hansen-Schwoebel. 1999. *Big Brothers Big Sisters School-Based Mentoring: Evaluation Summary of Five Pilot Programs.* Philadelphia, PA: Big Brothers Big Sisters of America.

Deci, E.L., and R.M. Ryan. 1985. *Intrinsic Motivation and Self-Determination in Human Behavior.* New York: Academic Press.

Deemer, E., L. Desimore, and M. Finn-Stevenson. "21C: A Decade of School-Based Child Care." *Principal* 77(3):43–46.

Dishion, T.J., D.C. French, and G.R. Patterson. 1995. "The Development and Ecology of Antisocial Behavior." In *Developmental Psychopathology, Vol. 2: Risk, Disorder, and Adaptation,* eds. D. Cicchetti and D.J. Cohen, 421–71. New York, NY: John Wiley & Sons, Inc.

Dryfoos, J.G. 1990. *Adolescents at Risk: Prevalence and Prevention.* New York: Oxford University Press.

———. 1994. "Full-Service Schools: A Revolution in Health and Social Services for Children, Youth, and Families." *The Jossey-Bass Health Series, The Jossey-Bass Social and Behavioral Science Series, and The Jossey-Bass Education Series.* San Francisco, CA: Jossey-Bass.

———. 2000. *Evaluation of Community Schools: Findings to Date.* http://www.communityschools.org/evaluation/evalprint.html (8 July 2002).

DuBois, D.L., R.D. Felner, H. Meares, and M. Krier. 1994. "Prospective Investigation of the Effects of Socioeconomic Disadvantage, Life Stress, and Social Support on Early Adolescent Adjustment." *Journal of Abnormal Psychology* 103(3):511–22.

Dusenbury, L., and M. Falco. 1995. "Eleven Components of Effective Drug Abuse Prevention Curricula." *Journal of School Health* 65(10):420–25.

Dusenbury, L., and A. Lake. 1996. *Making the Grade: A Guide to School Drug Prevention Programs.* Washington, DC: Drug Strategies.

Dweck, C.S., and C.B. Wortman. 1982. "Learned Helplessness, Anxiety, and Achievement Motivation: Neglected Parallels in Cognitive, Affective, and Coping Responses." *Series in Clinical and Community Psychology: Achievement, Stress, and Anxiety* 2:93–125.

Eccles, J.S., and R.D. Harold. 1993. "Parent-School Involvement during the Early Adolescent Years." *Teachers College Record.* 94(3):568–87.

Epstein, J.L. 1992. "School and Family Partnerships." In *Encyclopedia of Educational Research* (6th ed.), ed. M. Alkin, 1139–51. New York: Macmillan.

———. 1995. "School/Family/Community Partnerships: Caring for the Children we Share." *Phi Delta Kappan* 76(May):701–12.

———. 2001. *School, Family and Community Partnerships: Preparing Educators and Improving Schools.* Boulder, CO: Westview Press.

Epstein, J.I., K.C. Salinas, and B. Simon. 1996. "Effects of Teachers Involving Parents in Schoolwork (TIPS)—Interactive Homework in the Middle Grades." Paper presented at the annual meeting of the American Educational Research Association, New York.

Entwisle, D.R., and K.L. Alexander. 1990. "Beginning School Math Competence: Minority and Majority Comparisons." *Child Development Special Issue: Minority Children* 61(2):454–71.

Family and Community Trust. 2001. "Family and Community Trust Home." http://www.mofit.org (17 April 2002).

Felson, R.B., A.E. Liska, S.J. South, and T.L. McNulty. 1994. "The Subculture of Violence and Delinquency: Individual vs. School Context Effects." *Social Forces* 73(1): 155–73.

Fine, M. 1991. *Framing Dropouts: Notes on the Politics of an Urban Public High School.* Albany: State University of New York Press.

Finkelhor, D., and J. Dziuba-Leatherman. 1994. "Children as Victims of Violence: A National Survey." *Pediatrics* 94:413–20.

Finn-Stevenson, M., and B.M. Stern. 1996. "CoZi: Linking Early Childhood and Family Support Services." *National Association of Elementary School Principals.* May. http://www.naesp.org/comm/p0596a.htm (17 April 2002).

Fiqueria-McDonough, J. 1986. "School Context, Gender, and Delinquency." *Journal of Youth and Adolescence* 15(1):79–98.

Fox, J.A., and S.A. Newman. 1997. *After-School Crime or After-School Programs: Tuning in to the Prime Time for Violent Juvenile Crime and Implications for National Policy. A Report to the United States Attorney General.* Washington, DC: Fight Crime: Invest in Kids.

Freeman, E.M., and M. Pennekamp. 1988. *Social Work Practice: Toward a Child, Family, School, Community Perspective.* Springfield, KS: Charles C. Thomas, Publisher.

Furstenberg, F.F., T.D. Cook, J. Eccles, G.H. Elder, and A. Sameroff. 1999. *Managing to Make It: Urban Families and Adolescent Success.* Chicago: University of Chicago Press.

Gibelman, M., and P. Schervish. 1995. "Practice Areas and Settings of Social Workers in Mental Health." *Psychiatric Services* 46(12):12–37.

Gibson, R.L., and M.H. Mitchell. 1990. *Introduction to Counseling and Guidance* (3rd ed.). New York: Macmillan.

Gold, R.S. 1994. "The Science Base for Comprehensive Health Education." Volume 2 of *The Comprehensive School Health Challenge,* eds. P. Cortese and K. Middleton, 543–74. Santa Cruz, CA: ETR Associates.

Gortmaker, S.L., L.W. Cheung, K.E. Peterson, G. Chomitz, J.H. Cradle, H. Dart, M.K. Fox, R.B. Bullock, A.M. Sobol, G. Colditz, A.E. Field, and N. Laird. 1999. Impact of a School-Based Interdisciplinary Intervention on Diet and Physical Activity among Urban Primary School Children: Eat Well and Keep Moving." *Archives of Pediatrics and Adolescent Medicine* 153(9): 975–83.

Greenberg, M.T., C. Domitrovich, and B. Bumbarger. 2001. "The Prevention of Mental Disorders in School-Aged Children: Current State of the Field." *Prevention and Treatment.* 30 March. http://journals.apa.org/prevention/volume4/toc-mar30–01.htm (17 April 2002).

Greenberg, M.T., and C.A. Kusche. 1998. "Preventive Interventions for School-Age Deaf Children: The PATHS Curriculum." *Journal of Deaf Studies and Deaf Education* 3(1):49–63.

Grossman, D., H.J. Neckerman, T.D. Koepsell, P.Y. Liu, K.N. Asher, K. Beland, K. Frey, F.P. Rivera. 1997. "Effectiveness of a Violence Prevention Curriculum among Children in Elementary School—A Randomized Controlled Trail." *Journal of the American Medical Association* 277(20):1605–11.

Gysbers, N.C., and P. Henderson. 2000. *Developing and Managing Your School Guidance Program.* Alexandria, VA: American Counseling Association.

Hall, J.A., and P.L. Maza. 1990. "No Fixed Address: The Effects of Homelessness on Families and Children." *Child and Youth Services* 14(1):35–47.

Harkavy, I. 1999. "School-Community-University Partnerships: Effectively Integrating Community Building and Education Reform." *Universities and Community Schools* 6(1–2):7–24.

Hartford Public Schools. 2001. "Hartford Public Schools Home." http://www.hartfordschools.org (April 17 2002).

Haveman, R., and B. Wolfe. 1995. "The Determinants of Children's Attainments: A Review of Methods and Findings." *Journal of Economic Literature* 33:1829–78.

Hawkins, J.D., R.F. Catalano, and J.Y. Miller. 1992. "Risk and Protective Factors for Alcohol and Other Drug Problems in Adolescence and Early Adulthood: Implications for Substance Abuse Prevention." *Psychological Bulletin* 112(1):64–105.

Haynes, N.M., and J.P. Comer. 1996. "Integrating Schools, Families, and Communities through Successful School Reform: The School Development Program." *School Psychology Review* 25(4):501–06.

Helms, J.E. 1990. *Black and White Racial Identity: Theory, Research, and Practice.* Westport, CT: Greenwood Press.

Henderson, A.C. 1987. *Healthy Schools, Healthy Futures: The Case for Improving School Environment.* Santa Cruz, CA: ETR Associates.

Henson, K.T., and B.F. Eller. 1999. *Educational Psychology for Effective Teaching.* Belmont, CA: Wadsworth Publishing Company.

Hill, M.S., and G. Duncan. 1987. "Parental Family Income and the Socioeconomic Attainment of Children." *Social Science Research* 16:39–73.

Hinshaw, S.P. 1992. "Externalizing Behavior Problems and Academic Underachievement in Childhood and Adolescence: Casual Relationships and Underlying Mechanisms." *Psychological Bulletin* 111(1):127–55.

Holtzman, W.H. 1992. "Community Renewal, Family Preservation, and Child Development through the School of the Future." In *School of the Future* 3–18, ed. W.H. Holtzman. Austin, TX: American Psychological Association and Hogg Foundation for Mental Health.

Illback, R.J., J. Kalafat, and D. Sanders. 1997. "Evaluating Integrated Service Programs." In *Integrated Services for Children and Families: Opportunities for Psychological Practice*, eds. R.J. Illback and C.T. Cobb. Washington, DC: American Psychological Association.

Jessor, R., J. Van Den Bos, J. Vanderryn, and F.M. Costa. 1995. "Protective Factors in Adolescent Problem Behavior: Moderator Effects and Developmental Change." *Developmental Psychology* 31(6):923–33.

Kagan, S.L. 1990. *Excellence in Early Childhood Education: Defining Characteristics and Next-Decade Strategies.* Washington, DC: Information Services, Office of Educational Research and Improvement, U.S. Department of Education.

Kagan, S.L., E. Moore, and S. Bredekamp. 1995. "Reconsidering Children's Early Development and Learning: Toward Common Views and Vocabulary." Washington, DC: National Education Goals Panel. http://purl.access.gpo.gov/GPO/LPS2809 (8 July 2002).

Kann, L., C.W. Warren, W.A. Harris, J.L. Collins, B.I. Williams, J.G. Ross, L.J. Kolbe, and State and Local YRBS Coordinators. 1996. "Youth Risk Behavior Surveillance—United States, 1995." *CDC Surveillance Summaries: Morbidity and Mortality Weekly Report* 45:(SS-4).

Kellam, S.G., G.W. Rebok, L.S. Mayer, and N. Ialongo. 1994. "Depressive Symptoms over First Grade and Their Response to a Developmental Epidemiologically Based Preventive Trial Aimed at Improving Achievement." *Development and Psychopathology* 6(3):463–81.

Kennedy, D.V., and K.J. Doepke. 1999. "Multicomponent Treatment of a Test Anxious College Student." *Education and Treatment of Children. Special Issue: Level 1 Research: Improving Our Education and Treatment through Simple Accountability Procedures* 22(2): 203–17.

Kirby, D., L. Short, J. Collins, D. Rugg, L. Kolbe, M. Howard, B. Miller, F. Sonenstein, and L. Zabin. 1994. "School-Based Programs to Reduce Sexual Risk Behaviors: A Review of Effectiveness." *Public Health Reports* 109(3):339–60.

Kleinman, R.E., J.M. Murphy, M. Little, M. Pagano, C.A. Wehler, K. Regal, and M.S. Jellinek. 1998. "Hunger in Children in the United States: Potential Behavioral and Emotional Correlates." *Pediatrics* 101(1):E3.

Kolbe, L.J., J. Collins, and P. Cortese. 1997. "Building the Capacity of Schools to Improve the Health of the Nation: A Call for Assistance from Psychologists." *American Psychologist* 52(3):256–65.

Kovacs, M. 1992. *Children's Depression Inventory Manual.* North Tonawanda, NY: Multi-Health Systems.

Kowalski, T. 1995. "Chasing the Wolves from the Schoolhouse Door." *Phi Delta Kappan* 76(6):486, 488–89.

Larson, R., and M. Richards. 1989. "Introduction: The Changing Life Space of Early Adolescence." *Journal of Youth and Adolescence* 18:501–10.

Learning First Alliance. 2001. *Every Child Learning: Safe and Supportive Schools.* November. http://www.learningfirst.org/pdfs/safe-schools-report.pdf (8 July 2002).

Leiter, J., and M.C. Johnsen. 1997. "Child Maltreatment and School Performance Declines: An Event-History Analysis." *American Educational Research Journal* 34(3):563–89.

Lerner, R.M. 1984. *On the Nature of Human Plasticity.* New York: Cambridge University.

———. 1986. *Concepts and Theories of Human Development* (2nd ed.). New York: Random House.

———. 1995. *America's Youth in Crisis: Challenges and Options for Programs and Policies.* Thousand Oaks, CA: Sage.

———. 1998. "Theoretical Models of Human Development." Volume 1 of *Handbook of child Psychology* (5th ed.), ed. W. Damon. New York: John Wiley & Sons, Inc.

Lerner, R.M., M.E. Walsh, and K.A. Howard. 1998. "Developmental Contextual Considerations: Person-Context Relations as the Bases for Risk and Resiliency in Child and Adolescent Development." In *Comprehensive Clinical Psychology, Vol 4: Children and Adolescents: Clinical Formulation and Treatment,* ed. T. Ollendick. New York: Elsevier Science Publishers.

Littlejohn-Blake, S.M., and C.A. Darling. 1993. "Understanding the Strengths of African American Families." *Journal of Black Studies* 23(4):460–71.

Los Angeles Unified School District. 2001. http://www.lausd.k12.ca.us/welcome.html (17 April 2002).

Ludwig, J., G. J. Duncan, and P. Hirschfield. 2001. "Urban Poverty and Juvenile Crime: Evidence from a Randomized Housing-Mobility Experiment." *The Quarterly Journal of Economics* 116 (2):655–79.

Lykken, D.T. 2001. "Parental Licensure." *American Psychologist* 56(11): 885–94.

Maehr, M.L. 1991. "The 'Psychological Environment' of the School: A Focus for School Leadership." Volume 2 of *Advances in Educational Administration,* eds. P. Thurstone and P.Z. Greenwich, 51–81. CT: JAI Press.

Marshall, N.L., C.G. Coll, F. Marx, K. McCartney, N. Keefe, and J. Ruh. 1997. "After-School Time and Children's Behavioral Adjustment." *Merrill-Palmer Quarterly* 43(3):497–514.

Marx, E., and D. Northup. 1995. *Educating for Health: A Guide to Implementing a Comprehensive Approach to School Health Education.* Newton, MA: Educational Development Center, Inc.

Marx, E., S.F. Wooley, and D. Northrup, eds. 1998. *Health is Academic: A Guide to Coordinated School Health Programs.* New York: Teachers College Press.

Masten, A.S., K.M. Best, and N. Garmezy. 1991. "Resilience and Development: Contributions from the Study of Children Who Overcome Adversity." *Development and Psychopathology* 2:425–44.

Masten, A.S., and J.D. Coatsworth. 1998. "The Development of Competence in Favorable and Unfavorable Environments: Lessons from Research on Successful Children." *American Psychologist* 53 (2):205–20.

McGauhey, P.J., B. Starfield, C. Alexander, and M.E. Ensminger. 1991. "Social Environment and Vulnerability of Low Birth Weight Children: A Social-Epidemiological Perspective." *Pediatrics* 88(5): 943–53.

McGraw, S.A., D. Sellers, E. Stone, K.A. Resnicow, S. Kuester, F. Fridinger, and H. Wechsler. 2000. "Measuring Implementation of School Programs and Policies to Promote Healthy Eating and Physical Activity among Youth." *Preventive Medicine: An International Journal Devoted to Practice and Theory* 31(2, Pt. 2):S86-S97.

McKenzie, F.D., and J.B. Richmond. 1998. "Linking Health and Learning: An Overview of Coordinated School Health Programs." In *Health is Academic: a guide to coordinated school health programs,* eds. E. Marx and S.F. Wooley, 1–14. New York: Teachers College Press.

McLaughlin, M.W. 2000. *Community Counts: How Youth Organizations Matter for Youth Development.* Washington, DC: Public Education Network.

McLaughlin, M.W., M.A. Irby, and J. Langman. 1994. *Urban Sanctuaries: Neighborhood Organizations in the Lives and Futures of Inner-City Youth.* San Francisco: Jossey-Bass.

McLoyd, V.C. 1990. "The Impact of Economic Hardship on Black Families and Children: Psychological Distress, Parenting, and Socioemotional Development." *Child Development* 61: 311–46.

———. 1998. "Socioeconomic Disadvantage and Child Development." *American Psychologist* 53:(2):185–204.

Medrich, E.A., J. A. Roizen, V. Rubin, and S. Buckley. 1982. *The Serious Business of Growing Up: A Study of Children's Lives outside School.* Berkeley: University of California Press.

Miller, B. 1995. *Out of School Time: Effects on Learning in the Primary Grades* (Action Research Paper No. 4). Wellesley, MA: School-Age Child Care Project, Wellesley College Center for Research on Women.

Missouri Department of Elementary and Secondary Education. 2001. "Caring Communities—Description/Contact Information." http://www.dese.state. mo.us (17 April 2002).

Morris, D., B. Shaw, and J. Perney. 1990. "Helping Low Readers in Grades 2 and 3: An After-School Volunteer Tutoring Program." *Elementary School Journal* 91(2):133–50.

Murphy J.M., M.E. Pagano, C.A. Wehler, M. Little, R.E. Kleinman, and M.S. Jellinek. 1998. "Relationship between Hunger and Psychosocial Functioning in Low-Income American Children." *Journal of the American Academy of Child and Adolescent Psychiatry* 37(2):163–70

National Center for Children in Poverty. 2002. *Children Poverty Fact Sheet.* New York: National Center for Children in Poverty, Mailman School of Public Health, and Columbia University.

National Coalition for Parent Involvement in Education. 1995. *Why a Coalition for Parent Involvement?* Fairfax, VA: Author.

National Health and Education Consortium. 1993. *Eat to Learn, Learn to Eat: The Link between Nutrition and Learning in Children.* Washington, DC: Institute for Educational Leadership.

National Institute for Urban School Improvement. 2001. "Districts on the Move: Unified Student Service in Boston Public Schools; Building a Continuum of Services through Standard-Based Reform." April. http://www.edc. org/urban/Boston_DOM.pdf (9 July 2002).

National Institute on Out-of-School Time, Center for Research on Women at Wellesley College. 2001. *Fact Sheet on School-Age Children's Out-of-School Time.* Wellesley, MA: Author.

Needleman, H. L., A. Schell, D. Bellinger, A. Leviton, and E.N. Allred. 1990. "The Long-Term Effects of Exposure to Low Doses of Lead in Childhood. An 11-year Follow-up Report." *The New England Journal of Medicine* 322(2):83–88.

Newmann, F.M., and G.G. Wehlage. 1995. "Successful School Restructuring: A Report to the Public and Educators." Madison, WI: Center on Organization and Restructuring of Schools.

Nicklas, T.A., C.E. O'Neil, and G.S. Berenson. 1998. "Nutrient Contribution of Breakfast, Secular Trends, and the Role of Ready-To-Eat Cereals: A Review of Data from the Bogalusa Heart Study." *The American Journal of Clinical Nutrition* 67(4):757S-763S.

Nolen-Hoeksema, S., J.S. Girgus, and M.E. Seligman. 1986. "Learned Helplessness in Children: A Longitudinal Study of Depression, Achievement, and Explanatory Style." *Journal of Personality and Social Psychology* 51(2):435–42.

North Central Regional Educational Laboratory. 2000. "City schools: Kentucky's Family and Youth Service Centers Break New Ground." http://www.ncrel.org/sdrs/cityschl/city1_1e.htm (17 April 2002).

Ollendick, T.H., M.D. Weist, M.C. Borden, and R.W. Greene. 1992. "Socio-metric Status and Academic, Behavioral, and Psychological Adjustment: A Five-Year Longitudinal Study." *Journal of Consulting and Clinical Psychology* 60(1):80–87.

Overstreet, S., and S. Braun. 1999. "A Preliminary Examination of the Relationship between Exposure to Community Violence and Academic Functioning." *School Psychology Quarterly* 14(4): 380–96.

Parker, J.G., and S.R. Asher. 1987. "Peer Relations and Later Personal Adjustment: Are Low-Accepted Children At Risk?" *Psychological Bulletin* 102(3):357–89.

Patterson, C.J., J.B. Kupersmidt, and N.A. Vaden. 1990. "Income Level, Gender, Ethnicity, and Household Composition as Predictors of Children's School-Based Competence." *Child Development. Special Issue: Minority children* 61(2):485–94.

Pederson, J., A. de Kanter, L.M. Bobo, K. Weinig, and K. Noeth. 1998. *Safe and Smart: Making the After-School Hours Work for Kids.* Washington, DC: U.S. Department of Education and U.S. Department of Justice.

Pelham, W.E., and E.M. Gnagy. 1999. "Psychosocial and Combined Treatments for ADHD." *Mental Retardation and Developmental Disabilities Research Reviews* 5(3):225–36.

Perry, C.L., R.V. Luepker, D.M. Murray, M.D. Hearn, A. Halper, B. Dudovipz, M.C. Maile, and M. Smythe. 1989. "Parental Involvement with Children's Health Promotion: A One-Year Follow-up of the Minnesota Home Team." *Health Education Quarterly* 16(2):171–80.

Pettit, G., R.D. Laird, K.A. Dodge, and J.E. Bates. 1997. "Patterns of After-School Care in Middle Childhood: Risk Factors and Developmental Outcomes." *Merrill-Palmer Quarterly* 43 (3):515–38.

Philliber Research Associates. 1994. *An Evaluation of the Caring Communities Program at Wallbridge Elementary School.* New York: Accord.

Piaget, J. 1952. "The Origins of Intelligence in Children." New York: International Universities Press.

Pollitt, E. 1995. "Does Breakfast Make a Difference in School?" *Journal of the American Dietetic Association* 95(10):1134–39.

Portz, J. 2000. "Supporting Education Reform: Mayoral and Corporate Paths." *Urban Education* 34(4): 396–417.

Posner, J.K., and D.L Vandell. 1999. "After-School Activities and the Development of Low-Income Children." *Developmental Psychology* 35(3): 868–79.

Pumariega, A.J., and H.R. Vance. 1999. "School-Based Mental Health Services: The Foundation of Systems of Care for Children's Mental Health." *Psychology in the Schools* 36(5):371–78.

Quinn, J. 1999. "Where Need Meets Opportunity: Youth Development Programs for Early Teens." *Future of Children* 9(2):96–116.

Rafferty, Y., and N. Rollins. 1989. *Learning in Limbo: The Educational Deprivation of Homeless Children.* (Report No. UD027127). Long Island City, NY: Advocates for Children of New York, Inc.

Rendon, L.I., and R.O. Hope, eds. 1996. *Educating a New Majority: Transforming America's Educational System for Diversity.* San Francisco: Jossey-Bass.

Rigsby, L.C., M.C. Reynolds, and M.C. Wang, eds. 1995. *School-Community Connections: Exploring Issues for Research and Practice.* The Jossey-Bass Education Series. San Francisco: Jossey-Bass.

Riley, R. 1998. "School/Community/University Partnerships." In *Connecting Community Building and Education Reform: Effective School, Community, University Partnerships.* Washington, DC: Joint Forum of the U.S. Department of Education and the U.S. Department of Housing and Urban Development.

Roeser, R.W., and J.S. Eccles. 2000. "Schooling and Mental Health." In *Handbook of Developmental Psychopathology* (2nd ed.), eds. A.J. Sameroff et al., 135–56. New York: Kluwer Academic/Plenum Publishers.

Roeser, R.W., J.S. Eccles, and K. Strobel. 1998a. "Academic and Emotional Functioning in Early Adolescence: Longitudinal Relations, Patterns, and Predication by Experience in Middle School." *Development and Psychopathology* 10: 321–52.

———. 1998b. "Linking the Study of Schooling and Mental Health: Selected Issues and Empirical Illustrations at the Level of the Individual." *Educational Psychologist Special Issue: Schooling and Mental Health: Issues, Research, and Future Directions* 33(4):153–76.

Roeser, R.W., C. Midgley, and T.C. Urdan. 1996. "Perceptions of the School Psychological Environment and Early Adolescents' Psychological and Behavioral Functioning in School: The Mediating Role of Goals and Belonging." *Journal of Educational Psychology* 88(3):408–22.

Roth, J., J. Brooks-Gunn, L. Murray, and W. Foster. 1998. "Promoting Healthy Adolescence: Synthesis of Youth Development Program Evaluations." *Journal of Research on Adolescence* 8:432–59.

Rothman, M.L., J.L. Ehreth, C.S. Palmer, J. Collins, J.A. Reblando, and B.P. Luce. 1993. "The Potential Benefits and Costs of a Comprehensive Health Education Program." Paper presented at the meeting of the American Public Health Association, San Francisco.

Rutter, M. 1980. "School Influences on Children's Behavior and Development: The 1979 Kenneth Blackfan Lecture, Children's Hospital Medical Center, Boston." *Pediatrics* 65:208–20.

———. 1983. "School Effects on Pupil Progress: Research Findings and Policy Implications." *Child Development* 54(1):1–29.

Scales, P.C., and N. Leffert. 1999. *Developmental Assets: A Synthesis of the Scientific Research on Adolescent Development.* Minneapolis, MN: Search Institute.

School Mental Health Project/Center for Mental Health in Schools. 2001. "CSSS—Hawaii's Comprehensive Student Support System: A Multifaceted Approach That Encompasses and Enhances MH in Schools." *Addressing Barriers to Learning* 6(3):1–10. Los Angeles: Department of Psychology, UCLA.

Schorr, L.B. 1988. *Within Our Reach: Breaking the Cycle of Disadvantage.* New York: Doubleday.

———. 1997. *Common Purpose: Strengthening Families and Neighborhoods to Rebuild America.* New York: Anchor.

Sexton, E.T. 1999. "The Relationship between Child Maltreatment and Delinquent Behavior." *Reaching Today's Youth: The Community Circle of Caring Journal* 3(3):10–12.

Shavers, C.A. 2000. "The Interrelationships of Exposure to Community Violence and Trauma to the Behavioral Patterns and Academic Performance among Urban Elementary School-Aged Children." *Dissertation Abstracts International: Section B: The Sciences and Engineering* 61(4-B):1876.

Shirley, D. 1997. *Community Organizing for Urban School Reform.* Austin: University of Texas Press.

Shonk, S.M., and D. Cicchetti. 2001. "Maltreatment, Competency Deficits, and Risk for Academic and Behavioral Maladjustment." *Developmental Psychology, Special Issue* 37(1):3–17.

Short, R.J., and R.C. Talley. 1997. "Rethinking Psychology and the Schools: Implications of Recent National Policy." *American Psychologist* 52(3): 234–40.

Skurulsky, R.J. 2001. "The Impact of Intrafamilial and Community Violence on Children's Psychological Adjustment and Academic Achievement." *Dissertation Abstracts International: Section B: The Sciences and Engineering* 61 (10-B):5582.

Spencer, M.B. 1990. "Development of Minority Children: An Introduction." *Child Development* 61(2):267–69.

Stack, L.C. 1975. "Ecological Factors Related to First Psychiatric Admissions." *Journal of Community Psychology* 3(3):215–23.

Steinberg, L., S.D. Lamborn, S.M. Dornbusch, and N. Darling. 1992. "Impact of Parenting Practices on Adolescent Achievement: Authoritative Parenting, School Involvement, and Encouragement to Succeed. *Child Development* 63(5):1266–81.

Suarez-Orozco, C., and M. Suarez-Orozco. 2001. *Children of Immigration.* Cambridge, MA: Harvard University Press.

Sue, D.W., P. Arredondo, and R.J. McDavis. 1992. "Multicultural Counseling Competencies and Standards: A Call to the Profession." *Journal of Multicultural Counseling and Development* 20:644–88.

Talley, R.C., and R.J. Short. 1996. "Schools as Health Service Delivery Sites: Current Status and Future Directions." *Special Services in Schools* 10(2):37–55.

Taylor, H.G., N. Klein, and M. Hack. 2000. "School-Age Consequences of Birth Weight Less Than 750 g: A Review and Update." *Developmental Neuropsychology* 17(3):289–321.

Thies, K.M., and J.W. McAllister. 2001. "The Health and Education Leadership Project: A School Initiative for Children and Adolescents with Chronic Health Conditions." *Journal of School Health* 71(5):167–72.

Tyack, D.B. 1992. "Health and Social Services in Public Schools: Historical Perspectives." *The Future of Children* 2:19–31.

U.S. Department of Education. 1995. *School-linked Comprehensive Services for Children and Families.* Washington, DC: National Center for Educational Statistics, Office of Educational Research and Improvement.

U.S. Department of Education and U.S. Department of Health and Human Services. 1993. *Together We Can: A Guide for Crafting a Profamily System of Education and Human Services.* Washington, DC: U.S. Government Printing Office.

U.S. Department of Health and Human Services. 1999. *Mental Health: A Report of the Surgeon General.* Rockville, MD: Department of Health and Human Services, Substance Abuse and Mental Health Services Administration, Center for Mental Health Services, National Institutes of Health, National Institute of Mental Health.

U.S. Public Health Service. 2000. *Report of the Surgeon General's Conference on Children's Mental Health: A National Action Agenda.* Washington, DC: Department of Health and Human Services.

———. 2001. *Youth Violence: A Report of the Surgeon General.* Washington, DC: Department of Health and Human Services.

United Way of America. 2002. "The Way America Cares: Community by Community." http://national.unitedway.org (17 April 2002).

University of Pennsylvania. 2002. "The Center for Community Partnerships." 3 May. http://www.upenn.edu/ccp/wepic_hist.shtml (17 April 2002).

Urdan, T.C., and R.W. Roeser. 1993. "The Relations among Adolescents' Social Cognitions, Affect, and Academic Self-Schemas." Paper presented at the annual meeting of the American Educational Research Association, Atlanta, GA.

Vargas, L.A., and J.D. Koss-Chioino. 1992. *Working with Culture: Psychotherapeutic Interventions with Ethnic Minority Children and Adolescents.* San Francisco: Jossey-Bass.

Walberg, H.J. 1984. "Families as Partners in Educational Productivity." *Phi Delta Kappan* 65:397–400.

Walsh, M.E. 1992. *Moving to Nowhere: Children's Stories of Homelessness.* Westport, CT: Auburn House.

Walsh, M.E., and J.G. Barrett (in press). Roots of Violence and Aggression. In *The Handbook of Human Development for Health Professionals,* eds. K. M. Thies, and J. F. Travers, Thorofare, NJ: SLACK Inc.

Walsh, M.E., M.M. Brabeck, and K.A. Howard. 1999. "Interprofessional Collaboration in Children's Services: Towards a Theoretical Framework." *Children's Services: Social Policy, Research, and Practice* 2(4):183–208.

Walsh, M.E., M.M. Brabeck, K.A. Howard, F.T. Sherman, C. Montes, and T.J. Garvin. 2000. "The Boston College-Allston/Brighton Partnership: Description and Challenges." *Peabody Journal of Education* 75(3):6–32.

Walsh, M.E., J. Galassi, J.A. Murphy, and J. Park-Taylor. 2002. "A Conceptual Framework for Counseling Psychologists Working in Schools." *The Counseling Psychologist* 30(5): 682–704.

Walsh, M.E., and J. Park-Taylor. 2003. "Comprehensive Schooling and Interprofessional Collaboration: Theory, Research, and Practice." In *Meeting at the Hyphen: Schools-Universities-Communities-Professions in Collaboration for Student Achievement and Well Being*, eds. M. M. Brabeck, M. E. Walsh, and R. E. Latta, 8–44. Chicago: University of Chicago Press.

Walter, H.J., R.D. Vaughan, B. Armstrong, and R.Y. Krakoff. 1996. "Characteristics of Users and Nonusers of Health Clinics in Inner-City Junior High Schools." *Journal of Adolescent Health* 18(5):344–48.

Walter, H. J., R.D. Vaughan, and E.L. Wynder. 1994. "Primary Prevention of Cancer among Children: Challenges in Cigarette Smoking and Diet after Six Years of Intervention." In *Psychosocial Processes and Health: A Reader*, eds. A. Steptoe and J. Wardle, 325–35. New York: Cambridge University Press.

Wang, M.C., and E.W. Gordon, eds. 1994. *Educational Resilience in Inner-City America: Challenges and Prospects.* Hillsdale, NJ: Lawrence Erlbaum Associates, Inc.

Wang, M.C., G.D. Haertel, and H.J. Walberg. 1993. "Toward a Knowledge Base for School Learning." *Review of Educational Research* (fall):249–94.

———. 1997. "Fostering Educational Resilience in Inner-City Schools." In *Children and Youth: Interdisciplinary Perspectives* 119–42, eds. H.J. Walberg, O. Reyes, and R.P. Weissberg. Thousand Oaks, CA: Sage.

Wechsler, H., R.S. Devereaux, M. Davis, and J. Collins. 2000. "Using the School Environment to Promote Physical Activity and Healthy Eating." *Preventive Medicine: An International Journal Devoted to Practice and Theory* 31(2, Pt. 2):S121-S137.

Weiner, B. 1986. *An Attributional Theory of Motivation and Emotion.* New York: Springer-Verlag.

Wentzel, K.R., and S.R. Asher. 1995. The Academic Lives of Neglected, Rejected, Popular, and Controversial Children. *Child Development* 66(3):754–63.

Werner, H. 1948. *Comparative Psychology of Mental Development.* New York: Science Editions, Inc.

West, J., E. Germino-Hausken, and M. Collins. 1993. "Readiness for Kindergarten: Parent and Teacher Beliefs" (GPO Reference No. NCES 93–257). Washington, DC: National Center for Education Statistics.

White, K. 1982. "The Relation between Socioeconomic Status and Academic Achievement." *Psychological Bulletin* 91:461–81.

Yale University Bush Center in Child Development and Social Policy. 2002. "The School of the 21st Century." 14 February. http://www.yale.edu/21C/index2.html (20 October 2003).

———. 2002. "About the School Development Program." 14 February. http://info.med.yale.edu/ comer/about/overview.html (17 April 2002).

Young, B.S. 1986, January. "A Study of Visual Efficiency Necessary for Beginning Reading." Paper presented at the annual meeting of the Southwest Regional Conference of the International Reading Association, San Antonio, TX. (ERIC Document Reproduction Service No. ED 26B498).

2

History of School Health Services

Over the past century, programs and policy initiatives have reflected the growing recognition of the critical link between children's health and learning. Programs attempting to implement health and youth development programs connected to or located within schools have existed in one form or another since the establishment of public education. As early as the late nineteenth century, physicians began to offer their services to conduct in-school vaccinations, inspections, and hygiene lessons. At the same time, settlement houses and charitable organizations attempted to provide community-based comprehensive support services to children and families that, in many cases, developed working relationships with schools. Also, since the early twentieth century, school nurses in Boston, New York, and other cities led the battle against infectious diseases and poor sanitation. As another example, young girls who were trained as health educators employed these skills in their homes and communities (Marx, Wooley, and Northrop 1998).

The following chronology delineates the major events and policy initiatives that led to the current concept of comprehensive health services for school-aged children and youth in the United States. By examining these events throughout our nation's history, it becomes clear that many of these concepts have been recycled continually throughout the years. Additionally, programs and ideas have waxed and waned in their popularity according to the current political climate. It also becomes clear, throughout this historical chronology, that the success of these efforts largely depends on the support of government funding as well as the support of the general public.

THE LATE NINETEENTH AND EARLY TWENTIETH CENTURIES

Federal and state governments began taking an active role in the delivery of human services soon after the Civil War ended. At this time, the need for human service programs increased as emancipated slaves, orphans, and displaced families required housing, food, and health services. Additionally, immigration and industrialization created an increase in the numbers of people needing human services. During this time there was significant discussion about whether to coordinate and integrate services at the level of the client or at the administrative level (Burt, Resnick, and Novick 1998). This issue continues to be debated to this day.

One venue for the delivery of health and social services during this time period was the public school system. The emergence of health inspections and medical services in a few urban schools can be seen during the late 1800s. Although the idea of offering health services in the schools began during the late 1800s, it did not flourish as a nationwide initiative until the Progressive Era.

Late 1800s and Early 1900s State boards emerge to oversee human service institutions and to advise state legislatures on the needs of emancipated slaves and displaced families (Burt, Resnick, and Novick 1998).

1870 In New York, the Department of Health begins to collaborate with the Board of Education in providing vaccinations to all schoolchildren (Dryfoos 1994; Lear 1996).

1872 An epidemic of smallpox in New York motivates the Board of Education to hire a health officer to enforce laws on vaccination of schoolchildren. After the epidemic, the health officer is kept on to examine all children for disease and to conduct periodic surveys of health conditions in the school (Dryfoos 1994).

1877 The Charitable Organization Societies (COS) is instituted in an effort to streamline and coordinate the wide array of charitable organizations. The COS is founded upon the belief that improved organization of charitable groups would reduce poverty, in part by reducing duplicative services and payment to the poor, thereby removing disincentives to employment. The COS focuses on reforming private charities and, as a result, reinforces the concept of the state as a "provider of last resort." This orientation would contribute to the increased fragmentation of social services as it widens the gulf between the public and private sectors (Burt, Resnick, and Novick 1998).

THE PROGRESSIVE ERA

During the years from 1890 to World War I, often referred to as the Progressive Era, activists and writers like Jacob Riis, Robert Hunter, and John Spargo called on schools to offer a range of health services (Tyack 1992). Initially, school-based medical inspections were considered the most popular cure-alls of the Progressive Era. These inspections were considered the best way to eliminate barriers to students' learning (Tyack 1992). These screening efforts were succeeded by the establishment of nursing and home visiting services to help families address problems found during medical screenings (Lear 1996).

At the same time, dentists viewed schools as the ideal site for inspections and instruction in dental hygiene. Dentists, like other medical personnel, also regarded their work as a cure-all, claiming that eliminating cavities would bring good health, eliminate school failure, and prevent delinquency. Dentists, however, supported the idea of free clinics (Tyack 1992) while the medical profession attempted to discourage the idea of school-based free clinics preferring to limit their services to medical inspections and vaccinations.

While physicians and dentists took the lead in introducing health services in the schools, nonprofessional volunteer groups were often responsible for the promotion of reforms in social services. Women's clubs sometimes worked with elite society groups and socialist leaders to pioneer such reforms. These groups provided free lunch or breakfast, vacation schools, and playgrounds. Additionally, reformers working in settlement houses in urban slums pioneered new forms of school-linked social work and counseling (Tyack 1992).

The progressive movement and the increasing professionalism of the social work field were both factors in the greater role that state and federal governments took in providing services to the poor during the Progressive Era. The primary focus of social services during this time was on two issues: eliminating the root causes of poverty and providing a social safety net for older persons and widows with dependent children (as opposed to reforming or ameliorating individual problems) (Burt, Resnick, and Novick 1998).

1890s Physicians first propose that schoolchildren be given medical inspections, vaccinations, and instruction in hygiene. In some cases, they create school clinics to treat indigent students, but in the 1920s the American Medical Association (AMA) would denounce free clinics as socialized medicine (Tyack 1992).

1894 After several epidemics have swept through its schools, Boston places 50 physicians in schools to screen children for signs of infectious disease. Communicable disease rates decrease. Within a few years, the cities of New York, Chicago, and Philadelphia follow suit (Lear 1996).

1894 Later that same year, Boston establishes the first citywide system of medical inspection. The Boston commissioner of health appoints 50 school physicians as medical visitors, one to each of the 50 school districts, following epidemics of diphtheria and scarlet fever. These physicians visit the schools daily and examine all the children selected by the teachers. Communicable disease rates decrease and other cities began to set up similar systems for medical inspections (Dryfoos 1994).

1899 Connecticut requires teachers to test children's eyesight every three years (Lear 1996).

1900s Private charities and mutual aid societies emerge as the primary means of providing assistance to the poor.

1900s Settlement houses (such as Hull House in Chicago) are first established. These are organizations based in the community and designed to provide advocacy and a wide range of services to poor families (e.g., day care, health care, citizenship classes, and language instruction). These settlement houses are also seen as vehicles to mobilize communities (Burt, Resnick, and Novick 1998).

1904 Vermont mandated that each student have annual examinations of ears, eyes, nose, and throat (Lear 1996).

1904 Reformer Robert Hunter writes, "The time has come for a new conception of the responsibilities of the school." The lives of youth in cities are desperate, parents "bring up their children in surroundings which make them in large numbers vicious and criminally dangerous," and some agency must take charge of "the entire problem of child life and master it." Hunter makes it clear who should do so: "If the school does not assume this responsibility, how shall the work be done?" (Tyack 1992).

1909   Child advocates such as Jane Addams, Florence Kelley, and Lillian Wald influence Theodore Roosevelt to organize the first White House Conference on Children to address the problems of poor children living in the United States. These advocates are primarily concerned with issues around child labor and compulsory education (Burt, Resnick, and Novick 1998; Dryfoos 1994).

1910   Three hundred and twelve cities provided medical inspection as schools incorporate some of the new health programs initiated by physicians and dentists. During the next decade the practice becomes common in most cities that are home to large numbers of immigrants. Medical examinations performed by physicians or nurses who are employed by school boards become common in most districts. Health education classes appear in teacher education programs and are taught in most progressive high schools (Tyack 1992).

1911   The AMA and the National Education Association (NEA) come together to form the Joint Commission on School Health Policies. This commission is an attempt to bring together the professions of education and medicine to assist in developing and expanding health education in schools (Dryfoos 1994).

1912   The Children's Bureau by Congress is established. This organization conducts and supports research on child welfare, infant mortality, child employment, and neglect. Although the bureau is responsible for child well-being in the federal government, it is not authorized to provide services (Burt, Resnick, and Novick 1998; Dryfoos 1994).

1914   Hoag and Terman, among the earliest and most noted authors on school health, argue that for school health to reach its full potential the schools would have to take control of school health from local boards of health, expand school nursing, and establish medical clinics in schools. These authors also urge the inclusion of dental services, eye care, and psychological services.

1915   Draftees in World War I fail their medical examinations in such large numbers that all states soon mandate physical education (Tyack 1992).

1915   The Health Department's Bureau of Child Hygiene closes five special nose and throat clinics for schoolchildren, beginning a trend to separate the functions of public health and clinical services (Lear 1996).

1918   The NEA's "Cardinal Principles of Secondary Education" symbolizes the progressive consensus; it includes health, worthy home membership, vocation, worthy use of leisure, and ethical character as five of its seven guiding principles (Tyack 1992).

1920s In an effort to stem delinquency and promote mental health, foundations begin to subsidize school social workers. Despite the publicity given to these efforts, school districts do not invest much in mental health personnel. Summer school programs are also popular, even in small cities. However, this number would drop considerably during the 1930s (Tyack 1992).

1921   The Maternal and Infancy Care Act, the oldest and most important federal child initiative in our nation's history, was passed by Congress. The legislation would be allowed to lapse in 1929 (Dryfoos 1994).

1921   The Shepard-Turner Act authorizes federal matching grants to states for their efforts to reduce infant mortality (Burt, Resnick, and Novick 1998).

1923   School Superintendent of Gary, Indiana, William Wirt, states that the school should "serve as a clearing house for children's activities so that all child welfare agencies may be working simultaneously and efficiently, thus creating a child world within the city wherein all children may have a wholesome environment all of the day and every day" (Tyack 1992).

1923   The American Child Health Association conducts a survey that demonstrates that almost all major cities have established nursing services in their schools and, in many, physicians still conduct some physical examinations (Dryfoos 1994).

1927   The American School Physicians Association is established (Dryfoos 1994).

1928 Sociologist Thomas D. Eliot, advocating a uniting of education and other forms of child welfare, states that all efforts dealing with "neglected or behavior-problem children" should "be closely coordinated" under the aegis of the school. He goes on to state that this coordinated efforts should include "medical inspection, school nursing, attendance control, vocational guidance and placement, psychological testing, visiting teachers, and special schools and classes" (Tyack 1992).

1929 Lewis Terman, the coauthor of the leading text published on educational hygiene, advocates for an expanded role for medical personnel in the schools to protect children from the environment of poor and stressed families and communities. Terman states that the school should be "the educational center, the social center, and the hygiene center of the community in which it is located" (Dryfoos 1994).

THE 1930s THROUGH 1950s

The federal relief programs, also called the New Deal programs, were created to combat the effects of the Great Depression. These programs sought to create a permanent state structure that would take primary responsibility for social services. The programs used federal funds to establish the role of each state as a sovereign body and established the states' role as managers of federal money (Burt, Resnick, and Novick 1998).

The idea of the community school began gaining increased attention during this time period. Community school, at this time, referred to a school in which both the curriculum and the support services were designed to intersect with the community (Dryfoos 1994). The community school or full-service school movement would later prove to be one of the most promising initiatives to emerge from this era.

1933 The American School Physicians Association becomes the American School Health Association (Dryfoos 1994).

1935 Fifty school buildings in Flint, Michigan, are selected as part of the Flint Community School Initiative, funded by the Charles Mott Foundation (Dryfoos 1994).

1935 The Social Security Act authorizes federal support for dependent children, older persons, and blind persons; maternal and child health programs; child welfare services; and vocational rehabilitative and public health services. The act creates a "permanent state structure with primary responsibility for social welfare" and requires that state governments become significantly involved in categorical social programs (Burt, Resnick, and Novick 1998). Aid to Dependent Children is also created under this important act. Much of the funding from the Act is used to set up child health clinics for low-income families. This funding source would eventually become a major support for school-based clinics (Dryfoos 1994).

1937   In cities with more than 100,000 people, the ratio of mental health professionals and students is 2.82 psychologists, 17.54 psychiatrists, and 27.55 social workers per 100,000 students (Tyack 1992).

1939   The Federal Security Agency is established to administer and coordinate the many federal human services organizations. The agency is designed as an intergovernmental partnership and includes the Social Security Board, the National Youth Administration, the Civilian Conservation Corps, the Public Health Service, the Office of Education, and the U.S. Employment Service (Burt, Resnick, and Novick 1998).

1940   A survey found that in almost all cities with a population greater than 30,000 there is some form of public health service—usually the availability of school nurses and medical inspection. In 70 percent of the cities reporting, the school districts run the service; in 20 percent, the departments of health run it; and in 10 percent, the two agencies collaborate. In most cases, a physician is responsible for administering the program. Despite the Great Depression, medical budgets and staff increased during this decade. More and more dentists and dental hygienists become school employees, and school dental clinics experienced a steady growth (Tyack 1992).

After   School social workers and mental health professionals are phased
World   back into school settings. This is especially true in prosperous
War II   districts (Dryfoos 1994).

1944   William Schmidt, a consultant to the Children's Bureau, encourages the American Public Health Association and the American School Health Association to support health services in schools because of the high rejection rate among Selective Service registrants (Dryfoos 1994).

1945 The Selective Service findings stimulate more than 12 new bills affecting school health although almost none are passed. Leona Baumgartner, an advocate for children's services, talks about this period as one that shifted from comprehensive health efforts to building programs around individual children (Dryfoos 1994).

1945 The Astoria Plan for elementary school health services in New York City provides a successful example of an effective screening and referral program for children with health concerns. This program includes coordination with teachers and school nurses (Lear 1996). After being tested in a few schools, this plan is adopted by the entire New York City School system as well as by other cities (Dryfoos 1994).

1946 The National School Lunch Program is instituted. The free lunch policy overcomes many arguments before becoming a regular part of the public school program and budget. New Deal efforts and a federal law make subsidized lunches a familiar fixture in most school districts.

1947– Alfred Yankauer, a public health administrator and later editor
1962 of the *American Journal of Public Health*, contributes to the literature on school-based health services by publishing a series of evaluations of the Astoria Plan in New York City and other programs in Rochester and Albany. He demonstrates in his research that elementary school students show little evidence of illness and that, after an initial physical exam, difficulties could be determined by teachers and nurses (Dryfoos 1994).

THE 1960s

This time period was characterized by the states' becoming conduits for attaining clearly defined national objectives. This was a period of dramatic expansion in the number of federal categorical programs to meet specific needs. This decade also marked the beginning of the movement to improve the organization of social services (Burt, Resnick, and Novick 1998). During the 1960s, as during the Progressive Era, reformers targeted particularly disadvantaged populations, especially the urban poor and persons of color, as recipients of services. Reformers were also concerned with assisting the whole family, not only children. A time of vigorous social movements for African Americans,

Latinos, women, and the disabled, the 1960s viewed education as a vanguard institution in the war on poverty. The federal government passed Head Start legislation and the Elementary and Secondary Education Act (ESEA) of 1965 and developed programs to improve nutrition, job training and placement, and health. Federal policymakers who were focused on eradicating poverty often did not give credence to the ability of public educators to understand or assist the poor. Sometimes these reformers bypassed schools entirely and funneled money for services through community action agencies of various kinds.

1961   A National Institute of Child Health and Human Development is added to the National Institutes of Health to conduct more basic research than that produced by the Children's Bureau (Dryfoos 1994).

1961   President Kennedy establishes the Advisory Commission of Intergovernmental Relations. The new commission documents the fragmentation of federal programs at the state and local levels and blames this fragmentation on a lack of coordination at the federal level. The commission was motivated by a concern about waste, duplication, and misuse of federal resources and by a general desire to improve efficiency at the federal level (Burt, Resnick, and Novick 1998).

1961   The Juvenile Delinquency and Youth Offenses Control Act passes. The Act authorizes the award of grants for "experimental community projects" that focus on changing institutions; integrating and coordinating existing programs; involving local leadership and residents; and funding activities in the areas of education, vocational training, youth employment, legal aid, and community service (Burt, Resnick, and Novick 1998).

1961   The Ford Foundation begin its "gray areas" program, which awards grants to city governments and community agencies in New York, Oakland, New Haven, Philadelphia, Boston, Washington, D.C., and the state of North Carolina to improve conditions in low-income neighborhoods and prevent delinquency and crime (Burt, Resnick, and Novick 1998).

1961   President Kennedy establishes the President's Committee on Juvenile Delinquency and Youth Crime to review and coordinate federal activities related to juvenile delinquency and to stimulate innovative and experimental programming (Burt, Resnick, and Novick 1998).

1962– The number of federal categorical programs increases from 160
1966 to 349. Some programs transfer federal dollars to the states (Title IV of the Social Security Act); some programs transfer funds to local grantees (Head Start); and some programs transfer state dollars to local recipients (Title 1 of the Elementary and Secondary Education Act). The multitude of funding formulas, types of grants, and levels of administrative responsibility leads to confusion and fragmentation of services (Burt, Resnick, and Novick 1998).

1964 The Economic Opportunity Act launches President Johnson's War on Poverty. The Act is motivated by several ideas that still drive efforts to improve outcomes for poor children and families: reversing the causes of poverty, coordinating efforts, relying on developmental services, using local initiatives, and empowering the poor to solve their own problems. The Act breaks new ground by appropriating funds for the express purpose of reducing poverty. Despite its lofty ideals, the emphasis on involving the residents of poor neighborhoods in the local planning and decision-making process is reduced in 1965 after an organized protest by a group of mayors (Burt, Resnick, and Novick 1998).

The Act establishes the federal Office of Economic Opportunity and authorizes the creation of 500 Community Action Agencies (CAAs) around the country to improve coordination among local human service programs such as Head Start, Legal Services, Job Corps, and VISTA (Volunteers in Service to America) and to operate some of these programs directly. CAAs are designed as community-based, nongovernmental entities that could work across agencies and service sectors to mobilize public and private resources. They are not very effective because of lack of political support and are viewed as duplicative of existing community planning entities, radical, confrontational, and poorly managed. Local officials are successful in pressuring congress to reduce the power of CAAs. By the 1970s, they are reduced to small local agencies working outside the organized social service delivery system. Some rural areas still have CAAs (Burt, Resnick, and Novick 1998).

1965   The Elementary and Secondary Education Act is first enacted. The act supplements state and local efforts to provide all children with a high-quality education.

1965   The Advisory Commission of Intergovernmental Relations' work leads to the establishment of the U.S. Department of Housing and Urban Development (HUD). HUD is created to serve as a focal point for all federal policies and programs related to urban problems (Burt, Resnick, and Novick 1998).

Mid-   The Model Cities Program is launched with the twin goals of
1960s   helping the poor and coordinating the federal grant system. HUD funds this effort, which is designed to avoid the mistakes of the CAAs by encouraging the development of locally driven planning processes that would precede community action. This program enjoys moderate success in medium-sized cities. However, it is underfunded, it does not concentrate its efforts, and it does not lead to coordination of federal funding streams. Model Cities has been described as a "lesson in the dissipation of limited resources" (Burt, Resnick, and Novick 1998).

1965   Amendments to the Social Security Act are established, creating Medicaid and Medicare. Additionally, new kinds of maternal and child health efforts are developed, called Children and Youth (C&Y) Projects. These projects attempt to create comprehensive care through grants to local agencies such as hospitals and medical schools (Dryfoos 1994).

1967   The C&Y Grants fund a new Medicaid initiative called Early Periodic Screening Diagnosis and Treatment for all Medicaid Eligible Children (Dryfoos 1994).

THE 1970s

During the 1970s, significant federal interest in service integration was renewed, but efforts were more modest than those undertaken in the 1960s. President Nixon shifted the focus from direct intervention to reduce urban poverty to coordination and reform of the federal grant system, shifting power from federal to local government and improving the situation of all citizens. The term "service integration" came into use during this period to characterize efforts designed to counteract the "categorical excesses" of President Johnson's Great Society Programs. It also described efforts to meet the needs of the whole person, an approach that reflected new thinking in the field of developmental psychology. The Department of Health, Education, and Welfare (HEW), the lead agency for service integration efforts, developed an ambitious agenda of research and demonstration projects, proposed legislation, technical assistance efforts, and internal reforms (Burt, Resnick, and Novick 1998).

1972   HEW proposes the Intergovernmental Cooperation Act, later amended and renamed to become the Allied Services Act. This Act is intended to improve state and local planning and administrative capacities by waiving federal requirements and allowing the transfer of funds between programs. The legislation is eventually withdrawn from Congress for several reasons, including inadequate funding and perceptions that the bill gives too much control to governors and too little to local communities (Burt, Resnick, and Novick 1998).

1972   HEW launches the Services Integration Targets of Opportunity demonstration, focusing on forging interagency program links in the areas of budget, personnel, planning and programming, administrative support, core services, and case coordination at the local level. Forty-five project grants are given to agencies and groups with diverse purposes and goals, to test service integration in preparation for the introduction of an Allied Services Act in Congress (Burt, Resnick, and Novick 1998).

1973   The Department of Labor's Comprehensive Employment and Training Act (which consolidates 17 categorical training programs and would be replaced in 1982 by the Job Training Partnership Act) is created (Burt, Resnick, and Novick 1998).

1974   HUD's Community Development Block Grant (which consolidates a number of urban programs created during the Johnson administration) is created. This program typifies this new approach to federal funding, with local agencies performing planning functions and nongovernmental entities delivering actual services through contracts (Burt, Resnick, and Novick 1998).

1974   HEW launches the Partnership Grant Projects (PGP) with the goal of helping local government improve the planning, management, and accountability of human services programs. The PGP emphasize innovative program design (Burt, Resnick, and Novick 1998).

1974   The Allied Services Act is reworked and reintroduced. This new Act authorizes HEW demonstration grants and allows the transfer of up to 30 percent of funds from one HEW program to another. This bill does not pass because of opposition from supporters of categorical programs (Burt, Resnick, and Novick 1998).

1975   HEW funds five sites to participate in the Comprehensive Human Services Planning and Delivery System project, an attempt to develop and test the effect of several different models of local comprehensive management and planning on the efficiency and effectiveness of human service systems. The initial evaluation indicates that improved management techniques could reduce clients' waiting time and improve agencies' accountability and efficiency, but funding cuts prevents the project's full implementation, and a planned third-party evaluation would never be carried out (Burt, Resnick, Novick 1998).

1975   The Education Act for All Handicapped Children (Public Law 94–142) is passed. This law states that schools must provide free public education for all children and addresses the importance of special education and support services.

1975   The Allied Services Act is reintroduced to Congress with a number of changes but does not pass because of a number of issues, including the loss of White House support during the Watergate scandal (Burt, Resnick, and Novick 1998).

1975   Title XX of the Social Security Act (renamed the Social Services Block Grant in 1981) passes. Title XX, which becomes the first title of this social welfare act to fund services, is intended to facilitate states' development of comprehensive, integrated human service delivery systems. Title XX replaces parts of two categorical social service funding streams with a block grant that gives states significantly more flexibility to use the same level of funding. This Act remains an important source of funding for human services programs (Burt, Resnick, and Novick 1998).

Late 1970s   Initiatives begin in the late 1970s to create more modest coordinated partnerships between city, state, and federal agencies and state-level service-integration efforts. HEW supports the efforts of several states to develop umbrella human service agencies with centralized management of the major social services and public assistance agencies and with at least three other major human service programs to encourage service integration (Burt, Resnick, and Novick 1998).

THE 1980s

During the Carter administration, HEW became the Department of Health and Human Services (HHS). During this time, the department oversaw some moderate efforts to identify barriers to coordinated services and to outline national strategies to improve service delivery. By the early 1980s, however, interest in efforts to initiate service integration on a large scale had dropped off and federal initiatives were terminated. The Reagan administration launched reforms intending to reduce the federal role in social service provision, ease the burden of federal regulations on the states, and significantly reduce funding for human service programs. Overall, funding for social services programs declined significantly during the years of the Reagan presidency (Burt, Resnick, and Novick 1998).

Additionally, during the early 1980s, education reform efforts focused on graduating a productive workforce to ensure the nation's competitiveness in the world economy. The initial reform efforts concentrated on improving academic standards, holding schools and teachers accountable for student achievement, and emphasizing basic skills and the increased use of technology. Later, school reform efforts focused on structural change—specifically, more flexibility in program implementation, shared decision making within each school, links between curriculum standards and assessment and accountability, family involvement, and options for which programs students could attend. The connection between health and education was an issue that received attention in education reform discussions (Marx, Wooley, and Northrop 1998).

Finally, this decade saw a new emphasis in primary prevention programs. Practitioners and policymakers began to focus on the high cost and limited effectiveness of crisis intervention programs. However, the focus of these intervention programs remained on reducing risk behaviors, such as substance abuse, teen pregnancy, and dropping out of school, rather than on more comprehensive approaches.

1981   The Omnibus Budget Reconciliation Act creates nine new or revised block grants, decreases funding for social services and other programs by 25 percent, reduces federal reporting requirements for states, and gives states more discretion in the use of federal dollars. These block grants are seen as a way to reduce spending and shift more responsibility to the states (Burt, Resnick, and Novick 1998).

1984   The Deficit Reduction Act authorizes the Services Integration Pilot Projects with the explicit goal of reducing social welfare costs. In contrast to the focus of earlier efforts on improving management and delivery of human services as ends in themselves, this reduction is to be accomplished by increasing the accountability of the social service system, primarily through the use of case management to link all relevant services and providers in the community. Evaluation reveals that successful service integration required support at every level, including state and local policymakers, in-house power brokers, employees, case workers, clients, and community leaders (Burt, Resnick, and Novick 1998).

Mid-to-late 1980s   Federal agencies and foundations begin to fund community-level attempts to integrate services at the juncture where clients receive the services. This effort is made more urgent by increasingly complex social problems and a less-cohesive social service system. However, because there was no overarching theme guiding these interventions, this period has been described as one of "unplanned variation" (Burt, Resnick, and Novick 1998).

1986   The Drug Free Schools and Community Act launches federal support for drug education and treatment efforts in the schools.

1987   The Children's Aid Society, New York City's oldest and largest social service agency, conducts a needs assessment of Manhattan's Washington Heights neighborhood.

1987   A groundbreaking article by Diane Allensworth and Lloyd Kolbe is published in a special issue of the *Journal of School Heath*. This article discusses comprehensive school health programs and proposes that school health programs should include eight components: health education; physical education; health services; nutrition services; counseling, psychological, and social services; healthy school environment; healthy promotion for staff; and parent-community involvement (Marx, Wooley, and Northrop 1998).

1989   The Children's Aid Society collaborates with New York City's Public Schools and community-based partners to develop a comprehensive response to the pressing needs of children and families in the northern Manhattan neighborhood of Washington Heights. Out of this collaboration would grow the concept of a community school.

1990s AND EARLY TWENTY-FIRST CENTURY

Service integration and coordination efforts in the early 1990s continued to emphasize local systems reform. Federal initiatives attempted to reinvigorate service integration. Some of the efforts included reauthorizing previous initiatives, such as Head Start. Some efforts focused on the creation of new initiatives, such as the Family Preservation Act. The election of President Clinton in 1992, and his reelection in 1996, did not change the trend toward reducing the federal role in providing for the marginalized and underserved populations within the United States (Burt, Resnick, and Novick 1998). However, state and local governments continued to use federal funds to create opportunities for collaborative planning, cross-professional training, and coordinated service referral. All of these efforts sought to create comprehensive and coordinated service systems. Yet, at the same time, the federal government continued the trend toward reducing the role of the government in the provision of social services (i.e., passing welfare reform legislation).

Additionally, during this time, the youth development approach became more established. The idea that *all* children needed support and opportunities to grow into healthy adults began to replace the idea of intervention services only for children with serious difficulties. This decade saw a dramatic increase in the number of services to promote children's growth and development as well as funding efforts directed at these services.

1990   The National Institute of Mental Health issues a report estimating that 15–22 percent of the nation's 63 million children and adolescents have mental health problems severe enough to warrant treatment, yet fewer than 20 percent receive any type of mental health services.

1990   Two organizations representing diverse major interest groups, the AMA and the National Association of State Boards of Education, issue *Code Blue: Uniting for Healthier Youth*. Their recommendations stem from their agreement that education and health are inextricably intertwined. The commission strongly supports the establishment of health centers in schools, attention to school climate and to issues related to achievement, and the restructuring of public and private health insurance to ensure access to services (Dryfoos 1994).

1990   HHS funds a National Center for Service Integration to disseminate information and provide technical assistance to local governments and nonprofit organizations, but the center's funding would not be renewed when the Clinton administration arrives in 1992 (Burt, Resnick, and Novick 1998).

1992   The first of the National Education Goals (NEG), established by President Bush, are carried forward by President Clinton. The NEG are designed to emphasize the establishment of family, school, and community partnerships (Burt, Resnick, and Novick 1998).

1992   On the state and local levels, many integrated service efforts are made, including the use of federal Child Care Development Block Grant dollars as a catalyst for collaborative planning, integrated training, and coordinated service referral; the popularity of one-stop shopping for multiple social services; and community-based planning for comprehensive and coordinated service systems (Burt, Resnick, and Novick 1998).

1992   A federally sponsored effort to promote the integration of services is an outgrowth of the "reinventing government" effort begun by the Clinton administration. Additionally, as part of this effort, the 104th Congress focuses on changing government more directly by block granting and eliminating or reducing funding for a number of social service programs, including welfare, food stamps, and Supplemental Security Income. These changes shift the responsibility for serving vulnerable populations to the state and local governments and the private sector (Burt, Resnick, and Novick 1998).

1993   Education Reform Act; Section 94 directs the Departments of Social Services, Youth Services, Mental Health, and Mental Retardation to study and develop a plan to earmark 1–2 percent of their budgets for services in school-based centers.

1993 The Phi Delta Kappa/Gallup Poll of attitudes toward public schools finds that a majority of the American public would like public schools to provide student health services (Marx, Wooley, and Northrop 1998).

1993 The 21st Century Community Learning Centers Program is established by Congress to award grants to rural and urban public schools, or a group of such schools, to enable them to plan, implement, or expand projects that benefit the educational, health, social services, cultural, or recreational needs of the community.

1994 The Goals 2000: Educate America Act is signed into law by President Clinton on March 31.

1994 The reauthorization of the Drug Free Schools and Community Act expands the scope of funded activities to include violence prevention measures.

1994 The Gallup Organization finds that a majority of school administrators, students, and families support comprehensive school health education (Marx, Wooley, and Northrop 1998).

1994 The concept of an "enabling component" is introduced by Howard Adelman and illustrated by the New American Schools' Learning Center Model (Adelman 1996). This new concept refers to the school reforms' propensity to concentrate on improving instruction and school management, while ignoring the programs and services needed to address barriers to students' learning. The enabling component helps to support socioemotional services and is essential in any effort to reform and restructure schools. The enabling component intertwines all appropriate school, community, and home resources through policy reform and system restructuring (Marx, Wooley, and Northrop 1998).

1994 Forty-four percent of secondary schools in the United States develop individualized health plans as part of individualized education plans for students with special needs (Marx, Wooley, and Northrop 1998).

1994 The National Consensus Building Conference on School-Linked Integrated Service Systems (Ad Hoc Working Group on Integrated Services) develop several principles to guide further activity: the development of operating systems and techniques that promote interdisciplinary interagency collaboration; the creation of interdisciplinary teams and partnerships; and the continued focus on resource needs (Marx, Wooley, and Northrop 1998).

1994   "Joint Statement on School Health" is issued. The secretaries of education and health and human services attempt to foster cooperation and coordination between the education and health sectors. In this statement, the two secretaries recognize the link between education and health and the convergence of the national health and education goals. The secretaries also announce the establishment of the Interagency Committee on School Health and the National Coordinating Committee on School Health, both chaired by officials of the Departments of Education, Health and Human Services, and Agriculture (Marx, Wooley, and Northrop 1998).

1995   Vice President Al Gore announces awards of nearly $67 million in new grants to 125 communities throughout the nation to provide high-quality community learning centers in 517 schools. The school-based centers are designed to provide enriched learning opportunities to children outside of the regular school hours and during the summer in a community-school setting.

1995   The Office of Adolescent Health undertakes a major initiative to enhance mental health in schools. This initiative includes the initial step of establishing two national training and technical assistance centers. They are already pursuing a wide range of activities designed to improve how schools address barriers to learning and enhance healthy development (Marx, Wooley, and Northrop 1998).

1995   The Joint Committee on National Health Education Standards releases National Health Education Standards that are informed by health education theory and practice as well as by curriculum frameworks and standards from several states. The national standards are compatible with the Goals 2000: Educate America Act and provide a bridge to Healthy People 2000:

National Health Promotion and Disease Prevention Objectives (Marx, Wooley, and Northrop 1998).

1995   The U.S. Department of Agriculture creates the School Meals Initiative for Healthy Children, which requires that school meals meet the dietary Guidelines for Americans, supply certain proportions of recommended daily allowances of particular nutrients, include foods from different cultures, and appeal to the consumer (Marx, Wooley, and Northrop 1998).

1996   "Putting the Pieces Together: Comprehensive Schooling Strategies for Children and Families" is published by the U.S. Department of Education. This document outlines ways federal and state officials, communities, and private agencies can work together to set and achieve benchmarks for improving student well-being. (Marx, Wooley, and Northrop 1998).

1997   Centers for Disease Control and Prevention publishes *Guidelines for School and Community Programs to Promote Lifelong Physical Activity Among Young People,* suggesting broad strategies for a coordinated effort to increase the physical activity levels of young people (Marx, Wooley, and Northrop 1998).

1998   The U.S. Departments of Education and Justice publish a report titled, "Safe and Smart: Making After School Hours Work for Kids," that emphasizes research evidence on the potential of afterschool programs to increase the safety of children, reduce their risk-taking, and improve their chances of academic success.

1998   President Clinton announces the award of $60 million in new grants to 183 communities nationwide to help establish high-quality afterschool programs. The 21st Century Learning Centers program is designed to provide increased learning opportunities to children outside of regular school hours in a safe environment. This program would more than triple in its funding to schools in the next three years.

1999   The Educational Excellence for All Children Act of 1999 is President Clinton's proposal for reauthorizing the Elementary and Secondary Education Act (ESEA). This proposal is an extension of the commitment to the 1994 reauthorization of ESEA and the Goals 2000: Educate America Act.

1999   The first Surgeon General's Report on Mental Health is published. The report explores recent research on mental disorders, treatment, and the mental health care system.

2000   The House Education and Workforce Committees approve a bill to renew parts of ESEA. This bill, entitled the Literacy Involves Families Together (LIFT) Act, improves the quality of services under the Even Start Family Literacy Program (first authorized in 1989). The LIFT Act lowers the age of children served to birth; sets standards based on scientific research; encourages coordination with other federal programs to provide better services; and provides funding for training and technical assistance to local Even Start instructors.

2000   The Department of Education releases a report entitled "Hope for Urban Education." This report describes nine high-poverty, high-performing urban elementary schools. Each of these nine schools, including the Harriet A. Baldwin School in Boston, are recognized for impressive academic results where student achievement in math and reading is higher than the state average for all schools. These schools all focus on academic success, a collective sense of responsibility for school improvement, and building partnerships with parents.

2001   The Surgeon General's report on Children's Mental Health is released. The report states that the United States is facing a public health crisis in regards to addressing mental illness in children and, as one of its suggestions, advocates strongly for schools taking a central role in prevention and intervention efforts.

2002   President George W. Bush signs into law the No Child Left Behind Act of 2001. The Act is the most comprehensive reform of ESEA since it was enacted in 1965. The act redefines the federal role in kindergarten through twelfth-grade education and seeks to close the achievement gap between disadvantaged and minority students and their peers.

2002   The 21st Century Learning Centers program is converted from a federally administered discretionary grants program to a state administered program. Of the $1 billion appropriation, $325 million will flow to the states on a formula basis and the states will make competitive awards.

REFERENCES

Adelman, H. S. 1996. "Restructuring Education Support Services and Integrating Community Resources: Beyond the Full-Service School Model." *School Psychology Review* 25(4):431–45.

Burt, M., G. Resnick, and E. Novick. 1998. *Building Supportive Communities for At Risk Adolescents: It Takes More Than Services.* Washington, DC: American Psychological Association.

Dryfoos, J. 1994. *Full-Service Schools: A Revolution in Health and Social Services for Children, Youth, and Families.* San Francisco: Jossey-Bass.

Lear, J.G. 1996. "School-Based Services and Adolescent Health: Past, Present, and Future." *Adolescent Medicine: State of the Art Reviews* 7(2):163–80.

Marx, E., S. Wooley, and D. Northrop. 1998. *Health is Academic: A Guide to Coordinated School Health Programs.* New York: Teachers College Press.

Tyack, D. 1992. "Health and Social Service in Public Schools: Historical Perspectives." *Future of Children* 2(1):19–31.

3

Biographical Sketches

Pioneers and major contributors advancing a coordinated approach to children's health and learning have occupied a variety of professional roles, including educators, researchers, health care professionals, political leaders, lawyers, youth development professionals, and child care professionals. The collaboration of professionals from these diverse occupations is necessary for children and youth to experience optimal health and learning environments. While teachers and educators are central to the promotion of academic achievement and healthy development, their collaborators in comprehensive health services play a key role in sustaining their efforts. Practitioners and researchers in such fields as child development, pediatric health care, and program evaluation continually search for new prevention and intervention strategies that will lead to positive health and learning outcomes. Lawyers and policymakers develop and advocate for legislation that enhances the experiences and opportunities of our nation's youth. Parents, guardians, and community members, through their actions and advocacy, can influence the type of environment in which children in the community grow and learn.

Professionals in the field of youth development continue to remind us that a healthy young person needs more than a good education. While many individuals work to promote the positive change and advancement in young people's health and learning daily, the individuals described within this chapter are particularly known for their major contributions to the development of comprehensive school health services.

JANE ADDAMS (1860–1935)

Jane Addams was one of many reformers dedicated to social change during the turn of the twentieth century and is remembered primarily as a founder of the Settlement House Movement in the United States. She viewed children and families from a holistic perspective and understood the importance of linking health, education, and social supports. She is also remembered as the first American woman to receive the Nobel Peace Prize.

Jane Addams was born in Cedarville, Illinois, in 1860, and was the eighth of nine children. After graduating from the Rockford Seminary for Women in 1881, she hoped to earn a degree in medicine. However, discouragement from her family and poor health kept her from pursuing this goal. At the age of 27, while traveling in Europe, she visited a settlement house, Toynbee Hall, in London's East End. This visit prompted Ms. Addams to develop a similar house in an underprivileged area of Chicago. Subsequently, she and her friend, Ellen Starr, founded Hull House in Chicago in 1889. This center was dedicated to the mitigation of the harsh conditions of poverty found in the cities.

Hull House programs foreshadowed many contemporary programs linking health and learning. The center initially offered kindergarten classes and afterschool programming, including cooking and sewing lessons, as well as evening classes and clubs for adults. Later, an art gallery, a public kitchen, a coffee house, a gymnasium, a swimming pool, a cooperative boarding club for girls, a book bindery, an art studio, a music school, a drama group, a circulating library, an employment bureau, a theatre, and a labor museum were welcome additions. By its second year in existence, Hull House was host to two thousand people every week. In her book, *Twenty Years at Hull House,* Ms. Addams describes the importance of holistic health practices stating that "wisdom to deal with a man's difficulties comes only through some knowledge of his life and habits as a whole; and that to treat an isolated episode is almost sure to invite blundering."

In addition to her dedication to direct service to people living in poverty, Ms. Addams played a pivotal role in the areas of public and social policy reform. She was involved in policy changes regarding labor reform, laws governing the working conditions for children and women, the women's suffragist movement, and peaceful protests against World War I. She also assisted in founding the National Association for the Advancement of Colored People (NAACP) and the American Civil Liberties Union (ACLU).

During her life, Ms. Addams wrote many articles addressing social and health problems and their consequences. They were published in a variety of magazines, including *American Magazine, McClures, Crisis,* and *Ladies Home Journal.* Ms. Addams also wrote several books, including *Democracy and Social Ethics* (1902), *Newer Ideals of Peace* (1907), *Spirit of Youth* (1909), *Twenty Years at Hull House* (1910), *A New Conscience and an Ancient Evil* (1912), *Peace and Bread in Time of War* (1922), and *The Second Twenty Years at Hull House* (1930).

In recognition of her efforts, Jane Addams was awarded the Nobel Peace Prize in 1931 and remained president of the Women's International League for Peace and Freedom until her death on May 21, 1935.

HOWARD ADELMAN (1937-)

Howard Adelman is an important advocate for children's mental health and psychosocial concerns in the education reform agenda. His work provides schools with strategies for addressing mental health issues in ways that support the academic achievement of children. Dr. Adelman began his career as a remedial classroom teacher before going on to receive his Ph.D. in psychology from the University of California, Los Angeles (UCLA) in 1966. Since graduate school, his primary focus has been improving interventions for students with learning, behavioral, and emotional problems through educational reform. He established the UCLA Center for Mental Health in Schools as one of the two national training and technical assistance centers focused on mental health in schools. The center approaches mental health and psychosocial concerns from the broad perspective of addressing barriers to learning and promoting healthy development. Specific attention is given to policies and strategies that can counter service fragmentation and enhance collaboration between school and community programs. The Center was established in 1995 as part of a major initiative to foster mental health in schools (implemented by the U.S. Department of Health and Human Services, Public Health Service, Health Resources and Services Administration, Bureau of Maternal and Child Health, Office of Adolescent Health).

From 1970 to 1973, Dr. Adelman was a professor in the School of Education at the University of California at Riverside. In 1973, he returned to UCLA as a professor in the Department of Psychology and as director of the Fernald School and Laboratory. In 1986, along with Dr. Linda Taylor, he established the School Mental Health Project at UCLA to focus on school-based programs. In 1995, this project established a center with the objective of focusing on mental health in schools.

Dr. Adelman has continued to be involved with national initiatives focusing on enhancing school and community efforts to address barriers to student learning and promoting the healthy development of children, youth, and families as well as the professionals that work in child service agencies (including schools). He collaborates with the Los Angeles Unified School District's Early Assistance for Students and Families Project and with the district and the Los Angeles Educational Partnership on the Los Angeles Learning Centers project. These projects focus on restructuring education support programs and services and integrating them with community health and social services. He also currently serves as an Expert Panel Member for Safe, Disciplined, and Drug Free Schools through the U.S. Department of Education.

Dr. Adelman's most recent publications include *Learning Problems and Disabilities: Moving Forward* (1993); *On Understanding Intervention in Psychology and Education* (1994); and *Restructuring Education Support Services: Toward the Concept of an Enabling Component* (1996).

MARTIN J. BLANK (1944–)

Martin J. Blank, the Director of School/Family/Community Connections at the Institute for Educational Leadership, is a nationally recognized leader in the field of community schooling. Throughout his career, he has focused on promoting relationships among schools and other societal institutions that impact the education and development of our nation's children and youth. Currently working as Staff Director of the Coalition for Community Schools, an alliance of more than 170 organizations, he promotes a vision of schools as the centers of communities where children, youth, and families have access to an array of supports and services that improve student learning, strengthen families, and build communities.

Mr. Blank earned his bachelor's degree from Columbia University in 1965 and went on to earn a law degree from Georgetown University Law Center. He began his career as a VISTA (Volunteers in Service to America) volunteer in the Missouri Bootheel and subsequently worked with several community-based organizations. Before joining the Institute for Educational Leadership, he spent many years in the consulting business, primarily with A.L. Nellum and Associates, which is recognized as the nation's first African American owned company of its kind.

Mr. Blank currently consults with school districts and communities, in their efforts to integrate services and more effectively support youth's learning and development. Working with the United Way of America, he also is an integral player in the Extended Services School Movement, working to combine the resources of school facilities, community participation, and youth development. He has also developed a comprehensive map of community-school initiatives entitled, "Learning Together."

Mr. Blank participates in several initiatives in Washington DC. He serves as chairperson of the Management Team of the Early Childhood Collaborative (an initiative focusing on the development of a quality early childhood system) and as a member of the Steering Committee of DC VOICE, a community-driven education reform collaborative. He was also a managing partner of the Together We Can Initiative (TWC) and coauthored *Together We Can: A Guide for Crafting a Profamily System of Education and Human Services*, which is considered to be one of the primary resources in this field. He also is coauthor of *Education and Community: Connecting Two Worlds*, an analysis of the "sticking points that schools and community groups face in working together."

GILBERT J. BOTVIN (1947–)

Gilbert J. Botvin has a national reputation as a behavioral scientist involved in the areas of health promotion and disease prevention, with a particular emphasis on multi-ethnic drug abuse prevention and school-based prevention programs. He is widely recognized as an expert in the field of tobacco, alcohol, and drug abuse prevention and his classroom-based curriculum entitled "Life Skills Training" is being used in many schools across the country. Currently, Dr. Botvin is a professor of psychology and holds a joint appointment in the Departments of Public Health and Psychiatry at Cornell University's College of Medicine.

Gilbert Botvin was born in Trenton, New Jersey, on October 15, 1947. He earned his bachelor's degree from Colgate University in 1969. After working as a professional musician in New York City and Boston for a number of years, he went on to earn a doctorate from Columbia University in 1977 with training in developmental and clinical psychology.

Currently, Dr. Botvin serves as the Director of Cornell University Medical College's Institute for Prevention Research. The Institute's mission is to promote both physical and mental health and to reduce premature death and disability through a focus on behavioral risk factors related to public health dilemmas. Additionally, Dr. Botvin consults to a variety of state and federal agencies, advisory panels, and grant review committees, including the National Cancer Institute, the National Institute of Drug Abuse, the Center for Substance Abuse Prevention, and the U.S. Department of Education. Dr. Botvin has served as the principal investigator on 20 federally funded school-based prevention projects involving more than 300 schools and 40,000 students. He is currently the principal investigator on several grants, including a 10-year drug abuse prevention trial with urban youth and a center grant at Columbia University focusing on drug abuse prevention with multi-ethnic youth.

In 1994, Dr. Botvin was awarded the Federal Bureau of Investigation's (FBI's) National Leadership Award for his work in drug abuse prevention. In 1996, Dr. Botvin was the first prevention researcher to receive the prestigious Method to Extend Research in Time (MERIT) Award from the National Institute on Drug Abuse. Dr. Botvin was also recognized for his prevention research by the Society of Prevention Research's Disqu Dean Presidential Award in 1998.

Dr. Botvin is a productive researcher, publishing more than 140 journal articles and book chapters, and presenting numerous papers and invited addresses at national and international scientific meetings. Some of his publications include *Smoking Initiation and Escalation in Early Adolescent Girls: One-year Follow-up of a School-based Prevention Intervention for Minority Youth* (1999); *Prevention in Schools* (1999); *Preventing Drug Abuse* (1999); and *Adolescent Drug Abuse Prevention: Current Findings and Future Directions* (1999).

URIE BRONFENBRENNER (1917–)

Urie Bronfenbrenner, one of the most internationally renowned living psychologists, is best known for his groundbreaking theory of the ecology of human development. Over the last quarter of a century, Dr. Bronfenbrenner's theory of development, which proposes that progress from childhood through adulthood and old age is shaped by one's evolving personal history and by one's social, cultural, and economic environments, has dramatically transformed the way many scholars think about human development and the problems we confront as a society. Dr.

Bronfenbrenner is also known internationally for his cross-cultural studies on families and their support systems and research on the status of children.

Dr. Bronfenbrenner was born in Moscow, Russia, on April 29, 1917. In 1923, he immigrated to the United States with his family, and, in 1928, he became a naturalized United States citizen. He earned a bachelor's degree from Cornell University in 1938, and went on to earn a master's degree in education from Harvard University in 1940 and his first doctorate from the University of Michigan in 1942. Dr. Bronfenbrenner holds seven honorary doctoral degrees from universities throughout the world, and has been honored with numerous other awards over the decades for his contributions to his field.

Among his most notable accomplishments, Dr. Bronfenbrenner is the cofounder of the nation's Head Start program, a comprehensive child development program serving disadvantaged children from birth to age five, pregnant women, and their families. His theoretical contributions and ability to translate them into rigorous operational research models and effective social policies have also furthered the goals of Cornell's Life Course Institute, which has been renamed the Bronfenbrenner Life Course Institute in his honor. In 1996, Dr. Bronfenbrenner was honored by Division 7 of the American Psychological Association as the first recipient of the Bronfenbrenner Lifetime Contribution to Developmental Psychology in the Service of Science and Society award.

Dr. Bronfenbrenner is currently the Jacob Gould Schurman Professor Emeritus of Human Development and Family Studies and Psychology at Cornell University. Dr. Bronfenbrenner has authored and coauthored numerous publications, including *Two Worlds of Childhood: U.S. and U.S.S.R* (1970); *Influences on Human Development* (1972); *The Ecology of Human Development: Experiments by Nature and Design* (1979), and, more recently, *The Ecology of Developmental Processes* (1996); and *The State of Americans: This Generation and the Next* (1998).

PHILIP COLTOFF (1936–)

Philip Coltoff has been a national leader in advocating for the importance of linking educational and human service approaches in our nation's schools. Mr. Coltoff is the Executive Director and Chief Executive Officer of The Children's Aid Society, a 148-year-old child and family service agency and one of the largest and oldest voluntary, nonsectarian agencies in the nation. The collaboration of his human service agency with the New York City Public Schools has led to new models of intersecting health and learning.

Mr. Coltoff received his bachelor's degree from City College and went on to complete his master's degree in social work at New York University. Later he became the director of the Children's Aid Society (CAS), a voluntary, nonsecretarian agency that provides a broad spectrum of health, education, recreation, and emergency services to New York City's neediest children, youth, and families. Over the years of its existence, many CAS programs have served as national models in the area of human services. By the end of the nineteenth century, CAS had established the first industrial schools, parent-teacher associations (PTAs), visiting nurse services, nutrition programs, free dental clinics, and day schools for handicapped children.

The philosophy of CAS has been to identify the city's neediest communities and build a presence there for 30, 50, or 100 years through prevention and intervention programs. Under Mr. Coltoff's direction since 1981, CAS originated the first Head Start Program in New York City, initiated drug prevention programs, created a teen pregnancy prevention prototype, started a community mental health clinic, began to offer family mediation, provided services to homeless children and youth in welfare hotels, and began offering mobile medical and dental services. CAS also opened the first medical Foster Care Boarding Program for boarder babies and implemented one of the first transitional housing units for homeless families. In collaboration with the New York City Board of Education, CAS opened the first year-round community public school, which provided academic and full social services, 15 hours a day, for children and families in the Washington Heights/Inwood, Harlem, and South Bronx neighborhoods of New York City. This agency is one of the oldest and largest welfare agencies in the country and has an operating budget of $50 million, with more than 550 full-time and 800 part-time staff reaching 120,000 children and families through centers and schools in the city's poorest neighborhoods.

In addition to his work with CAS, Mr. Coltoff has written many articles in the field of social work, including a benchmark study on child abuse, which was published in three languages by the World Health Organization. He is an officer/member of many government and other advisory committees and task forces including the Mayor's Task Force on Child Abuse and Neglect, the Human Services Task Force, the Professional Board of the Boys and Girls Clubs of America, the Advisory Board of New York City's Human Resources Administration, and the U.S.

Domestic Policy Council as a nongovernment participant. Recently, Mr. Coltoff has also taken on the role of Chairman of the New York City Volunteer Youth Campaign, a coalition of more than 100 youth agencies aimed at providing volunteers/mentors to tens of thousands of youngsters in trouble at school or with the law.

Mr. Coltoff has received many awards, including the Federation of Alcohol and Chemical Dependency Award (1990), the 1991 Exemplars Award from the National Association for Social Work Managers, the New York City Council Award for service to the city's children and their families (1991), the Salome Urena Community School Award (1992), the East Harlem Residents Award (1992), and the Boys and Girls Clubs of America Thomas G. Garth Character and Courage Award (1999).

JAMES P. COMER (1934–)

James P. Comer has been a leading researcher and practitioner in empowering school staff and parents to build schools that are responsive to children's health and learning needs. He is an author and a psychiatrist as well as the founder of the Comer School Development Program (CSDP), a visionary approach to improving urban schools through addressing the needs of the whole child—health, mental health, and social services. This program is based on the theory that providing children and youth with experiences that promote their social, emotional, cognitive, and moral development is critically important to determining performance in school and in life. Dr. Comer currently serves as a Maurice Falk Professor of Psychiatry at the Yale University Child Study Center and Associate Dean of the Yale University School of Medicine. As both an author and a psychiatrist, Dr. Comer advocates the creation of a family-like atmosphere in the classroom to improve academic progress for urban children and youth.

The second oldest of five children, Dr. Comer was born in East Chicago, Indiana, in 1934. He graduated from Indiana University with a bachelor's degree in 1956. In 1960 he earned his medical degree from Howard University and followed with a master's in public health from the University of Michigan in 1964. Dr. Comer was trained in psychiatry at Yale University School of Medicine and Child Study Center between 1964 and 1967. In addition, he served as a lieutenant colonel in the U.S. Public Health Service from 1961 to 1968.

Dr. Comer established his first CDSP schools in New Haven, Connecticut, in 1968. The program's success there and around the country drew the attention of the Rockefeller Foundation, which funded Comer's efforts with $15 million over five years. The philosophy of this program consists of surrounding schoolchildren with an integrated network of services, such as medical clinics, mental health centers, libraries, and child care centers. By 1998, about 600 schools in the United States had adopted the CSDP model.

Dr. Comer served as consultant to the Children's Television Workshop, which produces "Sesame Street" and "Electric Company." In 1989 he was a consultant to the Pre-Education Summit. He has also been a member of the National Commission on Teaching and America's Future since 1994. From 1996 to 1997, Dr. Comer supervised the development of the Kidpreneurs Program sponsored by *Black Enterprise* magazine. The two-year program taught children and youth the essentials of entrepreneurship.

Dr. Comer has received more than 30 honorary degrees and has been recognized by many for his commitment to improving the lives of disadvantaged children and youth. He has received such awards as the Rockefeller Public Service Award (1980), Charles A. Dana Award for Pioneering Achievement in Education (1991), Heinz Award for the Human Condition (1996), and the James Bryant Conant Award given by the Education Commission of the United States (1991). Comer's publications include *Beyond Black and White* (1972); *Maggie's American Dream: The Life and Times of a Black Family* (1988); *Rallying the Whole Village: The Comer Process for Reforming Education* (1996); *Waiting for a Miracle: Why Schools Can't Solve our Problems;* and *How We Can* (1997), as well as many journal articles.

JOHN DEWEY (1859–1952)

John Dewey was an American psychologist, philosopher, educator, social critic, and political activist whose writings and teachings have had profound influences on education in the United States. Dewey believed that "education is not preparation for life; education is life itself." He was born in Burlington, Vermont, on October 20, 1852. Dr. Dewey graduated from the University of Vermont in 1879, and received his Ph.D. from Johns Hopkins University in 1884. He began teaching at the University of Michigan that same year. In 1894, he became chairman of the Department of Philosophy, Psychology, and Pedagogy at the University of Chicago. In 1899, Dr. Dewey was elected president of the American Psychological Association, and in 1905 he became president of the

American Philosophical Association. Dr. Dewey taught at Columbia University from 1904 until he retired in 1930, and was professor emeritus until 1939. During his years at Columbia University, he worked across the globe as a philosopher, social and political theorist, and educational consultant. He was outspoken about matters related to education, domestic and international politics, and numerous social movements. Dr. Dewey was an active supporter of the women's suffragist movement, progressive education, and world peace. His concern with environments for learning continues to be an inspiration for modern day educational practice.

Dr. Dewey made major contributions to nearly every domain of philosophy and was a primary founder of both functionalist and behaviorist psychology. Dewey was a prolific writer. The following list contains references to his most popular works on education: *My Pedagogic Creed* (1897), *The School and Society* (1900), *Child and the Curriculum* (1902), *Democracy and Education: An Introduction to the Philosophy of Education* (1916), and *How We Think: A Restatement of the Relation of Reflective Thinking to the Educative Process* (1933).

Dr. Dewey died on June 1, 1952, in New York City.

JOY G. DRYFOOS (1925–)

Joy G. Dryfoos has played a critical and national role in the development of full-service schools that address children's comprehensive health needs. As an independent researcher, writer, and lecturer from Hastings-on-Hudson, New York, she developed community strategies to improve the quality of life for disadvantaged youth and for implementing and studying the development of full-service community schools.

Born in Plainfield, New Jersey, in 1925, Ms. Dryfoos graduated from Antioch College with a bachelor's degree in sociology in 1951. In 1967, she earned a master's degree in urban sociology from Sarah Lawrence College. Ms. Dryfoos' research primarily focuses on programs for adolescents, with substantive contributions on the subject of high-risk youth, and the prevention of teen pregnancy, substance abuse, delinquency, and school dropouts. Her current work focuses on the development of full-service community schools.

Ms. Dryfoos serves on many task forces and advisory committees. She was one of the organizers of the national Coalition for Community Schools and sits on the Steering Committee. The National Research Council of the National Academy of Sciences appointed her to the panels on Adolescent Pregnancy and Childbearing (1985–87) and High-Risk Youth (1993). Ms. Dryfoos has also served as a member of the Committee on Comprehensive School Health, Institute of Medicine (1994), and the Carnegie Task Force on Youth Development and Community Programs (1990–93). She is a consultant to many foundations, including Milton S. Eisenhower Foundation, Charles Stewart Mott Foundation, Carnegie Foundation, The Wallace Foundation, Annie E. Casey Foundation, Ewing Marion Kaufman Foundation, Richard C. Stillman Foundation, Open Society Foundation, William T. Grant Foundation, Robert Wood Johnson Foundation, and The Wellness Foundation. Ms. Dryfoos has recently served on several advisory committees, including Achievement Plus of the Wilder Foundation, Academy for Educational Development, New York State Department of Health Robert Wood Johnson School-Based Services Project, Westchester Center for School Community Partnership, New Jersey School-Based Youth Centers Evaluation, Urban Institute-Robert Wood Johnson School Based Clinic Prevention Task Force, University of Kansas Pregnancy Prevention, and Public Private Ventures Extended School Evaluation.

Since 1981, Ms. Dryfoos has been supported primarily by the Carnegie Corporation. Her books include *Inside Full-Service Community Schools (2002), Safe Passage: Making it Through Adolescence in a Risky Society (1998), Full-Service Schools: A Revolution in Health and Social Services (1994), Adolescents at Risk: Prevalence and Prevention (1990),* and *Putting the Boys in the Picture (1988).* She also has written more than one hundred articles.

MARIAN WRIGHT EDELMAN (1939–)

Marian Wright Edelman is a leading policymaker advocating for healthy child development in the United States. She is the founder of the Children's Defense Fund (CDF), a private, nonprofit organization begun in 1973 that advocates on behalf of children living in poverty who are denied access to basic needs such as housing, health care, and adequate education. CDF supports and organizes a wide range of programs and is supported by foundations, corporation grants, and individual donations. Ms. Edelman's goal through CDF is to provide every American child with "a healthy start, a head start, and a fair start" in life. Ms. Edelman is also recognized as the first black woman on the Mississippi bar and is a civil rights lawyer with the NAACP.

Ms. Edelman was born in 1939 in the racially segregated town of Bennetsville, South Carolina. The daughter of a Baptist preacher, she was raised to believe that it was her duty to help others and make the world a better place. She graduated from Spelman College in 1960, spending her junior year abroad in Geneva, Switzerland, after winning the Merrill Scholarship. The following summer she traveled in the Soviet Union under a Lisle Fellowship. After spending some time as a volunteer worker at a local office of the NAACP, Ms. Edelman decided to study law. After graduating from Yale Law School in 1963, Ms. Edelman spent a year in New York working as a staff attorney for the NAACP Legal Defense and Education Fund before returning to Mississippi to head the Fund's Jackson office and becoming involved in efforts to establish a Head Start Program.

Convinced she could do more to help disadvantaged children and youth as an advocate and lobbyist, Ms. Edelman moved to Washington, D.C., and founded the CDF in 1973 as an organization that seeks aid for children and youth through research, lobbying, and advocacy. The CDF seeks to provide effective advocacy for all the children of America, with particular attention to the needs of poor children, children of color, and those with disabilities. The CDF researches topics such as health care, teenage pregnancy, education, juvenile justice, homelessness, substance abuse, and violence. The CDF makes budget proposals for federal, state, and local governments. Additionally, the CDF has been a leading advocate in Congress, state legislatures, and courts for children and youth's rights.

Ms. Edelman has earned several honors for her public service work and is the recipient of more than 30 honorary degrees. In 1979 she received a Presidential Citation from the American Public Health Association. Also in 1979 she received the Outstanding Leadership Award from the national Alliance of Black School Educators. She was the 1981 recipient of the Rockefeller Public Service Award and the 1989 Gandhi Peace Award.

Ms. Edelman's publications include *Guide My Feet: Meditations and Prayers on Loving and Working for Children* (1996), *The Measure of Our Success: A Letter to My Children and Yours* (1992), *Families in Peril: An Agenda for Social Change* (1987), and *Stand for Children* (1998). Ms. Edelman is also a consultant to lawmakers and journalists on many policy, research, and practice issues related to children and youth.

JOYCELYN ELDERS (1933–)

Joycelyn Elders, the first African American and second female to serve as the United States Surgeon General, led the country in supporting a comprehensive approach to the health needs of adolescents. Dr. Elders' pioneering research and advocacy interests in the areas of teenage pregnancy, AIDS prevention, and sexual abuse prevention has earned her national attention. Additionally, she has been particularly influential in the establishment of school-based health clinics in Arkansas. She has been tireless in her efforts to reduce teen pregnancy rates in the United States, often advocating controversial positions in regard to access to birth control and sex education. She asserts that to address teenage pregnancy, schools must depend on measures of prevention.

Dr. Elders was born in 1933 in Schaal, Arkansas, and was the first of eight children. As the daughter of a sharecropper in a poor, segregated section of the country, Dr. Elders and her brothers and sisters attended an all-black school 13 miles from home and worked in the cotton fields. She later earned a scholarship to Philander Smith College in Little Rock, Arkansas. She was trained by the U.S. Army as a physical therapist and entered the Arkansas School of Medicine in 1956. After an internship in pediatrics in Minnesota, Dr. Elders returned to Little Rock in 1961 for her residency and was quickly appointed chief pediatric resident. Her initial research work on juvenile diabetes slowly expanded into a keen interest in teenage pregnancy prevention. In 1987, she was named director of the Arkansas Department of Health. In 1993, President Clinton nominated Dr. Elders to serve as U.S. Surgeon General.

As U.S. Surgeon General, Dr. Elders was concerned with tobacco use, national health care, and alcohol and drug abuse. She also considered gun control a central issue to the health of the United States. In 1994 Dr. Elders resigned as Surgeon General in response to controversy surrounding her views. In 1995 Dr. Elders returned to the University of Arkansas as a researcher and professor. She continues to be a vigorous, albeit controversial, advocate for children, youth, and families.

Dr. Elders has earned numerous honors and awards. In 1980 she was named one of the One Hundred Outstanding Women in Arkansas and, in 1987, she received the Arkansas Professional Woman of Distinction Award. She was also awarded the American Medical Association's Dr. Nathan Davis Award and the Dr. Lee Humanitarian Award. Dr. Elders has also been awarded honorary doctor of medical science degrees from Morehouse College, University of Minnesota, and Yale University.

JOYCE EPSTEIN (1940–)

Joyce Epstein's groundbreaking work on how schools can partner with families and communities has led to collaborations that support and enhance the healthy development of schoolchildren. After receiving her doctorate in sociology from Johns Hopkins University, she established an organization in 1995 to demonstrate the importance of collaboration among researchers, policymakers, and practitioners for school improvement. Dr. Epstein currently serves as director of this organization, entitled the National Network of Partnerships-2000 Schools, as well as director of the Center on School, Family, and Community Partnerships at Johns Hopkins University. She is the principal research scientist and codirector of the Center for Research on the Education of Students Placed at Risk (CRESPAR) and a part-time professor of sociology at Johns Hopkins University.

Dr. Epstein's research focuses on the organization and effects of school, family, and community connections. She has published many papers and studies on the effects of school, classroom, family, and peer environments on student learning and development, with many of these studies focusing on school-family connections. Some of her publications include *School, Family, and Community Partnerships: Your Handbook for Action* (1998); *Education in the Middle Grades: National Practices and Trends* (1990); *Promising Programs in the Middle Grades* (1992); *The Quality of School Life* (1981); and *Friends in School: Patterns of Selection and Influence in Secondary Schools* (1978). Her most recent publication is entitled *School, Family and Community Partnerships: Preparing Educators and Improving Schools* Dr. Epstein serves on the editorial boards of *Phi Delta Kappan, Education and Urban Society, The Urban Review,* and *Social Psychology of Education* and has many advisory roles concerning parent involvement, middle school grades, and school improvement. The Academy for Educational Development awarded her the Alvin C. Eurich Education Award in 1991 and, in 1997, she received the Working Mother Magazine Award. Both of these honors were awarded for her work on school, family, and community partnerships.

MICHAEL FULLAN (1940–)

Michael Fullan is recognized for his work as an innovator and leader in education reform. He has developed a number of partnerships across schools and communities that are designed to bring about major school improvement and positive academic and social outcomes for children. Dr. Fullan is the dean of the Ontario Institute for Studies in Education at the University of Toronto. He has participated as a researcher, consultant, trainer, and policy advisor on a wide range of educational projects within school systems, teacher federations, research and development institutes, universities, and government agencies within Canada and around the world. Dr. Fullan has written extensively on the topic of education reform. His publications include *Leading in a Cultural Change* (2001); *Change Forces: The Sequel* (1999); *Change Forces: Probing the Depths of Educational Reform* (1994); *What's Worth Fighting For Series* (1998); and *New Meaning of Educational Change* (2001).

Dr. Fullan received his doctorate in sociology from the University of Toronto in 1969. He spent a number of years conducting research, graduate teaching, and leading in-service programs on educational change. He has been recognized by many for his hands-on approach to understanding the complex issues involved in education. In 1990, he became the first recipient of the Annual Award for Excellence of the Canadian Association for Teacher Educators. In 1993, he received the Colonel Watson Award for outstanding leadership from the Ontario Association of Curriculum Development. He also received the Contribution to Staff Development Award from the National Staff Development Council in 1995. In 1997, Dr. Fullan was recognized by the Canadian Education Association with the Whitworth Award for Educational Research. He is a Laureate Chapter Member of Kappa Delta Pi, an international honor society in education, and holds an honorary doctorate degree from the University of Edinburgh.

ROBERT JOHNS HAGGERTY (1925–)

The primary focus of Robert Johns Haggerty's career is the promotion of healthy children and youth through the establishment of effective, integrated services and public policy that will improve the life chances of children and youth throughout the world. His work reflects his keen understanding that children's development is holistic with psychosocial health and academic domains constantly impacting one another. Dr. Haggerty is a professor emeritus of pediatrics at the University of Rochester School of Medicine and Dentistry. He received his bachelor's degree from Cornell University in 1946 and his medical degree from Cornell University in 1949.

Dr. Haggerty's career in pediatrics began at Harvard Medical School and its affiliate, Children's Hospital in Boston, where he developed a training and research program in family pediatrics. It was during this time that he developed his lifelong interest in the effects of psychosocial stress as a cause of many children's illnesses. Later, he went on to take a position as professor and chairman of the Department of Pediatrics at the University of Rochester's School of Medicine and Dentistry. During this time, he and his colleagues developed community-based health services for children and youth and coined the phrase "the new morbidity" for psychosocial problems of children. He then returned to Boston, where he was the Roger I. Lee Professor of Health Services at Harvard School of Public Health, and chairman of the Department of Health Services. In 1994, he coauthored the Institute of Medicine's report on the status of children's health, including mental health.

Dr. Haggerty has served as president of several notable organizations and associations such as the American Association of Poison Control Centers and American Academy of Pediatrics. He served as the executive director of the International Pediatric Association from 1993 to 1998. He has held other positions, including clinical professor of pediatrics at Cornell University Medical Center and professor of pediatrics at Harvard Medical School. He was formerly president of the William T. Grant Foundation, which supports research on ways to improve the mental health of school-aged children and youth and to assist them in achieving their full potential.

Dr. Haggerty has served on many prestigious boards and committees dedicated to improving children's quality of life. He served as chairperson for the Mayor's Committee on Child Health in New York City, the Subcommittee on Adolescents, and the Committee on Neonatal AIDS of New York State Governor's Commission on AIDS. He was a member of the New York State Council of Graduate Medical Education, the Carnegie Council on Children and the Board of Alliance for Healthcare for All, as well as a member of the MacArthur Foundation Committee on Successful Adolescence.

Dr. Haggerty is editor of *Pediatrics in Review,* the continuing education journal of the American Academy of Pediatrics, as well as a past president of that organization. He is the editor-in-chief of the *Bulletin of the New York Academy of Medicine: A Journal of Urban Health* and executive director of the International Pediatric Association. He is also a member of the Institute of Medicine, the American Pediatric Society, and a Fellow of the American Association for the Advancement of Science.

Dr. Haggerty has received numerous awards, including the Martha Eliot Award in Maternal and Child Health of the American Public Health Association, the Clifford C. Grulee Award, the Abraham Jacobi Award, the Dale Richmond Award of the American Academy of Pediatrics, the Joseph St. Geme Award for the Future of Pediatrics of the American Pediatric Society, the Gustav Leinard Award for contributions in health services from the Institute of Medicine, the Primary Care Achievement Award for Education of Pew Charitable Trust's Center for Health Professions Commission, and the John Howland Award.

Dr. Haggerty is author of more than 150 original papers, editor or author of three books, and author of nearly 200 book chapters, editorials, and abstracts.

BEATRIX ANN HAMBURG (1923–)

Beatrix Ann Hamburg is known nationally and internationally as a medical educator and researcher who has made substantial contributions to the field of youth health.

Dr. Hamburg earned her bachelor's degree from Vassar College in 1944 and went on to earn her medical degree from Yale University in 1948. Dr. Hamburg began her career studying stress and conflict at Stanford University, and eventually shifted her focus to issues of school public health and child and adolescent welfare.

Dr. Hamburg served as president of the William T. Grant Foundation in New York City from 1992 to 1998. She is the author of *Behavioral and Psychosocial Issues in Diabetes* (1980) and *School Age Pregnancy and Parenthood* (1986). Dr. Hamburg served as an editor of *Violence in American Schools—A New Perspective* (1998) and has also made contributions to numerous other scientific and professional journals.

Currently, Dr. Hamburg serves on the Advisory Committee for the Healthy People 2010 Library Initiative, which aims to increase the quality and length of health for all minority groups, including African Americans, Hispanic Americans, Asian Americans, and Native Americans. Dr. Hamburg also serves as a visiting scholar for the Department of Psychiatry at the Weill Medical College of Cornell University

DAVID ALLEN HAMBURG (1925–)

David Allen Hamburg is a researcher who has worked over the last 50 years to improve the well-being and education of young people and the underprivileged. Dr. Hamburg is also recognized as a leader in promoting public policy by helping to strengthen the role of science and technology in government. Dr. Hamburg is president emeritus of Carnegie

Corporation of New York, having served as the corporate president from 1983 to 1997.

Dr. Hamburg earned his medical degree from Indiana University in 1947, and also holds 10 honorary degrees from universities across the country. During his long and illustrious career, Dr. Hamburg has worked as an educator, author, and psychiatrist, maintaining a private practice as well as various appointments with many institutions, including the Center for Advanced Study in the Behavioral Sciences, the National Institute of Mental Health's adult psychiatry branch, the National Academy of Sciences Institute of Medicine, and Harvard University's Division of Health Policy Research and Education. During his career, Dr Hamburg has also held tenure as the Reed-Hodgson Professor of Human Biology at Stanford University and the John D. MacArthur Professor of Health Policy at Harvard University.

Dr. Hamburg began his career at the Walter Reed Army Institute of Research in Washington, D.C., investigating stress and anxiety, but switched his focus when four of his students at Stanford were kidnapped by rebels from Zaire will working at the Gombe Station in Tanzania. Dr. Hamburg spent 10 weeks in Gombe negotiating the release of his students, and when he returned, he devoted his energies to using science to help meet social needs, focusing primarily on violence prevention, human resource development, and child and adolescent development. For his considerable contributions to public well-being, Dr. Hamburg has been honored with numerous awards, including the Presidential Medal of Freedom, the nation's highest civilian honor, and the National Academy of Sciences' Public Welfare Medal, the Academy's most prestigious award.

Currently, Dr. Hamburg serves as president emeritus of Carnegie Corporation of New York and as a member of the Defense Policy Board of the U.S. Department of Defense and the President's Committee of Advisors on Science and Technology.

KAREN KRAMER HEIN (1944–)

Karen Kramer Hein is recognized nationally and internationally as a researcher and policymaker advocating for health care reform. Dr. Hein has assumed a multitude of roles, including health care program development, teaching, and clinical research. Dr. Hein earned her bachelor's degree from the University of Wisconsin in 1966, attended Dartmouth Medical School for two years, and received her medical degree from

Columbia University College of Physicians and Surgeons in 1970. From 1973 to 1978, she served as a founding member of the Dartmouth Medical School Board of Overseers.

Over the last two decades, Dr. Hein has worked to benefit the health of young people by founding the nation's first adolescent HIV/AIDS program and expanding AIDS education within the New York City public school system. Dr. Hein has also served as a consultant or advisor to many local, state, and federal health organizations, as well as a year-long term as president of the Society for Adolescent Medicine in 1992. A prolific writer, Dr. Hein has authored more than 150 articles, chapters, and abstracts related to adolescent health, paying particular attention to high-risk youth.

Dr. Hein currently serves as president of the William T. Grant Foundation, where she is committed to supporting and improving research on public health and youth development. She also currently serves as an editorial advisory board member for five journals, as a member of the board of directors for five national organizations, and as chair of the Center for Health Care Strategies.

SHARON LYNN KAGAN (1943–)

Sharon Lynn Kagan is nationally and internationally renowned for her research and advocacy work on the care and education of young children. She has been a leader in advocating for the importance of collaboration across professions when working with young children and their families. Dr. Kagan is the Virginia and Leonard Marx Professor of Early Education and Family Policy at Teachers College, Columbia University, and a senior research associate at Yale University's Child Study Center.

Dr. Kagan received her bachelor's degree from the University of Michigan in 1965 and her master's degree in education from Johns Hopkins University. She earned her doctorate in education (curriculum and teaching) from Teachers College, Columbia University, in 1979. She has worked as a Head Start teacher and director, a fellow in the U.S. Senate, an administrator in the public schools, and director of the New York City Mayor's Office of Early Childhood Education. More recently, she has served as a consultant to many government agencies and organizations, including the White House, Congress, National Governors' Association, U.S. Department of Education, and U.S. Department of Health and Human Services.

Dr. Kagan is a governing board member of the highly respected National Association for the Education of Young Children (NAEYC) as well as the president of the Family Resource Coalition. She is also the vice president of the Institute for Responsive Education. Her research and publications focus on the facilitation of home-to-school transition for children and families, preparation of teachers and schools for effective involvement of young children and parents, and preparation and assessment of young children for school.

Dr. Kagan has published more than 120 works, including the authorship or editorship of 12 volumes and the guest editorship of numerous journals. Her writing focuses on the development of policy for children and families, family support, early childhood pedagogy, strategies for collaboration and service integration, and the evaluation of social programs. She has recently completed a national study, *Not by Chance* (1997), the report of the Quality 2000 Initiative, and coedited new volumes on *Reinventing Early Care and Education,* and *Children, Families, and Government* (1996). Her publications have been supported by research grants from national foundations, including the U.S. Departments of Education and Health and Human Services.

MICHAEL W. KIRST (1939–)

Michael W. Kirst is a nationally recognized leader in bridging the world of government education policymaking and the world of schools and classrooms. As a researcher and professor of education and business administration at Stanford University in California, he has been involved for many years in government education policymaking at both state and federal levels. At Stanford, he is a faculty affiliate with the Department of Political Science and has a courtesy appointment with the Graduate School of Business. He currently serves as codirector of Policy Analysis for California Education (PACE), a research consortium including Stanford, University of California at Berkeley, and University of Southern California.

Dr. Kirst was born in West Reading, Pennsylvania, in 1939 and earned his bachelor's degree from Dartmouth College in 1961. In 1963, he received a Masters of Public Administration in government and economics from Harvard University and earned his doctorate in political economy and government the following year. Before joining the Stanford faculty, Dr. Kirst held several positions with the federal government, including staff director of the U.S. Subcommittee on Manpower, Employment, and Poverty and director of Program Planning and Evaluation (now the U.S. Department of Education). Dr. Kirst was also a program analyst for the Title I Elementary and Secondary Education Act (ESEA) when it began in 1965.

Dr. Kirst has participated in various capacities in state and national organizations, including as the president of the California State Board of Education (1977–1980), as a member of the National Advisory Council on Education of Disadvantaged Children (1966), for the U.S. Office of Education (1977), as a policy analyst for the California Education Department, and for the U.S. National Academy of Science (1994–). Kirst's publications include "Bridging Education Research and Education Policymaking" in the *Oxford Education Review* (2001); "Bridging the Remediation Gap" in *Education Week* (1998); "New Demands for Educational Accountability" in the *Handbook of Research on Educational Administration* (1998); and "Redefining the Role and Responsibilities of Local School Boards" in *The New American Urban School District* (1995). His current research focuses on the relationship between state education reform efforts and educational outcomes.

LLOYD KOLBE (1948–)

Lloyd Kolbe has spent a significant portion of his career working to improve the health and educational performance of young people. He has led a major initiative to promote comprehensive health education for schoolchildren. Dr. Kolbe's vision was responsible for initiating a now classic book on coordinated school health programs—*Health is Academic* (Marx, Wooley, and Northup, 1998). Dr. Kolbe is the director of the Center for School Health at the World Health Organization and the founding director of the Division of Adolescent and School Health, in the National Center for Chronic Disease Prevention and Health Promotion, at the U.S. Centers for Disease Control and Prevention. Born in Baltimore, he earned his bachelor's degree from Towson University in 1973. He went on to earn his master's degree in education in 1975 and his doctorate in 1978, both from the University of Toledo.

Dr. Kolbe has served as the director of numerous programs, including the director of school health education and director of evaluation at the National Center for Health Education. He was also the associate director at the Center for Health Promotion Research at the University of Texas.

Dr. Kolbe has received recognition for his contributions to the field. In 1988, he received the Distinguishing Service Award from the State Directors of Health Education. In 1989, he received the Honor Award of Eta Sigma Gamma and was also recognized as an Outstanding Alumnus by the University of Toledo. Dr. Kolbe is the coauthor of *School Health in America* (1999). Dr. Kolbe coauthored a groundbreaking 1987 article in a special issue of the *Journal of School Health* where he proposed an eight-component conceptual model for comprehensive school health programs.

EVA MARX (1932–)

Eva Marx has been a consistent and strong advocate for comprehensive school health programs and for the interprofessional collaboration that these programs require. Following her role as the associate director of the Center for School Health Programs at the Education Development Center (EDC) in Newton, Massachusetts, she became a private consultant in the field of comprehensive school health. Ms. Marx earned a bachelor's degree in philosophy from Antioch College and a master's degree in human services management from the Florence Heller School of Social Welfare at Brandeis University.

Before her involvement with EDC, Ms. Marx organized a partnership of student services organizations to pilot the dissemination of the coordinated school health program concept at the national and state level. She also coordinated the development and management of the Comprehensive School Health Education Network, an organization designed to provide training and technical assistance for school health education and HIV prevention to education agencies. She also worked for the New England Resource Center for Children and Families at the Judge Baker Children's Center, a nonprofit organization dedicated to improving the lives of at-risk children and their families, providing technical assistance to public and private child welfare agencies, developing program implementation manuals, and helping to create the National Parent Aide Association.

In her initial work with EDC, Ms. Marx coordinated the integration of HIV materials into nationally recognized health education curricula (*Growing Healthy* and *Teenage Health Teaching Modules*), and coauthored *Schools Face the Challenge of AIDS*. She also developed an implementation manual for Project Drug Awareness Resistance Program (DARE) and directed the initial implementation efforts of this prevention program in the state of Massachusetts.

Ms. Marx created and coedits a nationally distributed newsletter, *School Health Program News*. She is also the coauthor of several books: *Educating for Health: A Guide for Implementing Comprehensive School Health Education* (1995), *Choosing the Tools: A Review of Selected K-12 Health Education Curricula* (1995), and *Health Is Academic: A Guide to Coordinated School Health Programs* (1998).

FLORETTA DUKES MCKENZIE (1935–)

Floretta Dukes McKenzie, over many decades, has helped to shape policy initiatives that link youth development and education. She is the president of the McKenzie Group, Inc., a comprehensive education consulting firm that works with both public and private organizations. Dr. McKenzie received her bachelor's degree from Teachers College, Washington, D.C., a master's degree from Howard University, and a doctorate in education from George Washington University.

Earlier in her career, Dr. McKenzie served as superintendent of schools for the District of Columbia Public Schools. From 1979 to 1981, she served as deputy assistant secretary in the Office of School Improvement, U.S. Department of Education. During this time, she administered 15 federal education discretionary programs and initiatives and directed the department's efforts to improve schools in areas ranging from basic skills instruction to women's educational equity. Dr. McKenzie represented the department at the Twenty-first General Conference of the United Nations Educational, Scientific, and Cultural Organization and the Third Conference of Ministries of Education. She also served as deputy superintendent of the Montgomery County, Maryland, Public Schools, and assistant deputy superintendent of the Maryland State Department of Education.

Dr. McKenzie is active on many organizational boards, including Howard University, the University of Maryland Board of Visitors, the Lightspan Partnership, Inc., the Foundation for Teaching Economics, the Association of Governing Boards of Universities and Colleges, and Reading Is Fundamental.

WALTER H. PALMER (1924–2003)

Walter Palmer was a Boston business man and civic leader who created public-private partnerships across schools, communities, and businesses to enhance the life chances of children living in poverty. He has served as president of the Boston Urban Coalition, Public Affairs Director of Associated Industries of Massachusetts, and Executive Director of the Republican State Committee. From 1970 to 1992, Mr. Palmer held several positions at Raytheon Company, including director of affirmative action programs; director of public affairs/community relations; vice president of public and financial relations; and vice president of external affairs.

Mr. Palmer was director of charitable affairs at the Harcourt General Charitable Foundation from 1993 to 1997. He worked with the newly created Barr Foundation in 1998 and 1999, and he served as a consultant to Boston Public Schools Superintendent Thomas Payzant. Mr. Palmer was instrumental in the funding of several community programs, including the model "Connect 5," which is taking the full-service school model to scale across a geographic cluster of Boston Public Schools. He served as chairman of the board of Cambridge College and chairman of the New England Foundation for the Arts, as well as on the boards of the New England Conservatory of Music, the Massachusetts Society for Prevention of Cruelty to Children, and the Charles River Museum of Industry.

KAREN J. PITTMAN (1952–)

Karen Pittman is a policy researcher and widely published author and speaker on youth issues. She is the senior vice president of the International Youth Foundation (IYF), an organization working toward improving conditions for children and youth worldwide by enabling them to care more responsibly for themselves, their families, their communities, and the world. In 1999, she expanded IYF to include a branch that is committed to bringing international lessons and perspectives to U.S. conversations about youth development and youth policy.

Ms. Pittman received her bachelor's degree in sociology and education at Oberlin College and her master's in sociology at the University of Chicago. Early in her career, Ms. Pittman initially worked for the Urban Institute, conducting numerous studies on social services for children and families in the United States. She then spent six years at the CDF promoting an adolescent policy agenda through the development of a bimonthly report series that linked pregnancy prevention to broader youth development strategies. In 1990, Ms. Pittman left CDF, and founded the Center for Youth Development and Policy Research. In 1995, she accepted a position with the Clinton administration as director of the President's Crime Prevention Council.

Ms. Pittman has written many books and articles on youth issues and contributes regularly to the periodical, *Youth Today,* a publication of the American Youth Works Center. This periodical is an important resource for communicating a variety of research- and practice-related information to practitioners involved in youth development. During her career, she has served on numerous boards and panels, including the E.M. Kaufman Foundation, the Carnegie Council on Adolescent Development, the Search Institute, and the Family Resource Coalition. Recently, she has given presentations to the Chief State School Officers, Learning First Alliance, White House Conference on Teenagers, U.S. Department of Education, Aspen Institute, and Carnegie Corporation's High Schools for a New Society Initiative. Currently, she serves on the boards of the Educational Testing Service, American Youth Work Center, High/Scope Foundation, and National Center for Children and Poverty, and is a member of W.K. Kellogg Foundation's Youth Initiative Partnership Advisory Council, California Tomorrow's Equity and Access in Afterschool Project Advisory Group, and National Academy of Science's Forum on Adolescence.

JANE QUINN (1944–)

Jane Quinn is a national leader in promoting links between academic and social development. She currently serves as assistant director for community schools with the Children's Aid Society (CAS), New York City's oldest and largest youth-serving organization. Before joining the CAS staff in January 2000, she served for seven years as program director of the DeWitt Wallace-Reader's Digest Fund, a national foundation that invests in programs fostering improvement of educational and career development opportunities for school-age children and youth. Quinn graduated with a bachelor's degree in economics from New Rochelle College in 1966. In 1969, she received a master's degree from the University of Chicago School of Social Service Administration.

Ms. Quinn has long supported the active collaboration of educators and human service workers in school contexts. While program director at the DeWitt Wallace-Reader's Digest Fund (now called The Wallace-Foundation), Ms. Quinn funded several school-university partnerships to prepare preservice social workers and teachers to collaborate in school settings. She was a national leader in funding the establishment of full-service community schools modeled on those developed by the CAS.

Before her position with DeWitt Wallace, Ms. Quinn worked with the Carnegie Council on Adolescent Development. She headed a study of youth development programs and services in the United States that resulted in the publication of a book entitled *A Matter of Time: Risk and Opportunity in the Nonschool Hours.* Ms. Quinn was the director of program services for Girls Clubs of America in New York from 1981 to 1990. She has held positions within the Washington, D.C. Health Department and Center for Population Options. She has also been a caseworker for the Juvenile Protection Association for Chicago and Family Counseling Center, Catholic Charities of Buffalo, New York. She is a member of the National Association of Social Workers and the Academy of Certified Social Workers.

JULIUS BENJAMIN RICHMOND (1916–)

Julius Benjamin Richmond has long understood the inextricable link between children's health and learning and believes that "if schools do not address children's needs by design, they will do so by default." Dr. Richmond is the John D. MacArthur Professor of Health Policy Emeritus in the Department of Social Medicine at Harvard Medical School. He holds a doctor of medicine (M.D.) and a master's degree in science from the University of Illinois at Chicago. He served from 1942 to 1946 in the U.S. Army Airforce as a captain. In 1965, Dr. Richmond was chair of the Pediatrics Department and dean of the School of Medicine at the State University of New York at Syracuse, when he was asked to direct the Head Start Program in Washington, D.C. He also served as director for U.S. Health Affairs, which, under his leadership, initiated the Neighborhood Health Centers Program for the Office of Economic Opportunity. In 1971, Dr. Richmond joined the faculty at Harvard Medical School as professor of child psychiatry and human development and became director of the Judge Baker Children's Center and chief of psychiatry at Children's Hospital.

From 1977 to 1981, Dr. Richmond served as assistant secretary for health in the U.S. Department of Health and Human Services, and Surgeon General of the U.S. Public Health Service. Under his leadership, the agency published *Healthy People: The Surgeon General's Report on Health Promotion and Disease Prevention.*

Dr. Richmond is a member of the American Pediatric Society, American Psychiatric Association, American Public Health Association, Child Welfare League of America, and many other notable organizations. His publications focus on pediatrics, child health, child development, and public health policy. He has received the Aldrich Award of the American Academy of Pediatrics, the Martha May Elliot Award of the American Public Health Association, the Ronald McDonald Children's Charities Prize, the Gustave Lienhard Award of the Institute of Medicine, the Howland Award of the American Pediatric Society, the Sedgwick Medal of the American Public Health Association, and the Ittleson Award of the American Orthopsychatric Association. He is also a member of an expert advisory panel on maternal and child health at the World Health Organization.

LISBETH B. SCHORR (1931-)

Lisbeth B. Schorr is recognized for bringing together her experiences with public policy, community building, education, and social services to work toward improving the future of disadvantaged children and their families and neighborhoods. She is a lecturer in social medicine at Harvard University and director of the Harvard University Project on Effective Interventions. She cochairs the roundtable on Comprehensive Community Initiatives for Children and Families of the Aspen Institute and the Boundaries Task Force of the Harvard Children's Initiative.

Ms. Schorr received her bachelor's degree from the University of California at Berkeley in 1952. She has held leadership positions in many of the major national efforts on behalf of children and youth, including the National Center for Children in Poverty, City Year, National Academy of Science's Board on Children and Families, Children's Program Advisory Committee of the Edna McConnell Clark Foundation, and Foundation for Children's Development. Ms. Schorr has worked as an adjunct professor of maternal and child health at the University of North Carolina and has served on the board of directors of Eureka Communities. Ms. Schorr is a member of the Brookings Children's Roundtable, the Education Commision of the States (ECS), National Commission on Governing America's Schools, and the National Selection Committee for the Ford Foundation/Kennedy School Awards for Innovations in American Government. Currently, she works with the Annie E. Casey Foundation, where she works on developing new approaches to building a stronger knowledge base about effective practices for improving outcomes for children, families, and communities.

Ms. Schorr's 1988 book, *Within Our Reach: Breaking the Cycle of Disadvantage,* carefully assessed social programs that were successful in improving the life chances of disadvantaged children. She followed up with her 1997 publication of *Common Purpose: Strengthening Families and Neighborhoods to Rebuild America.* In this book, she advocated for changing funding patterns and building new alliances to have more success with strengthening and supporting families and communities in their efforts to raise healthy children.

ROGER WEISSBERG (1951–)

Roger Weissberg has been an articulate spokesperson for school-based prevention and intervention efforts with children and adolescents. He is a professor of psychology and education at the University of Illinois at Chicago. He is also the chair of the Division of Community and Prevention Research and directs a Predoctoral and Postdoctoral Prevention Research Training Program in Urban Children's Mental Health and AIDS Prevention.

Dr. Weissberg received his doctorate in clinical psychology from the University of Rochester in 1980. He began his career as the reach director and clinical consultant for the Primary Mental Health Project, a school-based program for the early detection and prevention of school maladjustment. From 1982 to 1992, he was a professor at Yale University and also directed Yale University's National Institute of Mental Health-funded Prevention Research Training Program for Predoctoral and Postdoctoral Trainees. He also collaborated with the New Haven Public School System to establish New Haven's kindergarten through twelfth grade Social Development Project.

Dr. Weissberg's research focus is on preventative interventions with children and adolescents and he has published more than 80 articles and chapters focusing on this topic. He has also coauthored nine curricula on school-based programs promoting social competence and prevention of risk behaviors, including drug use, high-risk sexual behaviors, and aggression.

Dr. Weissberg has served as the president of the American Psychological Association's Society for Community Research and Action. He is a recipient of the William T. Grant Foundation's Five-Year Faculty Scholars Award in Children's Mental Health and he received the Lela Rowland Prevention Award from the National Mental Health Association. In

1997, he received the University Scholar Award for distinction as a member of the faculty of the University of Chicago. In addition he was recognized by the American Psychological Foundation for Distinguished Contributions of Applications of Psychology to Education and Training.

SUSAN F. WOOLEY (1945–)

Susan F. Wooley has contributed significantly to the development of comprehensive and coordinated approaches to school health. She is the executive director of the American School Health Association and has served as a consultant in health education for many local, state, and national organizations, including the Society of State Directors of Health, Physical Education, and Recreation; the American Association for Health Education; the U.S. Centers for Disease Control and Prevention (CDC); and the Delaware Department of Public Instruction. She received her bachelor's degree from Case Western Reserve University in 1967 where she received a National Science Foundation grant for biological research. She went on to receive her master's degree in health education from the University of North Carolina at Greensboro, and, in 1987, she earned her doctorate in health education from Temple University.

In the past, Dr. Wooley worked as a health education specialist for the CDC Division of Adolescent and School Health (DASH). During this time, Dr. Wooley managed cooperative agreements with state and local education agencies and national organizations. Additionally, she edited publications supported by DASH and coordinated a project for pinpointing curricula that address at-risk behaviors in youth.

Dr. Wooley also worked on developing a curriculum for elementary schools entitled *Science for Life and Living: Integrating Science, Technology, and Health*. She also served as the editor of the health newsletter *Snooper*, for kindergarten through fifth grades, assisted in the development of a kindergarten through twelfth-grade curriculum in health education for the state of Delaware, and is a coauthor of *Health is Academic: A Guide to Coordinated School Health Programs* (1998). She has extensive experience with community health education, currently serving as the director of safety programs and of nursing and health programs for the Red Cross.

EDWARD F. ZIGLER (1930–)

Edward F. Zigler is a developmental psychologist and professor who has focused on maximizing the potential of young children from disadvantaged backgrounds. He is best known for his contribution to national programs for children, particularly as cofounder of Project Head Start. Project Head Start combined early childhood education with nutrition counseling, health screenings, and parental involvement and sought to better prepare children and youth for later educational challenges. The Head Start initiative is now considered one of the most widely supported antipoverty programs in the nation.

Dr. Zigler was born in Kansas City, Missouri, in 1930. After attending a vocational high school in Kansas City, he received his bachelor's degree from the University of Missouri at Kansas City in 1954 and his doctorate in developmental psychology from the University of Texas at Austin in 1958. Dr. Zigler then taught for a year at the University of Missouri at Columbia before going to Yale in 1959, where he became director of the Yale University Department of Child Development in 1961. Dr. Zigler has been a professor of psychology at the Yale Child Study Center since 1967, serving as chairman of the department in 1973 and 1974. Throughout his career he has held many noteworthy positions, some of which include director of the Office of Child Development (1970–72), director of Health Education and Welfare (1970–72), and director of the Bush Center in Child Development and Social Policy (1977).

While director of the Office of Child Development in Washington, D.C., Dr. Zigler cofounded and administered the nation's Head Start Program, which was established by the U.S. Congress in 1965. A federally funded project, Head Start provides learning materials, nutrition, parent education, and before- and afterschool programs in an effort to better prepare children and youth for challenges of the future. Throughout its history, more than 12 million children have participated in Head Start. Dr. Zigler works continuously to improve the program, favoring strong parental involvement and currently advocating for a three-year transition period for all participants. In 1970, Dr. Zigler was appointed by President Nixon to the post of first director of the Office of Child Development, which has since been renamed the Administration of Children, Youth, and Families. He was also appointed as chief of the U.S. Children's Bureau. Dr. Zigler is also credited with conceptualizing and initiating other programs, such as Health Start, Home Start, Education for Parenthood, the Child Development Associate Program, and the Child and Family Resource Program.

Dr. Zigler has been a consultant to many governmental committees at the federal, state, and local level, and he has received academic and scientific awards from nearly all psychology-related professional organizations over the years. In 1985 he received the National Achievement Award from the Association for the Advancement of Psychology. He was also awarded the McGraw Prize in Education for his commitment to the success of children and youth in education and life. In 1998 he was awarded the Bronfenbrenner Lifetime Contribution Award (division 7) and the Lifetime Achievement Award from the American Association of Applied and Preventive Psychology.

4

Facts and Statistics

Economic conditions, cultural and ethnic identity, and gender-related issues have a substantial impact on children and their ability to learn. This chapter presents some of the important facts and statistics about the conditions that affect children's health and their capacity to learn. After reviewing statistics about economic indicators, such as family income and the impact of poverty, the chapter will examine data about selected health indicators, for example, rates of infant mortality, low birthweight, HIV/AIDS, substance use and abuse, and school and youth violence. The chapter concludes with data on indicators of learning, including measures of student achievement and teacher standards. The facts and data presented in this chapter are intended to illustrate the multiple and complex influences that bear on children's health and schooling.

CURRENT DEMOGRAPHIC DATA FOR CHILDREN

To provide a context for understanding the factors that are affecting children's learning and health, it is important to review the general demographic data for today's children, including data on the total population of children in the United States, ethnic diversity, utilization of child care, family information, and information on out-of-home youth.

- *Numbers:* In 2000, 26 percent of the total United States population (70.4 million) were children under the age of 18. Of this number, there were approximately the same number of children (between 23 and 24 million) in the 0 to 5, 6 to 11, and 12 to 17 age groups (Federal Interagency Forum on Child and Family Statistics 2001).

- *Diversity:* In 2000, the reported racial and ethnic diversity of U.S. children was continuing to increase, with 64 percent white, non-Hispanic; 16 percent Hispanic; 15 percent Black, non-Hispanic; 4 percent Asian or Pacific Islander; and 1 percent American Indian or Alaska Native (Federal Interagency Forum on Child and Family Statistics 2001).

- *Child Care:* An increasing number of families are using nonparental child care, with 54 percent of children (birth to three years old) in 2000 receiving some form of child care on a regular basis (Federal Interagency Forum on Child and Family Statistics 2001).

- *Unmarried Mothers:* In 1999, 33 percent of births were to unmarried mothers; this is an increase from 26.6 percent in 1990 (Annie E. Casey Foundation 2001).

- *Single-Parent Households:* There was a 13 percent increase in the number of families with children headed by a single parent between 1990 and 1998 (Annie E. Casey Foundation 2002).

- *Out-of-Home Children and Youth:* In 2000, 588,000 children resided in the nation's foster care system (U.S. Department of Health and Human Services 2001).

Economic Indicators

One vehicle for the way in which poverty impacts learning is the home environment or living arrangements of the child. Living arrangements that are crowded, unhealthy, or unsafe can lead to poor academic outcomes for school-age children. Economic data regarding family income and the impact of poverty is critical in light of the link between these factors and learning. It is widely recognized that successful, happy, and healthy children need families that are strong and provide love, nurturing, and support. However, families can find it very difficult to remain strong in high-poverty neighborhoods where few opportunities and supports are available. Children's health and ability to learn can be seriously compromised when some of the child's most basic needs are not being met because of pervasive poverty. What follows is a list of relevant statistics about poverty in the United States.

FAMILY INCOME AND THE IMPACT OF POVERTY

- As of 1999, the median income of families with children was $47,900 (Annie E. Casey Foundation 2002)

- The overall percent of children (under the age of 18) living in poverty in 2000 was 16.1 percent (Annie E. Casey Foundation 2002).

- Twenty-three percent of children under age five were living in poverty in 1996 (Annie E. Casey Foundation 2000).

- In 1999, 7 percent of children were living in extreme poverty (defined as income below 50 percent of poverty level) (Annie E. Casey Foundation 2002).

- Thirty-five percent of female-headed families received child support or alimony in 1999 (Annie E. Casey Foundation 2002).

- In 1999, 25 percent of children were living with parents who did not have full-time, year-round employment (Annie E. Casey Foundation 2001).

- In 1999, 17 percent of children were living below the poverty line (Dalaker and Proctor 2000).

- In 1995, 22 percent of children were living in poverty in the United States. This was found to be the highest level of poverty among 17 developed countries (Rainwater and Smeeding 1995).

- The number of children receiving Child Care and Development Fund subsidies was 1.8 million in 1999, an increase of 0.8 million since 1996. However, among families that left welfare and were working, less than one-third were receiving child care subsidies (Greenberg et al. 2002).

- In 1999, there were 6.7 million children living in working poor families. Working poor is defined as families where at least one parent worked 50 or more weeks a year and family income was below the poverty level (Annie E. Casey Foundation 2001).

Figure 4.1
Child Poverty in 17 Developed Countries

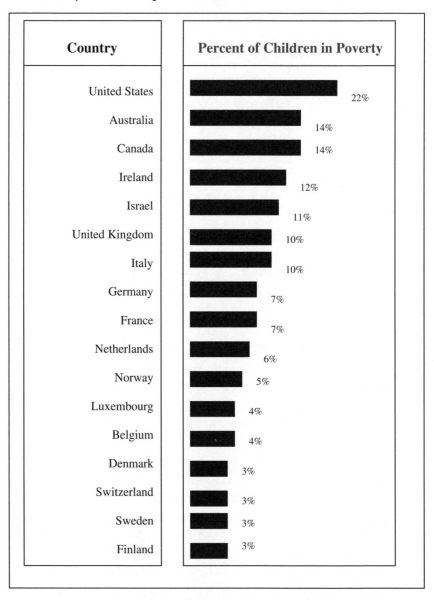

Source: Lee Rainwater and Timothy M. Smeeding, 1995, "Doing Poorly: The Real Income of American Children in a Comparative Perspective," Working paper No. 27, Luxembourg Income Study, Maxwell School of Citizenship and Public Affairs, Syracuse University, Syracuse NY. Annie E. Casey Foundation (2000) *Kids Count Data Book I*, page 32, figure 15.

- In 1994, the child poverty rate was 22 percent, and, in 1999, it dropped to 17 percent. However, the share of poor children receiving assistance also fell from 62 percent in 1994 to 40 percent in 1999 (Greenberg et al. 2002).

- According to the 1999 U.S. Census Bureau data, 8 out of every 100 children in very high poverty neighborhoods were not living with either parent (Annie E. Casey Foundation 2000).

- Data from the 1997 U.S. Census Bureau indicate that the percent of children living in a family that does not own a car or other vehicle was 50 percent for children living in low-income urban areas, as compared to 13 percent for all children (Annie E. Casey Foundation 2000).

- In 1998, the percent of households in urban areas that did not have a computer was 84 percent. In 1998, the percent of households without a phone in very high poverty neighborhoods was 17 percent (Annie E. Casey Foundation 2000).

- Children who live in poverty are twice as likely to repeat a grade in school as those children not living in poverty and are three times more likely to be expelled from school. Children from poverty are also half as likely as children not living in poverty to graduate with a bachelor's degree from college (Children's Defense Fund 1997).

- The average intelligence quotient (IQ) scores for children living in poverty at age five were an average of 9 points lower than their peers. Average achievement scores for children in poverty ages 3 or older were an average of 11 to 25 percentile points lower. Children living in poverty are also more likely to have a learning disability, receive special education services, and be held back a grade in school. Also, these children are at least twice as likely to drop out of school between the ages of 16 and 24 (Children's Defense Fund 1997).

- 1989–90 National Maternal and Infant Health Survey reported that for those families living in poverty 25.9 percent had missed at least one mortgage payment in the last 12 months; 8.5 percent had lost phone service; 16 percent had utilities shut off; 21.9 percent were afraid to travel in their neighborhood; 23 percent had no place to go for routine health issues; and 11 percent lived in families that indicated that they did not have enough food at least once in the last four months (Children's Defense Fund 1997).

Figure 4.2
Percent of Children in Central Cities Not Living with Either Parent, 1999

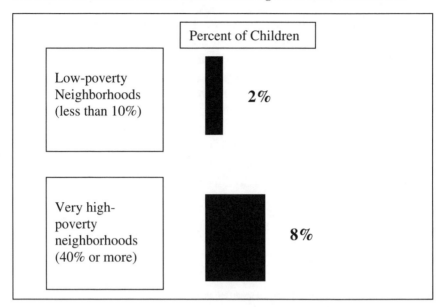

Source: 2002 Kids Count Data Book, Annie E. Casey Foundation, Baltimore, MD, www.aecf.org.

Figure 4.3
Percent of Children in Central Cities Not Living with Either Parent, 1998

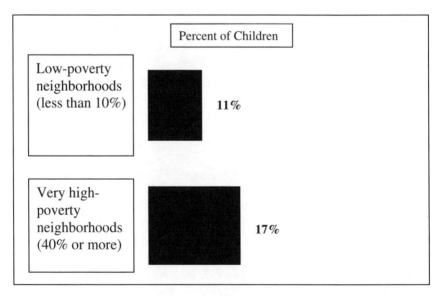

Source: 2002 Kids Count Data Book, Annie E. Casey Foundation, Baltimore, MD, www.aecf.org.

Figure 4.4
Health Status of Children under 18 by Race and Ethnicity, First Half of 1996

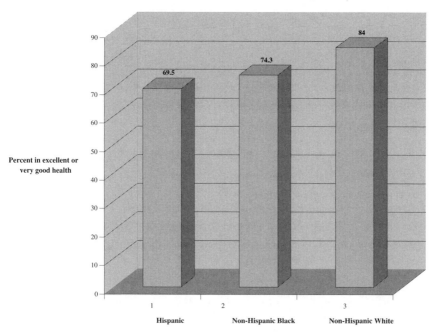

Source: M. E. Weigers and S. K. Drilea, "Health Status and Limitations: A Comparison of Hispanics, Blacks, and Whites, 1996." MEPS Research Findings No. 10 (Rockville, MD: U.S. Department of Health and Human Services, Agency for Health Care Policy and Research, 1996). Children's Defense Fund (2000) *The State of America's Children Yearbook*, page 34.

- In 1998, 3.4 million children lived in households that experienced hunger, while another 11 million children lived in homes at risk for hunger (Children's Defense Fund 2000).

- In 2000, approximately one-third of children living in poverty experienced food insecurity (Federal Interagency Forum and Family Statistics 2001).

- The income gap between rich and poor families is at its widest point in 50 years (Children's Defense Fund 2000).

CHILDREN'S LIVING ARRANGEMENTS

- In 2000, 69 percent of children lived with two parents (Federal Interagency Forum on Child and Family Statistics 2001).

- Over nearly 20 years (1980–1999), family structures have increasingly become more diverse, with an increase in children living with one parent (20 percent in 1980, 26 percent in 2000) (Federal Interagency Forum on Child and Family Statistics 2001).

- In 1999, 22 percent of children lived with their mothers only; 4 percent of children lived with their fathers only; and 4 percent of children lived with neither parent (Federal Interagency Forum on Child and Family Statistics 2001).

- Of the 2.6 million children living with neither parent in 1996, 50 percent lived with grandparents; 21 percent lived with other relatives; and 22 percent lived with nonrelatives (Federal Interagency Forum on Child and Family Statistics 2001).

- According to data from the 1999 U.S. Census Bureau, one-quarter of children living in high poverty neighborhoods had moved within the last year (Annie E. Casey Foundation 2000).

- Many families with children experience housing problems, such as physically inadequate or crowded housing, and high costs associated with housing. In 1999, it was reported that 35 percent of children experience one or more housing problems (Federal Interagency Forum on Child and Family Statistics 2001).

- In 1995, 10 percent of poor children in New York City spent time in homeless shelters. Homeless children are exposed to a variety of risks, including communicable diseases, increased mortality rate, diarrhea, asthma, family separation, and missed school (Children's Defense Fund 1997).

Health Indicators

Good health is vital to positive academic outcomes. There is little question among policymakers that the key to maintaining children's health is adequate health insurance. When Medicaid was introduced in 1965, infant mortality rates decreased and these rates continue to decrease today. While much has been done to increase health insurance coverage for children, many children are still not covered. Lack of adequate health insurance coverage is a particular problem for children of color and often results in significant health problems.

Other health-related issues also have a bearing on a child's success in school and in life, including teen pregnancy rates, immunization rates,

Figure 4.5
Income and Children's Health Status, 1996

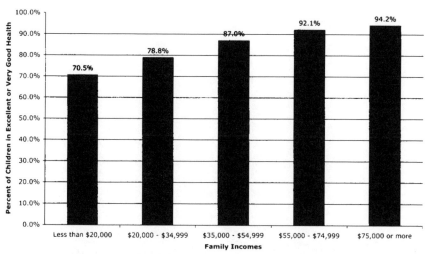

Source: P. F. Adams, G. E. Henershot, and M. A. Marano, "Current Estimates from the National Health Interview Survey, 1996," Vital and Health Statistics, Series 10. No.200 (Hyattsville, MD: U.S. Department of Health and Human Services, National Center for Health Statistics, 1999). Children's Defense Fund (2000) *The State of America's Children Yearbook*, page 35.

nutrition, substance abuse, school violence along with general school safety, child care issues, and parental abuse and neglect.

Child health varies by family income. Children living below the poverty line are less likely than children in higher income families to be in very good or excellent health. In 1997, only 68 percent of children in families below the poverty line were in very good or excellent health compared with 86 percent of children in families living at or above the poverty line (Federal Interagency Forum on Child and Family Statistics 2000).

HEALTH INSURANCE

- The U.S. Census Bureau found in 1998 that 17 % of children living in very high poverty neighborhoods were without health insurance (Centers for Disease Control 2000).

Figure 4.6
Child Care Arrangements for Children Younger Than Age Five with Working Mothers, 1994 (percent)

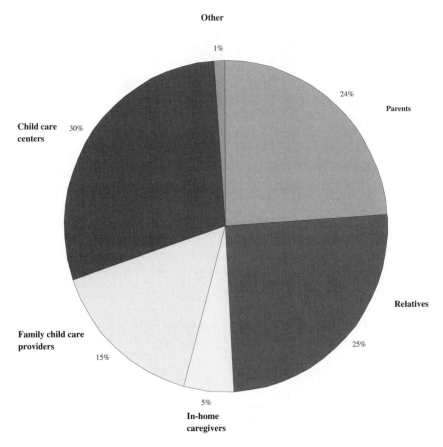

Source: Lynne Casper, "Who's Minding our Preschoolers?" Current Population Reports. P70-62 (Washington, DC: U.S. Department of Commerce, Bureau of the Census, 1997). Children's Defense Fund (2000) *The State of America's Children Yearbook*, page 47.

- In 1999, almost 12 million children lacked health insurance (Centers for Disease Control 2000).

- In 1999, one in five black children and one in three Hispanic children were uninsured, compared with one in nine white children (Centers for Disease Control 2000).

- In 1999, approximately 21 million children were enrolled in Medicaid, and more than 2 million children were enrolled in CHIP (Children's Health Insurance Program) (Centers for Disease Control 2000).

- In 1997, while Congress was debating CHIP, roughly 11.3 million children (or one of every seven) were uninsured (Children's Defense Fund 2000).

- In 1999, the U.S. Census Bureau reported that a total of 44.3 million Americans, including an estimated 10.8 million children under the age of 19, were uninsured. This represents a record number of uninsured Americans, despite the fact that there was the highest rate of employment and most robust economy in decades (U.S. Bureau of the Census 2000).

IMMUNIZATION

- Childhood immunizations have reached a record level of 80 percent as of 1999 (Children's Defense Fund 2001).

- There are still differences regarding immunization rates across different racial groups. In 1999, among two year olds, only 75 percent of black children and 77 percent of Hispanic children had received the adequate numbers of vaccinations for diphtheria, tetanus, pertussis, polio, measles, and Hib, while the rate for white children was 82 percent (Centers for Disease Control and Prevention 2000).

- Among all children entering school since 1980, at least 95 percent have had appropriate immunization, which is one of the requirements for school entry in all 50 states (Children's Defense Fund 2000).

- Exemptions from immunization requirements for medical reasons are legitimized in all 50 states, for religious reasons in 48 states, and for philosophical reasons in 15 states (Children's Defense Fund 2000).

- Between 1985 and 1992, exemptions from immunization for religious or philosophical reasons increased the risk of children contracting measles by 35 times (Children's Defense Fund 2000).

INFANT MORTALITY AND LOW BIRTHWEIGHT

- In 1999, approximately 7.6 percent of infants were born with low birthweight and 1.4 percent were born with very low birthweight. Low birthweight is defined as less than 5.5 pounds, and very low birthweight is defined as less than 3.3 pounds (Ventura et al. 2001).

- The United States has made progress in reducing the infant mortality rate over the last two decades. However, the United States still ranks twenty-second among industrialized countries and shows a disparity among different racial and ethnic groups. In 1998, the infant mortality rate stalled at 7.2 deaths per 1,000 births. This was the first year in more than 40 years in which the rate had not declined at all (Children's Defense Fund 2000).

- In 1998, the death rate for children ages 1 to 4 was 34 per 100,000 children and for children ages 5 to 14 it was 20 per 100,000 (Federal Interagency Forum on Child and Family Statistics 2001).

- The mortality rate among black infants is twice as high as that of white infants. Black infants are also four times more likely to have low birthweight involved in their death than are white infants (Children's Defense Fund 2000).

- Mothers without a high school diploma are 50 percent more likely to have infants with low birthweight. One explanation for this finding is that education is almost directly linked to income, therefore, the lower the level of education one attains, the less likely one is to earn a high income and have adequate health coverage (Children's Defense Fund 2000).

- In 1997, the adolescent mortality rate for youth ages 15 to 19 was 71 per 100,000 (Federal Interagency Forum on Child and Family Statistics 2001).

TEEN BIRTHRATES

- Bearing a child during adolescence often leads to long-term difficulties for the mother, her child, and society. Babies born to adolescent mothers are at higher risk for low birthweight and infant mortality. Furthermore, the children born to adolescent mothers are more likely to grow up in homes that offer lower levels of emotional support and cognitive stimulation, and they are less likely to earn high school diplomas (Sandefur and McLanahan 1994).

- In 1998, the adolescent birthrate was 30 per 1,000 young women ages 15 to 17. There were 173,231 births to these young women in 1998, a new national record low (Federal Interagency Forum on Child and Family Statistics 2000).

- Between 1991 and 1998 there was a substantial decrease in the teen birthrate, which followed a period of substantial increase from 1986 to 1991 (Ventura et al. 2001).

- There are significant racial and ethnic disparities in birthrates among adolescents aged 15 to 17. In 1998, the rate per 1,000 for this group was 18 for whites, 44 for Native Americans, 59 for blacks, and 62 for Hispanics (Ventura et al. 2001).

- Twice as many teens in the United States become pregnant as in England, Wales, and Canada. U.S. rates are nine times higher than in the Netherlands and Japan (Children's Defense Fund 2000).

- Every year almost 1 million teens become pregnant, or approximately 10 percent of sexually active teens between the ages of 15 and 19 (Children's Defense Fund 2000).

- Although 70 percent of teen mothers graduate from high school, they are less likely to go to college than other young women, and 83 percent of the teens who give birth are from low-income families (Children's Defense Fund 2000).

HIV/AIDS

- Between 1992 and 1996, 43 percent fewer children contracted AIDS through mother-to-child transmission with the use of zidovudine (ZDV or AZT) in pregnancy (Children's Defense Fund 2000).

- In 2000, HIV infection and AIDS ranked sixth as the cause of death for 15- to 24-year-old people. The actual epidemic among teens is more severe than what available statistics indicate because of the 8- to 10-year average incubation between HIV infection and AIDS. The fact that not all states collect data on new infection rates also contributes to underestimating the severity of the epidemic (Children's Defense Fund 2000).

- The year 2000 goal of HIV and sexually transmitted disease (STD) education was to reach 90 percent of all college students on campuses, but only 50 percent of college students actually received educational programs and services (Children's Defense Fund 2000).

ASTHMA

- In the last decade, asthma has become more prevalent all over the world. The rate of asthma in the United States has doubled and the rate of asthma among children of color in low-income communities is larger than it is for all other populations in America (Children's Defense Fund 2001).

- Despite the Healthy People 2000 goal, children's hospitalization rates for asthma increased. The rates for asthma-related emergency room visits and hospitalizations are higher among blacks than among whites for all ages, and especially for children under the age of four (Children's Defense Fund 2001).

- Nearly half of all the homeless children in cities were found to be asthmatic (Children's Defense Fund 2000).

LEAD POISONING

- The risk of having elevated blood-lead levels is eight times higher in children from low-income families than in other children, and five times higher in black children than in white children. Houses built before 1978 with lead paint put all children living in them at potential risk for lead poisoning (Centers for Disease Control and Prevention 2000).

- Children on Medicaid are three times more likely to suffer from lead poisoning than other children, but only 25 percent of them are tested for blood-lead levels (Children's Defense Fund 2000).

- Since 1999, all states are responsible to give annual blood-lead tests to children under two years old who enrolled in the Medicaid program. Those with high blood-lead levels will be treated effectively with Medicaid funds (Children's Defense Fund 2000).

DENTAL HEALTH

- Among all children ages 6 to 8, more than half need treatment for their dental problems, and with all 15 year olds, the amount increases to two-thirds (Children's Defense Fund 2000).

- Compared with children living above 200 percent of the federal poverty level those who live below it have twice as many dental pains and cavities but receive half as many dentist visits (Children's Defense Fund 2001).

- The Medicaid coverage of dental service is only about 10 percent of the actual costs, and only 18 percent of the children enrolled have dentist visits for preventive purposes (Children's Defense Fund 2000).

- Almost 29 million children are not insured for dental visits, and only two states have CHIP programs that cover some dental costs (Children's Defense Fund 2000).

BIRTHRATES TO UNWED MOTHERS

- In 1999, there were 44 births for every 1,000 unmarried women (ages 15 to −44). This is a marked increase from 1980, when the birthrate for unmarried women ages 15 to 44 was 29 in every 1,000. (Federal Interagency Forum on Child and Family Statistics 2001).
- In 1998, 33 percent of all births were to unmarried women (Federal Interagency Forum on Child and Family Statistics 2000).

NUTRITION

- The percentage of children under age 18 in households experiencing food insecurity with moderate or severe hunger in 1999 was 3.8 percent, compared with 4.7 percent in 1998 (Children's Defense Fund 2000).
- In 1996, only about one-quarter of children aged 2 to 5 had a "good diet" (Children's Defense Fund 2000).
- The U.S. Department of Agriculture reported in 1999 that 19.7 percent of children experienced hunger in 1998 compared with 14.6 percent in 1997, which is an increase of 3.7 million children (Children's Defense Fund 2000).
- The Urban Institute's National Survey of America's Families reported that, among families with children living below 200 percent of the poverty line, more than half have problems affording sufficient food or are worried about being able to provide adequate food for their children (Children's Defense Fund 2000).
- The National Assessment of Educational Progress reading assessment of 1998 collected information for the federally funded free/reduced-price lunch program, which provides children near or below the poverty line with nourishing meals. At all three grade levels assessed, students who were eligible for the free/reduced-price lunch program had lower average reading scores than students who were not eligible for the program (National Center for Education Statistics 1999a).

SUBSTANCE USE AND ABUSE

- Today, more than 4 million children between the ages of 12 and 17 smoke cigarettes. Nine out of every ten adults who die from smoking-related causes each year started smoking as teens. If this trend continues, nearly 5 million children who are alive today will die of smoking-related disease (Centers for Disease Control and Prevention 2000).

- As of 1999, about 70 percent of students have tried smoking cigarettes, and 25.3 percent have had a daily consumption of at least one cigarette in 30 days (Centers for Disease Control and Prevention 2000).

- Among high school seniors, smoking rates are highest among whites (26 percent) and lowest among blacks (about 8 percent) (Johnston, O'Malley, and Bachman 2000).

- In the 1999 Youth Risk Behavior Survey, 8 percent of eighth graders, 16 percent of tenth graders, and 23 percent of twelfth graders reported smoking cigarettes daily in the previous 30 days. Females and males report similar rates of daily smoking, between 7 and 8 percent for eighth graders, 16 percent for tenth graders, and 22 and 24 percent for twelfth graders (Centers for Disease Control and Prevention 2000).

- Nationwide, 7.8 percent of students have used smokeless tobacco at least once in the 30 days preceding the Youth Risk Behavior Survey. In the 30 days prior to the Youth Risk Behavior Survey, 17.7 percent of students nationwide had smoked cigars on at least one day (Centers for Disease Control and Prevention 2000).

- Alcohol is the most commonly used psychoactive substance during adolescence. In 2000, heavy drinking remained unchanged from 1999, with 30 percent of twelfth graders, 26 percent of tenth graders, and 14 percent of eighth graders reporting heavy drinking (i.e., at least five drinks at one sitting within the prior two weeks) (Johnston, O'Malley, and Bachman 2000).

- Males have a higher proportion of drinking than females do. In 1999, among all twelfth graders, 38 percent of males and 24 percent of females reported drinking heavily. And among tenth graders, the percentages for males and females were 30 percent and 22 percent respectively (Johnston, O'Malley, and Bachman 2000).

- Among secondary school students, Hispanic and white students are much more likely to drink heavily. The percentages of heavy drinking among twelfth graders are 13 percent of blacks; 35 percent of whites; and 31 percent of Hispanics (Johnston, O'Malley, and Bachman 2000).

- As of 2000, the percent of students using illegal drugs in the previous 30 days was 25 percent for twelfth graders; 23 percent for tenth graders; and 12 percent for eighth graders (Johnston, O'Malley, and Bachman 2000).

- From 1992 to 1996, more students reported using illicit drug in the previous 30 days in all grade levels. The percentage grew from 14 to 25 percent for twelfth graders, 11 to 23 percent for tenth graders, and 7 to 15 percent for eighth graders. The growth rate has stabilized or dropped since 1996 (Johnston, O'Malley, and Bachman 2000).

- A 1999 study of high-school students found that more twelfth-grade males (29 percent) used illicit drugs than females (23 percent) (Johnston, O'Malley, and Bachman 2000).

- In 2000, researchers looked at the illicit drug use of twelfth graders among racial groups and found that 26 percent of white, 20 percent of blacks, and 27 percent of Hispanics were using drugs (Johnston, O'Malley, and Bachman 2000).

- A recent nationwide study of drug use among adolescents found that 47.2 percent of students had used marijuana during their lifetime; 51 percent of these students were male and 43.4 percent were female. One-fourth of the students (26.7 percent) reported that they used marijuana at least once in the 30 days prior to their participation in the Youth Risk Behavior Survey (Centers for Disease Control and Prevention 2000).

- In 2000, an estimated 9.5 percent of students had used cocaine at least once in their lifetime. White students (15.3 percent) and Hispanic students (9.9 percent) are more likely to have used cocaine than black students (2.2 percent) (Centers for Disease Control and Prevention 2000).

- "Sniffing" or "puffing" is one way that young people get high. At least once during their life, 14.6 percent of students have sniffed glue, breathed the contents of aerosol spray cans, or inhaled paint with this intention (Centers for Disease Control and Prevention 2000).

- Among other illicit drugs, 9.1 percent of students reported methamphetamine use during their lifetime, 3.7 percent of students reported illicit steroid use, and 2.4 percent had reported using heroin (Centers for Disease Control and Prevention 2000).

- A significant number of students had initiated their substance use before the age of 13. The figures were 24.7 percent for cigarette smoking; 32.2 percent for alcohol use; and 11.3 percent for marijuana (Centers for Disease Control and Prevention 2000).

- Roughly 30.2 percent of students nationwide reported having been offered, sold, or given an illegal drug on school property at some time during the 12 months prior to the Youth Risk Behavior Survey. Seven percent had used marijuana on school property, and 4.9 percent had had at least one alcoholic drink on school property (Centers for Disease Control and Prevention 2000).

SCHOOL AND YOUTH VIOLENCE

- Every 2.5 hours during 1998, one American child or teen was killed by gunfire. In total, the lives of 3,761 children and teens were taken in this way (Children's Defense Fund 2001).

- The juvenile violent crime arrest rate was 394 per 100,000 youths ages 10 to 17 in 1998 (Annie E. Casey Foundation 2001).

- The juvenile property crime arrest rate was 2,130 per 100,000 youths ages 10 to 17 in 1998 (Annie E. Casey Foundation 2001).

- The rate of teen deaths by accident, homicide, and suicide per 100,000 teens ages 15 to 19 was 54 in 1998, a decrease of 24 percent from 1990. Juvenile arrests for violent crime have decreased by 19 percent since 1994 (Annie E. Casey Foundation 2001).

- American children under age 15 are 12 times more likely to die from gunfire than children in 25 other industrialized countries combined (Children's Defense Fund 2000).

- Children ages 12 to 17 are twice as likely as adults to be victims of violent crime (Children's Defense Fund 2000).

- Perpetrators of sexual assault often victimize children. In fact, one-third of all sexual assaults reported to law enforcement between 1991–1996 involved a child under age 12. In 365 out of 1,000 cases, the perpetrators were unknown to the child. More commonly, the offender is a friend or relative (45 percent) (Children's Defense Fund 2000).

- Only 28 percent of violent crime against juveniles aged 12 to 17 are reported to the police, with an additional 16 percent reported to authorities other than the police. More than half of all violent crimes against children are unreported and largely unknown (Children's Defense Fund 2000).

- Although girls are less likely than boys to become involved in the juvenile justice system, the arrest rate for females age 17 and under increased 103 percent between 1981 and 1997. By contrast, arrest rates for males the same age rose 27 percent (Children's Defense Fund 2000).

- Despite the recent tragic school shootings, overall school violence rates are in decline. In 1999, it was estimated that there was less than a one in a million chance that a student would suffer a school-associated violent death (Children's Defense Fund 2001).

- Theft is the most frequent crime committed against students and teachers, accounting for 61 percent of the total crimes. Although violent crime, weapon possession, and physical fights have decreased in schools, the level of fear has increased. Students are feeling unsafe more than ever at school and while traveling to and from school. Also, based on student reports, the presence of gangs nearly doubled between 1989 and 1995 (Children's Defense Fund 2000).

- In 1997, 7.2 percent of white high school students; 6.8 percent of black high school students; and 2.4 percent of Hispanic high school students felt unsafe while going to school. In addition, 10.4 percent of white students, 9.2 percent of black students, and 7.8 percent of Hispanic students reported carrying a gun onto school property. Nine percent of white students, 9.9 percent of black students, and 6.2 percent of Hispanic students were threatened or injured with a weapon on school property. Nineteen percent of white students, 20.7 percent of black students, and 13.3 percent of Hispanic students were in a physical fight on school property (Children's Defense Fund 2000).

- By the end of elementary school, the average child will have witnessed more than 100,000 acts of violence on television, and an average of 26 violent acts per hour during Saturday morning children's programs (Children's Defense Fund 2000).

Figure 4.7
Reading Skills of First-Time Kindergartners, Fall 1998

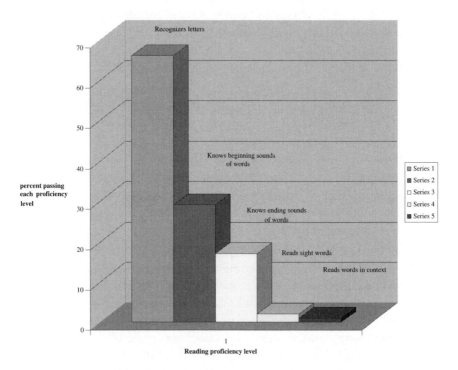

Source: National Center for Education Statistics, U.S. Department of Education. Early Childhood Longitudinal Study, "Kindergarten Class of 1998–99" Fall 1998. National Center for Education Statistics (2000) *The Condition of Education*, page xx, 16, figure 1.

- In 1998, an astounding 77 percent of juveniles, ages 13 to 17, who were murdered, were killed with a firearm (Children's Defense Fund 2000).

- In 1997, homicide accounted for more than 2,500 deaths among children age 19 and younger. Further, homicide is the third leading cause of death among children ages 5 to 14 and the second leading cause of death among young people ages 15 to 24 (Children's Defense Fund 2000).

- In the year 2000, accidental shootings accounted for 7 percent of deaths among children. More than 300 children died in gun accidents, almost one child every day (Children's Defense Fund 2001).

CHILD CARE

- According to the Children's Defense Fund, each day, an estimated 13 million children under age six spend some or all of their day being cared for by someone other than their parents (Children's Defense Fund 2001).

- Nearly 75 percent of preschool children were in some form of nonparental care in 1995 (Children's Defense Fund 1999).

- Nearly 60 percent of all children under age five, regardless of their mother's work status, were in some form of nonparental care in 1995 (Children's Defense Fund 1999).

- A 1999 Children's Defense Fund study found low-income children who received comprehensive, quality early childhood educational intervention had higher scores on cognitive, reading, and math tests than a comparison group of children who did not receive the intervention. These effects persisted through age 21 (Children's Defense Fund 1999).

- In 1998, two out of three (65 percent) women with children under 6 years of age, and three-quarters of women with children ages 6 to 17, were in the labor force according to the Children's Defense Fund (Children's Defense Fund 1999).

- In 1999, 64 percent of mothers with children younger than 6 and 78 percent of mothers with children ages 6 to 13 worked outside of the home. Nearly 60 percent of mothers with infants (under age 1) were in the labor force (Children's Defense Fund 2001).

- In the year 2000, 6 out of 10 children under age 6, and 7 out of 10 children ages 6 to 13, had both parents or their single parent in the labor force (Children's Defense Fund 2000).

- National studies have found serious problems with the quality of child care. Twelve percent of child care centers studied provided less than minimal quality care and only 14 percent received a rating of good quality care (Children's Defense Fund 1999).

- A study of family child care programs found that low-income and minority children in family-based settings were more likely to be in lower-quality programs than other children (Children's Defense Fund 1999).

- School-age programs are scarce in many low-income communities. In 1993, only 33 percent of schools in low-income neighborhoods offered before- and afterschool programs, compared with more than 50 percent of schools in affluent neighborhoods (Children's Defense Fund 1999).

- According to the Children's Defense Fund, full-day child care costs $4,000–$10,000 per year, yet one out of three families with young children earns less than $25,000 a year, and a family with both parents working full time at the minimum wage earns only $21,400 a year (Children's Defense Fund 1999).

- In the homes of American children, 5 million school-age children are without supervision each week (Children's Defense Fund 2001).

- More mothers than ever before are employed outside of the home, and provide critical financial support for their children. In fact, 55 percent of working women contribute 50 percent or more of their family's earnings. A 1999 report indicated that 30 percent of working mothers were single parents of children under six. For these children, the financial support provided by their mothers is vital (Children's Defense Fund 2000).

- In 1998, Congress expanded the 21st Century Community Learning Centers program. The program touches the lives of approximately 400,000 children who attend school in rural and inner-city environments. The program spans more than 1,600 schools in 471 communities (Children's Defense Fund 2000).

ABUSE AND NEGLECT

- In 1998, an estimated 2.9 million children were reported as suspected child abuse victims or neglect victims, and some 903,000 were confirmed as victims of abuse or neglect (Children's Defense Fund 2001).

- Only about 50 percent of child abuse cases reported nationally are investigated; in approximately one-third of these cases, investigators find sufficient evidence to make a claim of child abuse or neglect. Furthermore, of the cases investigated, only half of these abused and neglected children receive services following the investigation (Children's Defense Fund 2001).

- Among cases of suspected child abuse and neglect, twice as many children (55 percent) are victims of neglect as are victims of abuse (25 percent) (Children's Defense Fund 2000).

- Out of these same cases, 12 percent of children were sexually abused. Child victims of emotional and psychological abuse, medical neglect, and other types of maltreatment accounted for 6 percent, 2 percent, and 11 percent of these cases, respectively (Children's Defense Fund 2000).
- Black and Native American children are overrepresented among child victims of abuse and neglect. Abused children in these racial groups, represent two times their proportion in the general population (Children's Defense Fund 2000).
- Young children are most at risk for abuse and neglect, with more than 4 out of every 10 victims being under the age of six (Children's Defense Fund 2000).
- According to the Children's Defense Fund, children whose parents abuse drugs and alcohol are nearly three times more likely to experience abuse and more than four times more likely to experience neglect than children whose parents do not abuse drugs and alcohol (Children's Defense Fund 2001).

FAMILY HOMELESSNESS

- Recently, the U.S. Department of Education reported a national estimate of 850,000 homeless children and youths. Of these, 625,330 are school-aged, and 216,391 are younger than five (Children's Defense Fund 2000).
- The 1999 Better Homes Fund report, "Homeless Children: American's New Outcasts," estimated that 12 percent of homeless children were placed in foster care, compared with just over 1 percent of other children. Moreover, 22 percent of homeless children were separated from their immediate family, at some point, and reside with foster care families or relatives. Of these children, 9 percent are infants and toddlers, 19 percent percent are three to six year olds, and 34 percent were school-age children (Children's Defense Fund 2000).
- In 1997, approximately 2.8 percent of children had at least one parent serving jail sentences. Of these, approximately 200,000 children, or 1 in 359, had an incarcerated mother; and more than 1.7 million children, about 1 in 40, had an incarcerated father. An astounding two-thirds of the women in state prisons and one-half of the women in federal prisons had young chil-

dren living with them prior to entering prison (Children's Defense Fund 2000).

- The Orphan Project reported that, as of 2000, the parents of an estimated 72,000 to 125,000 American children died of AIDS. More than 90 percent of these children were black or Hispanic (Children's Defense Fund 2000).

- In 1998, 2.13 million children lived in households headed by adults other then their biological parents. As an alternative, extended family members provided care and guardianship of these children. This type of arrangement rose by 51.5 percent since 1990 (Children's Defense Fund 2000).

Education Indicators

Education is vital to ensure that our young people develop into happy, healthy, productive adults. Our nation's schools have an enormous

Figure 4.8
The Nation's Reading and Writing Performance

	4th Grade	8 th Grade	12 th Grade
Reading			
At or above Basic	62%	74%	77%
At or above Proficient	31%	33%	6%
Advanced	7%	3%	6%
Writing			
At or above Basic	84%	84%	78%
At or above Proficient	23%	27%	22%
Advanced	1%	1%	1%

Sources: National Center for Education Statistics, U.S. Department of Education. National Assessment of Educational Progress 1998 Reading Report for the Nation and the States (March 1999); National Assessment of Educational Progress 1998 Writing Report Card for the Nation and the States (September 1999). Children's Defense Fund (2000) *The State of America's Children Yearbook*, page 69.

impact on the development of children, yet there are many factors that are impeding student's progress in our schools. School resources are not evenly distributed, drop-out rates continue to be disparate between the cities and the suburbs and accountability in the classroom is an issue that is being debated nationally. The following information is meant to encompass some of the particularly salient issues facing children in schools today. Data is provided on topics such as school readiness, difficulty speaking English, measures of school achievement, teacher training, physical education, and mental health issues in school.

SCHOOL READINESS

- In 1999, 53 percent of children ages 3 to 5 were read to daily by a family member (Federal Interagency Forum on Child and Family Statistics 2000).

- In 1998, 66 percent of children entering kindergarten were able to recognize letters, while 29 percent knew the sounds of the letters that begin words. These skills are recognized as important for developing the ability to read (Federal Interagency Forum on Child and Family Statistics 2000).

DIFFICULTY SPEAKING ENGLISH

- In 1995, 5 percent of all school-aged children (2.4 million children) in the United States spoke a language other than English at home and had difficulty speaking English (Federal Interagency Forum on Child and Family Statistics 2000).

DISPARITY IN RESOURCES ALLOTTED TO POOR SCHOOL DISTRICTS

- The importance of computer literacy has grown tremendously in recent years. Poor children have little or no access to computers at school or home. Additionally, third-grade teachers in the poorest schools are 50 percent more likely to report inadequate supplies of textbooks, workbooks, and audiovisual equipment than teachers in the wealthiest schools (Children's Defense Fund 1997).

- In 1997, the U.S. Department of Education reported that students in the wealthiest school districts were allocated 56 percent more resources than students in the poorest districts (Children's Defense Fund 2001).

- More than 70 percent of teachers in schools with a high concentration of low-income students reported lacking some necessary materials for their classes (Children's Defense Fund 2001).

- The richest school districts spend 56 percent more per student than the poorest school districts spend (Children's Defense Fund 2001).

MEASURES OF STUDENT ACHIEVEMENT

- Nearly two-thirds of the nation's high school graduates do not have a college degree. As the job market becomes more specialized and competitive, economic success, even viability, becomes increasingly difficult to attain for individuals without a college education (Children's Defense Fund 2000).

- The ability of American students to compete at an international level in the subjects of math and science decreases as they approach graduation. According to the 1995 Third International Math and Science Study (TIMSS), American fourth graders scored above a 26-nation average and eighth graders scored close to the international average on math and science. However, by the twelfth grade, American students scored below the international average and among the lowest of 21 countries (Children's Defense Fund 2000).

- In a comparison of 27 countries, the United States ranked second in reading literacy scores for 9 year olds and ninth for 14 year olds (Children's Defense Fund 2000).

- Achievement levels being reached by young students in the United States are unsatisfactory. According to the National Education Goals Panel, only 31 percent of fourth graders were performing at a "proficient" reading level and only 7 percent were performing at an "advanced" reading level (Children's Defense Fund 2000).

- In 1999, most American children were writing at a substandard level. Only 23 percent of fourth graders achieved proficiency in writing and 1 percent wrote at an advanced level (Children's Defense Fund 2000).

- In an attempt to ameliorate student deficits in reading ability, Ohio adopted a Fourth Grade Reading Guarantee, which mandated that, by 2001–02, students who did not meet the required reading levels would not graduate to the fifth grade. As part of the initiative, students were provided with the individual assistance needed to reach this goal (Children's Defense Fund 2000).

- In 1999, $94 million was invested by the California state legislature to improve reading among students from kindergarten through third grade and to enhance the quality of teachers (Children's Defense Fund 2000).

- White students consistently score higher in reading and math than black or Hispanic students at ages 9, 13, and 17. In the 1980s, the discrepancy of obtained scores between racial groups decreased in each subject in some age-groups (National Center for Education Statistics 1999b).

- Since 1980, average reading scores have not improved among students ages 13 and 17. Among 9 year olds, scores have declined slightly (National Center for Education Statistics 1999b).

- In families, parent education is positively correlated to the academic performance of children. When reading and math scores of students (ages 13 and 17) are compared, higher scores are obtained by students whose parents completed more years of school than students whose parents have less formal education (Federal Interagency Forum on Child and Family Statistics 2000).

- Girls of all ages consistently obtain higher reading scores than their male peers. An exception to this trend occurred in 1996, when boys outperformed girls at every age level. Math scores among 9 to 13 year olds obtained from 1980 to 1996 were not significantly different between the sexes, however boys slightly outperformed girls at age 17 (National Center for Education Statistics 1999b).

TEACHER TRAINING AND STANDARDS

- An estimated 2.2 million teachers will be needed to meet enrollment increases in the next 10 years (Children's Defense Fund 2000).

- The American Council on Education found that 56 percent of seventh through twelfth graders were taught physical science by teachers who lacked degrees in the subject. This was true of 70 percent of seventh through twelfth graders in the poorest schools (Children's Defense Fund 2000).

- Nationally, more than one-third of newly hired teachers are put in a classroom without having completed their state's licensing requirements. Eleven percent of newly hired teachers do not have a license, and 15 percent hold only temporary, provisional, or emergency licenses (Children's Defense Fund 2001).

- A recent U.S. Department of Education survey of 4,000 teachers found that only 38 percent of all teachers have an undergraduate or graduate major in an academic field, 18 percent have a major in a subject area of education, and 37 percent have a major in general education (Children's Defense Fund 2000).

- In 1994, Congress required states to develop both content- and performance-based standards to measure students' academic achievements. As of spring 1998, only 21 states had implemented performance-based standards, and many states had failed to develop distinct assessments for students with disabilities and for those for whom English is their second language, despite the law requiring them to do so (Children's Defense Fund 2000).

DROP-OUT RATES

- In 1998, the overall high school completion rate for young adults (ages 18 to 24) was 85 percent (Federal Interagency Forum on Child and Family Statistics 2000).

- According to figures compiled by the U.S. Department of Education, in 1998 62.8 percent of Hispanic students; 88.2 percent of black students; and 93.6 percent of white students completed high school. In 1998, 85 percent of all young adults ages 18 to 24 had completed high school. This rate has fluctuated slightly since 1980, when it was 84 percent (Federal Interagency Forum on Child and Family Statistics 2000).

- The rate at which blacks and non-Hispanics completed high school increased significantly between 1980 and 1990, from 75 percent to 83 percent. Hispanics consistently have had a lower high school completion rate than either blacks or whites. This rate increased from 57 percent in 1980 to 67 percent in 1985, then declined to 57 percent again in 1991 (Federal Interagency Forum on Child and Family Statistics 2000).

- According to figures supplied by the U.S. Department of Education, in 1999 about 8 percent of the nation's 16 to 19 year olds were neither enrolled in school nor working. This rate has been declining since 1991, when it was at 11 percent. Young males make up the majority of this group (Federal Interagency Forum on Child and Family Statistics 2000).

- Black and Hispanic youth are considerably more likely to be neither in school nor working. In 1999, 13 percent of black and 14 percent of Hispanic students were neither in school nor working, compared with 6 percent of their white counterparts. However, these rates have decreased since 1984, according to data from the U.S. Department of Education (Federal Interagency Forum on Child and Family Statistics 2000).

- According to the Children's Defense Fund, children from poor backgrounds were twice as likely to drop out of school between the ages of 16 to 24 than middle-income youths, and 11 times more likely than wealthy youths (Children's Defense Fund 1997).

MENTAL HEALTH ISSUES AFFECTING EDUCATION

- According to the 1999 Youth Risk Behavior Survey, 28.3 percent of students had felt so sad or hopeless every day for at least two consecutive weeks that they stopped doing some form of usual activities. Females were significantly more likely than male students to have felt sad or hopeless for at least two weeks (Centers for Disease Control and Prevention 2000).

- Nationwide, 19.3 percent of students had seriously considered attempting suicide during the 12 months preceding the Youth Risk Behavior Survey. Female students were significantly more likely than male students to have made a suicide plan. Approximately 8.3 percent of students had attempted suicide at least once during the previous 12 months (Centers for Disease Control and Prevention 2000).

- Nationwide, 1 in 10 children and adolescents suffer from mental illness serious enough to cause some level of impairment. It is estimated that fewer than one in five of these children receives the needed treatment (National Institute of Mental Health 1999).

- According to the National Institute of Mental Health (NIMH), an estimated 3 percent to 5 percent of school-age children are diagnosed each year with Attention Deficit Hyperactivity Disorder (ADHD), and boys are three times more likely to be diagnosed than girls (National Institute of Mental Health 1999).

- Nearly 4 million children suffer from learning disabilities in the United States. Of these, at least 20 percent have a type of disorder that leaves them unable to focus their attention. About 17 percent of children under 18 years of age have been diagnosed with a developmental disability (National Institute of Mental Health 1999).

- Large-scale studies by NIMH have reported that up to 3 percent of children and up to 8 percent of adolescents in the United States suffer from depression. In 1996, suicide was the third leading cause of death for young people 15 to 24 years of age, and the fourth leading cause for children 10 to 14 years of age (National Institute of Mental Health 1999).

- Anxiety disorders are the most common mental health disorder found with children and adolescents in this country. According to one recent large scale study at the NIMH for young people aged 9 to 17, as many as 13 percent of young people experience an anxiety disorder in any given year (National Institute of Mental Health 1999).

- Among adolescent and young women in the United States, between 0.5 percent and 1.0 percent suffer from anorexia nervosa; 1 percent to 3 percent have bulimia nervosa; and 0.7 percent to 4 percent suffer from binge-eating disorder. Data is limited for eating disorder rates among males (National Institute of Mental Health 1999).

- One percent of adolescents aged 14 to 18 have suffered from bipolar disorder sometime in their life, according to NIMH data (National Institute of Mental Health 1999).

- Autism and other developmental brain disorders may occur in as many as 2 out of 1,000 children (National Institute of Mental Health 1999).

PHYSICAL EDUCATION AND ACTIVITY

- According to the 1999 Youth Risk Behavior Survey, only 64.7 percent of students surveyed had participated in activities that made them sweat and breathe hard for at least 20 minutes on at least three of the preceding seven days (Centers for Disease Control and Prevention 2000).

- Nationwide, 53.6 percent of students had done strengthening exercises on at least three of the seven days preceding the Youth Risk Behavior Survey (Centers for Disease Control and Prevention 2000).

- According to the Youth Risk Behavior Survey, 57.2 percent of students watched television for at least two hours during an average school day (Centers for Disease Control and Prevention 2000).

- In 1999, 56.1 percent of students were enrolled in a physical education (PE) class nationwide (Centers for Disease Control and Prevention 2000).

- During the 12 months preceding the Youth Risk Behavior Survey, 55.1 percent of students nationwide had played on sports teams (Centers for Disease Control and Prevention 2000).

REFERENCES

Annie E. Casey Foundation. 2000. *Kids Count Data Book: State Profiles of Child Well-Being.* Baltimore, MD: Annie E. Casey Foundation.

———. 2001. *Kids Count Data Book: State Profiles of Child Well-Being.* Baltimore, MD: Annie E. Casey Foundation.

———. 2002. *Kids Count Data Book: State Profiles of Child Well-Being.* Baltimore, MD: Annie E. Casey Foundation.

Centers for Disease Control and Prevention. 2000. *Youth Risk Behavior Surveillance–United States, 1999.* Atlanta, GA: U.S. Department of Health and Human Services.

Children's Defense Fund. 1997. *Poverty Matters: The Cost of Child Poverty in America.* Washington, DC: Children's Defense Fund.

———. 1999. *Key Facts: Essential Information about Child Care, Early Education, and School-Age Care.* Washington, DC: Children's Defense Fund.

———. 2000. *The State of America's Children Yearbook.* Washington, DC: Children's Defense Fund.

———. 2001. *The State of America's Children Yearbook.* Washington, DC: Children's Defense Fund.

Dalaker, J., and B. Proctor. 2000. "Poverty in the United States: 1999." *Current Population Reports, Series P60–210.* Washington, DC: U.S. Census Bureau.

Federal Interagency Forum on Child and Family Statistics. 2000. *America's Children: Key National Indicators of Well-Being 2000.* Washington, DC: Federal Interagency Forum on Child and Family Statistics.

————. 2001. *America's Children: Key National Indicators of Well-Being 2001*. Washington, DC: Federal Interagency Forum on Child and Family Statistics.

Greenberg, M.H., J. Levin-Epstein, R.Q. Hutson, T.J. Ooms, R. Schumacher, V. Turetsky, and D.M. Engstrom. 2002. "The 1996 Welfare Law: Key Elements and Reauthorization Issues Affecting Children." *The Future of Children* 12(1):27–57.

Johnston, L.D., P.M. O'Malley, and J.G. Bachman. 2000. *Monitoring the Future-National Survey Results on Drug Use, 1975–1999* (NIH Publication No. 00–4802). Bethesda, MD: National Institutes of Health, National Institute on Drug Abuse, and Institute of Social Research, University of Michigan.

National Center for Education Statistics. 1999a. *NAEP 1998 Reading. A Report Card for the Nation and the States*. (NCES 1999–500). U.S. Department of Education, Washington, DC: National Center for Education Statistics.

————. 1999b. *NAEP 1999 Trends in Academic Progress*. U.S. Department of Education, Washington, DC: National Center for Education Statistics.

National Institute of Mental Health. 1999. *Brief Notes on the Mental Health of Children and Adolescents*. Bethesda, MD: National Institute of Mental Health.

Rainwater, L., and T.M. Smeeding. 1995. *Doing Poorly: The Real Income of American Children in a Comparative Perspective*. Working Paper No. 127, Luxembourg Income Study. Syracuse, NY: Maxwell School of Citizenship and Public Affairs, Syracuse University.

Sandefur, G., and S.S. McLanahan. 1994. *Growing Up with a Single Parent: What Hurts, What Helps*. Cambridge, MA: Harvard University Press.

U.S. Department of Health and Human Services. 2001. "The AFCARS Report." Washington, DC. Available from http://www.acf.dhhs.gov/programs/cb/publications/afcars/apr2001.htm (November, 2001).

U.S. Bureau of the Census. 2000. *Current Population Survey*. Washington, DC: U.S. Bureau of the Census.

Ventura, S.J., J.A. Martin, S.C. Curtin, F. Menacker, and B.E. Hamilton. 2001. "Births: Final Data for 1999." *National Vital Statistics Report* 49:1. Hyattsville, MD: National Center for Health Statistics.

5

Key Organizations

This directory provides a guide to organizations and associations that are focused on comprehensive student health services in schools. The chapter is divided into three sections entitled National Organizations, Federal Agencies, and Funding Opportunities. Researchers, student support staff in schools, teachers, community-based human service providers, youth development workers, educational administrators and policymakers, and concerned citizens committed to children's health and well-being will benefit from information and assistance provided by key organizations in the field. The organizations included here address the many aspects of a comprehensive student health model. Not every organization included in this chapter deals with all aspects of comprehensive student health; however, each of these organizations deals with at least one of the key elements of a comprehensive student health model, for example, violence prevention or health education. Because the field is continually developing, this list is not exhaustive. These organizations, however, have established reputations and this list will be a good starting point for an information search.

NATIONAL ORGANIZATIONS

Academy for Educational Development
1825 Connecticut Avenue, NW
Washington, DC 20009-5721

(202) 884-8000
(202) 884-8400 (FAX)
http://www.aed.org

The Academy for Educational Development (AED) is an independent, nonprofit organization committed to solving critical social problems in the United States and throughout the world through education, social marketing, research, training, policy analysis, and program design and management. AED was founded in 1961 and is dedicated to improving people's lives by increasing knowledge and promoting democratic and humanitarian ideals. To this end, AED works with businesses, schools, community organizations, corporations, policy leaders, and government agencies to support the development of educational institutions. AED provides assistance to organizations interested in exploring new educational initiatives or supporting current efforts.

Advocates for Youth
1025 Vermont Avenue, NW, Suite 200
Washington, DC 20005
(202) 347-5700
(202) 347-2263 (FAX)
http://www.advocatesforyouth.org

Advocates for Youth (AFY) is dedicated to the promotion of a society where adolescents are valued and where public health policy, on issues such as adolescent sexuality, is driven by scientific research. AFY is committed to creating programs and promoting policies to help young people make informed and responsible decisions about their reproductive and sexual health. The organization provides information, training, and advocacy to schools, youth organizations, policymakers, youth activists, and the media in the United States as well as internationally. Programs include peer education, HIV/AIDS and sexually transmitted disease awareness, and sex education. The organization's mission is to offer information and support to educators, health care professionals, and other youth-serving professionals. These support services include technical assistance, education programs, research articles, referrals, resources, training, policy analysis, and curriculum review and development.

American Academy of Child and Adolescent Psychiatry
3015 Wisconsin Avenue, NW
Washington, DC 20016-3007

(800) 333-7636
(202) 966-2891 (FAX)
http://www.aacap.org

The American Academy of Child and Adolescent Psychiatry (AACAP) is a nonprofit organization founded in 1953. AACAP is a membership-based organization and comprises more than 6,500 child and adolescent psychiatrists. AACAP's mission is to promote the mental health of children and youth through research, training, advocacy, prevention, comprehensive diagnosis and treatment, peer support, and collaboration. It is the leading national professional medical association dedicated to treating and improving the quality of life for children, youth, and families affected by mental health concerns. AACAP accomplishes its mission through the distribution of information, acting as a liaison between state and local governments and community health concerns, and interfacing with managed care organizations. This organization also works to promote an understanding of mental illnesses and remove the stigma associated with these disorders.

American Academy of Pediatric Dentistry
211 E. Chicago Avenue, #700
Chicago, IL 60611-2663
(312) 337-2169
(312) 337-6329 (FAX)
http://www.aapd.org

The American Academy of Pediatric Dentistry (AAPD) was established to work toward improving the oral and dental health of children, adolescents, and those young people with special health care needs. The mission of AAPD is accomplished through information dissemination to teachers, nurses, dentists, and parents about the oral health of young people. The organization also includes a foundation that provides financial support and educational and research projects dedicated to the oral health of children. Their Web site contains information that teachers, nurses, and parents can use to educate themselves and their children.

American Academy of Pediatrics
141 Northwest Point Boulevard
Elk Grove Village, IL 60007

(847) 228-5005
(847) 228-5097 (FAX)
http://www.aap.org

The American Academy of Pediatrics (AAP), founded in 1930, is committed to the promotion of optimal physical, mental, and social health and well-being of all children and adolescents. AAP plays a valuable role in the development of comprehensive health care policies for all children and youth. AAP has approximately 55,000 members, who include pediatricians, pediatric medical subspecialists, and pediatric surgical specialists. AAP provides continuing education courses, annual scientific meetings, seminars, and publications. AAP conducts research and promotes the funding of research as well as seeks to ensure that children and youth's health care needs are taken into consideration as legislative and public policy are developed.

American Association for Active Lifestyles and Fitness
1900 Association Drive
Reston, VA 20191
(800) 213-7193
http://www.aahperd.org/aaalf/template.cfm

The American Association for Active Lifestyles and Fitness (AAALF) has as its primary mission the promotion of healthy and active lifestyles for all people across the lifespan. Toward this end, AAALF collaborates with other professional organizations and distributes information relating to health and physical fitness. AAALF seeks grants and sponsorships to reach a wider range of people with their mission and AAALF communicates with members through brochures, newsletters, and other publications.

American Association for Health Education
1900 Association Drive
Reston, VA 20191-1599
(703) 476-3437
(703) 476-6638 (FAX)
http://www.aahperd.org/aahe/template.cfm

The American Association for Health Education (AAHE) seeks to provide support and resources to health educators and other professionals who are concerned with the health of all people. This mission is accomplished through a comprehensive approach that encourages and supports health professionals concerned with health promotion through education and other systemic interventions. Specifically, AAHE serves community agencies, businesses, schools (kindergarten through twelfth grade), and higher education. AAHE develops standards, resources, and services regarding health education; fosters the development of national research priorities in health education; facilitates communication among members of the profession, the public, and other national and international organizations; provides technical assistance; provides leadership in promoting policies and evaluation procedures; and assists in the development and mobilization of resources for effective health education.

American Association of School Administrators
1801 North Moore Street
Arlington, VA 22209
(703) 528-0700
(703) 841-1543 (FAX)
http://www.aasa.org

The American Association of School Administrators (AASA), founded in 1865, is a professional organization for educational leaders and school administrators. AASA currently has more than 14,000 members around the world. The mission of AASA is to support effective educational leaders dedicated to providing the best quality public education for all children. The main areas of focus for AASA include improving the condition of children and youth, preparing schools and school systems for the twenty-first century, building links between schools and communities, and enhancing the quality and effectiveness of school leaders. The organization provides career advice and connections, facilitates conferences, publishes reports and newsletters, and advocates for educational issues in legislation and public policy.

American Counseling Association
5999 Stevenson Avenue
Alexandria, VA 22304
(703) 823-9800
(800) 347-6647
(703) 823-0252 (FAX)
http://www.counseling.org

The American Counseling Association (ACA), founded in 1952, is the world's largest private, nonprofit organization for professional counselors. ACA has been actively involved in developing professional and ethical standards for the profession of counseling. The association also is committed to promoting public confidence in the counseling profession and provides leadership, training, continuing education, and advocacy services. ACA publishes books, journals, and videos used by counselors, educators, administrators, and students; conducts professional development seminars; and provides liability insurance to those in the counseling profession. ACA members include professionals in education, community agencies, government agencies, and businesses in the United States and worldwide.

American Dietetic Association
216 West Jackson Boulevard
Chicago, IL 60606
(800) 877-1600
http://www.eatright.org

The American Dietetic Association (ADA), founded in 1917, is concerned with advocating healthy eating habits for all people and carries out this mission through supporting and educating its members. ADA is the leading source of health and nutrition information in the United States, and the organization distributes this information through books, journals, and conferences. Members include food service professionals, dietetic consultants, educators, dietetic researchers, and students. In their efforts to provide nutrition information for the public, ADA sponsors publications, national events, and media and marketing programs. The association establishes standards of quality for professional practice and lobbies for federal legislation that will contribute to the nutritional health of children, youth, and adults.

American Federation of Teachers
555 New Jersey Avenue, NW
Washington, DC 20001
(202) 879-4400
(202) 393-8648 (FAX)
http://www.aft.org

The American Federation of Teachers (AFT) is a teachers' union that was founded in 1916 to support the professional interests of teachers and educators. AFT benefits teachers by working to create strong local unions affiliated with the labor movement. AFT also seeks to influence standards and professional practices in the workplace. Its overall mission is to improve the lives of its members and their families, strengthen the institutions in which teachers work, improve the quality of services that teachers provide, and bring teachers together to support and assist one another.

American Medical Association
515 N. State Street
Chicago, IL 60610
(312) 464-5000
http://www.ama-assn.org

The American Medical Association (AMA) was founded in 1847 and is the nation's leader in promoting professionalism in medicine and setting standards for medical education, practice, and ethics. AMA also advocates on behalf of medical professionals and the patients it serves. AMA strives to provide timely and accurate information on matters that are important to the delivery of health services as well as to the overall health of Americans.

American Nurses Association
600 Maryland Avenue, SW, 100W
Washington, DC 20024
(202) 651-7000
http://www.nursingworld.org

The American Nurses Association (ANA) is a professional organization representing the nation's registered nurses. The association is dedicated to ensuring that an adequate number of well-trained nurses is available, as well as to meeting the needs of nurses and health care consumers. The organization seeks to promote the health of the public at large by supporting research and disseminating all association initiatives among its members. ANA regularly lobbies the U.S. Congress and other regulatory agencies for the implementation of policies to support nurses and the general health of the public. ANA is also at the forefront of policy initiatives pertaining to health care reform. The primary focus of ANA, for policy initiatives, is a restructured health care system that delivers health care in community-based settings and provides an expanded role for registered nurses and advanced practice nurses in the delivery of basic and primary health care.

American Psychological Association

750 First Street, NE
Washington, DC 20002-4242
(800) 374-2721
(202) 336-5500
http://www.apa.org

The American Psychological Association (APA), which was founded in 1892, is the largest scientific and professional organization representing psychology in the United States. APA works to advance psychology as a science, as a profession, and as a means of promoting human welfare. The organization seeks to promote research, improve research methods, and improve the qualifications and usefulness of psychologists. APA also strives to establish and maintain the highest standards of professional ethics and conduct, and to increase the dissemination of psychological knowledge through meetings, professional contacts, reports, papers, discussions, and publications.

American Public Health Association

800 I Street, NW
Washington, DC 20001-3710
(202) 777-APHA
(202) 777-2534
http://www.apha.org

The American Public Health Association (APHA), founded in 1872, is the largest and oldest organization of public health professionals in the world. The association's mission is to work closely with national and international agencies to improve health worldwide. APHA's members include researchers, health service providers, administrators, teachers, and other health workers in a unique multidisciplinary environment of exchange, study, and action. APHA advocates for a broad range of issues affecting personal and environmental health, pollution control policies related to infectious diseases, a smoke-free society, and professional education in public health.

American Public Human Services Association

810 First Street, NE, Suite 500
Washington, DC 20002-4267
(202) 682-0100
(202) 289-6555 (FAX)
http://www.aphsa.org

The American Public Human Services Association (APHSA), founded in 1930, is a nonprofit organization of individuals and agencies dedicated to human services. The association seeks to develop and enact public human service policies that improve the health and well-being of all people, but especially children and families. The organization seeks to develop social policy, provide training and technical assistance to states and localities, disseminate information, and promote dialogue through publications, conferences and training, and promote research and demonstration projects in human services. Members include many state and territorial human service agencies, and several thousand individuals who work in the human service professions. APHSA educates Congress, the media, and the public on such topics as welfare, child care reform, health care reform, and child care.

American School Counselor Association
801 N. Fairfax Street, Suite 310
Fairfax, VA 22314
(703) 683-2722
(703) 683-1619 (FAX)
http://www.schoolcounselor.org

The American School Counselor Association (ASCA), founded in 1953, is the national organization representing the school counseling profession. The association's focus is on providing professional development, enhancing school counseling programs, and researching effective school counseling practices. The association has 13,000 members—including school counselors, students, and other interested individuals—and works to promote academic, occupational, personal, and social growth among members and to ensure human rights, children's welfare, healthy learning environments, and positive interpersonal relationships. ASCA also works to advocate for its members' interests in governmental and public relations.

American School Food Service Association
700 S. Washington Street, Suite 300
Alexandria, VA 22314
(703) 739-3900
(703) 739-3915 (FAX)
http://www.asfsa.org

The American School Food Service Association (ASFSA), founded in 1946, promotes the availability, quality, and acceptance of school nutrition programs as a critical component of every student's education. The primary activities of the association are providing education and training, setting standards through certification, gathering and transmitting information, and representing the nutritional interests of all children. As one of the leading associations on school nutrition, ASFSA extends its services beyond traditional school meal programs and creates programs that increase awareness of global hunger issues, assist low-income families in obtaining skills to become food service workers, and promote good nutrition.

American School Health Association
7263 State Route 43
Kent, OH 44240
(330) 678-1601
(330) 678-4526 (FAX)
http://www.ashaweb.org

The American School Health Association (ASHA) brings together the efforts of many professionals working with or in schools who are dedicated to promoting the health of school-aged children. This multidisciplinary organization—comprising school physicians and nurses, nutritionists, health educators, school-based professionals, and public health workers—advocates for high-quality school health instruction, health services, and a healthy school environment. ASHA promotes comprehensive school health programs and health services that are linked to the family and community as well as programs that promote both the health of students and the professionals that serve them. The association also works to integrate school counseling, psychological and social services, food services, and physical education programs into the overall mission of school health programs.

The Association of State and Territorial Health Officials
1275 K Street, NW, Suite 800
Washington, DC 20005-4006
(202) 371-9090
(202) 371-9797
http://www.astho.org

The Association of State and Territorial Health Officials (ASTHO) is a national nonprofit organization representing the state and territorial agencies concerned with public health. ASTHO is dedicated to creating sound public health policy and to ensuring excellence in state-based public health practice. The agency is engaged in a wide range of legislative, scientific, educational, and programmatic issues and activities on the behalf of public health.

The Association for Supervision and Curriculum Development
1703 North Beauregard Street
Alexandria, VA 22311
(703) 578-9600
(800) 933-ASCD
(703) 575-5400 (FAX)
http://www.ascd.org

The Association for Supervision and Curriculum Development (ASCD), founded in 1943, is an international, nonprofit association of professional educators whose professions span all of the grade levels and a wide variety of subject areas. The ASCD's mission is to create partnerships in teaching and learning with the goal of success for all learners. Each year the ASCD Board of Directors chooses certain goals and these goals become the focus of special actions or development. ASCD provides a forum in education issues, shares research news and information, and forms partnerships with other agencies to achieve the overall goal of creating successful learners.

Coalition for Community Schools
1001 Connecticut Avenue, NW, Suite 310
Washington, DC 20036
(202) 822-8405
(202) 872-4050 (FAX)
http://www.communityschools.org

The Coalition for Community Schools (CCS) works toward improving education and helping students learn and grow while supporting and strengthening their families and communities. The Coalition's goal is to use the resources of many sectors and institutions to create a coordinated movement for community schools. The mission is accomplished through dialogue across professions, helping to shape public policy, use of the Internet, and by securing sustainable funding. Community schools bring together many agencies and disciplines to offer a range of supports and opportunities to children, youth, and families before, during and after school hours, seven days a week.

Collaborative for Integrated School Services
G-05 Larsen Hall
Cambridge, MA 02138
(617) 496-4570
(617) 496-5066
http://www.gse.harvard.edu/~ciss/

The Collaborative for Integrated School Services (CISS) is located in the Harvard Graduate School of Education. CISS is a practitioner-driven, development program with the mission of helping schools meet the needs of children, youth, and families. CISS advocates for greater awareness of the importance of school guidance, counseling, and other support services with a primary focus on supporting those in the helping professions. CISS also hosts several workshops, conferences, and forums throughout the year where professionals from across different professions can share their ideas about integrated school services. The organization also provides individualized technical assistance, consultation, and advocacy.

Children's Defense Fund
25 E Street, NW
Washington, DC 20001
(202) 628-8787
http://www.childrensdefense.org

The Children's Defense Fund (CDF), founded in 1973, is a private, nonprofit organization supported by foundations, corporate grants, and individual donations. Its mission is to ensure that every child is provided with a safe, healthy start in life. The CDF seeks to provide strong and effective advocacy on behalf of all children in the United States with a particular focus on the needs of poor and minority children and those with disabilities. The CDF has worked to inform the nation about the needs of children and youth and encourages preventive interventions to reduce health problems, at-risk behaviors, school difficulties, and family disintegration. The organization is involved in child care programs, child health programs, child welfare and mental health programs, violence prevention and youth development, and family income programs.

Committee for Children
2203 Airport Way S., Suite 500
Seattle, WA 98134-2027

(206) 343-1223
(206) 343-1445 (FAX)
http://www.cfchildren.org

The Committee for Children (CFC) is a nonprofit organization dedicated to promoting the safety, well-being, and social development of children. CFC provides professional training and technical assistance for teachers and school administrators who are concerned with school and family violence. CFC also develops social skills curricula for families and children concerning child abuse and violence prevention. CFC has earned an international reputation for the original research that it conducts and for its unique educational materials and training programs.

Communities in Schools, Inc.
277 South Washington Street, Suite 210
Alexandria, VA 22314
1-800-CIS-4KIDS
(703) 519-8999
(703) 519-7213 (FAX)
http://www.cisnet.org

Communities in Schools (CIS) promotes the connection of community resources and agencies with schools to assist children and youth with the multiple tasks related to successful learning and life preparation. CIS serves more than 1,500 school sites throughout the United States and operates 154 local and 15 state offices. CIS promotes high standards for its members and rigorous training as it seeks to serve more than 1 million young people. The CIS philosophy focuses on providing every child with a personal one-on-one relationship with a caring adult, a safe place to learn and grow, a healthy start and a healthy future, a marketable skill to use upon graduation, and a chance to give back to peers and community. To this end, the agency promotes tutoring and mentoring programs, before- and afterschool programs, mental health counseling, family strengthening initiatives, drug and alcohol education, physical and dental exams, eye care and immunizations, help for teen parents, technology training for the future, career counseling and employment skills, college preparation and scholarship opportunities, community service opportunities, and junior Reserve Officer Training Corps programs. CIS has more then 25 years experience forming partnerships with programs, businesses, and activities across the nation.

The Council for Exceptional Children
1110 N. Glebe Road, Suite 300
Arlington, VA 22201-5704
(730) 620-3660
(888) CEC-SPED
(703) 264-9494 (FAX)
http://www.cec.sped.org

The Council for Exceptional Children (CEC) is a professional organization that is dedicated to improving educational outcomes for children with exceptionalities, students with disabilities, and gifted students. CEC advocates for governmental policies, sets professional standards, provides professional development, and advocates for children and youth with exceptionalities. CEC promotes the needs of the underrepresented and supports those who work with these young people by lobbying Congress and other governmental agencies to promote effective policies.

Council of Chief State School Officers
One Massachusetts Avenue, NW, Suite 700
Washington, DC 20001-1431
(202) 408-5505
(202) 708-8072 (FAX)
http://www.ccsso.org

The Council of Chief State School Officers (CCSSO) is a nationwide, nonprofit organization consisting of public officials who head departments responsible for elementary and secondary education in the United States and its jurisdictions. CCSSO works on behalf of the state agencies that serve pre-kindergarten through twelfth-grade students throughout the nations. CCSSO is a major lobbying organization that seeks to promote positive educational policies to Congress, federal agencies, and the public. Because CCSSO includes members from all states, it has a broad reach and is influential in creating change across the spectrum of elementary and secondary schools.

Council of the Great City Schools
1301 Pennsylvania Avenue, NW, Suite 702
Washington, DC 20004
(202) 393-2427
(202) 393-2400 (FAX)
http://www.cgcs.org

The Council of the Great City Schools (CGCS) is a coalition of 58 of the nation's largest urban public schools systems. The Council's main focus is the promotion of policies to help improve education in our urban city schools. CGCS is governed by superintendents and board of education members from various school districts. The Council prides itself on acting as a voice for urban education in the United States with an overall mission of promoting the cause of urban schools and to advocate for urban students. The goals of CGCS are accomplished through legislation, education, research, and media relations. The organization provides a network for school districts confronting similar challenges to exchange information and to address, as a group, the new challenges as they emerge to provide the best possible education for urban youth.

Education Development Center, Inc.

55 Chapel Street
Newton, MA 02458-1060
(617) 969-7100
http://www.edc.org

The Education Development Center, Inc. (EDC), founded in 1958, was formed by a group of scientists at Massachusetts Institute of Technology who teamed with teachers and technical specialists to develop a new high school physics curriculum. EDC has adopted an interdisciplinary approach and has applied it to many other subject areas, including child development, violence prevention, substance abuse, health promotion, and institutional development. EDC has also developed a large selection of educational videos and software.

The Education Trust

1725 K Street, NW, Suite 200
Washington, DC 20006
(202) 293-1217
(202) 293-2605 (FAX)
http://www.edtrust.org

The Education Trust was founded to promote the academic achievement of all students at all levels (kindergarten through college) with the specific focus of closing the achievement gaps that separate low-income students and students of color from other children and youth. The Education Trust focuses primarily on the institutions most often left behind in plans to improve education, namely those serving concentrations of low-income Latino, African American, or Native American students.

Family Support America
20 North Wacker Drive, Suite 100
Chicago, IL 60606
(312) 338-0900
(312) 338-1522 (FAX)

The mission of Family Support America (FSA) is to bring about a new societal response to children, youth, and families. More specifically, the mission is to empower families and communities so they can foster the optimal development of children, youth, and adult family members. FSA envisions a future society in which all people work together to provide healthy and safe environments for children and families to live and work.

Food Research and Action Center
1875 Connecticut Avenue, NW, Suite 540
Washington, DC 20009
(202) 986-2200
(202) 986-2525
http://www.frac.org

The Food Research and Action Center (FRAC), founded in 1970, is a national organization that seeks to eradicate hunger and undernourishment in the United States. FRAC is a public, nonpartisan organization that influences public policy and distributes vital information to thousands of nutrition professionals throughout the country regarding hunger. FRAC strives to help the United States to better use its resources to help those who cannot help themselves.

Girls Inc.
120 Wall Street, 3rd Floor
New York, NY 10016-5394
(800) 374-4475
http://www.girlsinc.org

Girls Inc. is a national nonprofit youth organization dedicated to inspiring girls to be strong, smart, and bold. Founded in 1945, Girls, Inc. works to provide educational programs to American girls, particularly those in high-risk, underserved areas. The organization spearheads innovative programs designed to help girls confront subtle societal messages about their value and potential, and prepare them to lead successful, independent, and fulfilling lives. Girls, Inc. develops research-based informal education programs that encourage girls to take risks and master physical, intellectual, and emotional challenges. Some of the organization's programs address math and science education, pregnancy and drug abuse prevention, media literacy, economic literacy, adolescent health, violence prevention, and sport participation.

Institute for Youth Development
P.O. Box 16560
Washington, DC 20041
(703) 471-8750
http://www.youthdevelopment.org

The Institute for Youth Development (IYD), founded in 1996, is a nonprofit organization that promotes a comprehensive risk-avoidance message to children and youth. The organization focuses on five harmful risk behaviors: alcohol, drugs, sex, tobacco, and violence. IYD provides parents, government and community leaders, and other youth-serving professionals with information and resources so they may successfully promote and communicate this message. The organization conducts original research and compiles outside research on youth attitudes, beliefs, perceptions, and behaviors. IYD assists in creating sound public policy that promotes youth risk-avoidance and evaluates current government and private programs addressing these issues.

International Association of Pupil Personnel Workers
2940 N. Stratham Point
Hernando, FL 34442-5442
(352) 637-0653
(352) 637-0926 (FAX)

The International Association of Pupil Personnel Workers (IAPPW) believes that all children should have the right to an excellent education. The organization is made up of school administrators, teachers, counselors, and social workers. Some goals of the organization include helping teachers, improving attendance and behavior, and improving social and employment opportunities for children.

Learning First Alliance
1001 Connecticut Avenue, NW, Suite 335
Washington, DC 20036

(202) 296-5220
(202) 296-3246 (FAX)
http://www.learningfirst.org

Learning First Alliance (LFA) works to improve the quality of education in the United States. The Alliance strives to deliver a strong and
consistent message to all parts of the education system and to help
design strategies on a national level to address the gaps in the education system. Another major goal of LFA is to encourage collaboration among professionals, at all levels of education, to come to the table
and to discuss strategies for promoting learning that are based on
sound research.

National Assembly on School-Based Health Care
666 11th Street, NW
Suite 735
Washington, DC 20001
(888) 286-8727
(202) 638-5879 (FAX)
http://www.nasbhc.org

The National Assembly on School-Based Health Care (NASBHC) is
dedicated to promoting accessible school-based primary health care for
children and youth through collaboration with professionals from other disciplines. The NASBHC believes the institutionalization of health care is an
effective strategy for improving the lives of children and optimizing their
chances for success in school and society. NASBHC supports its members
through advocacy, information exchange, and technical assistance.

The National Association of Community Health Centers
1330 New Hampshire Avenue, Suite 122
Washington, DC 20036
(202) 659-8008
(202) 659-8519 (FAX)
http://www.nachc.com

The National Association of Community Health Centers (NACHC) is
the national trade organization representing the nation's community
health centers. The mission of NACHC is to serve the interests of
America's poor and medically underserved. NACHC is committed to
bringing doctors, nurses, and medical technology to the uninsured and

their families, the vulnerable, and those most at risk in our society. Part of this mission is accomplished through affecting positive change in public policy.

The National Association of Elementary School Principals
1615 Duke Street
Alexandria, VA 22314
(800) 386-2377
(800) 396-2377 (FAX)
http://www.naesp.org

The National Association of Elementary School Principals (NAESP) was founded in an effort to ensure that all of our nation's students receive the world's best elementary and middle school education. NAESP's mission rests on the belief that children's early years in school are the most crucial to their future, not only in the classroom but also in life, and that the key figure in ensuring a top-quality school and educational program is the principal. NAESP aims to strengthen the principalship and the profession by working with the institutions that prepare school administrators, as well as with government bodies at all levels. NAESP also strives to help principals attain their professional goals through training programs, publications, conferences, and professional meetings.

National Association of Partners in Education
901 North Pitt Street, Suite 320
Alexandria, VA 22314
(703) 836-4880
(703) 836-6941
http://www.napehq.org

The National Association of Partners in Education (NAPE) is committed to developing school volunteer, community service, and business partnership programs throughout the United States. Currently, the NAPE is the only national organization devoted to educational partnerships. The NAPE seeks to increase awareness about the importance of partnerships for healthy schools and healthy student outcomes. The NAPE also works to increase the number, quality, and scope of partnerships, as well as to increase funding for these programs. The NAPE accomplishes this through training and technical assistance, research, and its member network. The NAPE is devoted to working with grass-roots organizations, local school districts, and community leaders to form a comprehensive network of community partners, who can help ensure the delivery of quality education services to children and their families.

National Association of Pupil Services Administrators
P.O. Box 783
Pittsford, NY 14534-0783
(716) 223-2018
(716) 223-1497 (FAX)
http://www.napsa.com

The goal of the National Association of Pupil Services Administrators (NAPSA) is to provide leadership, support, and professional development for school administrators. NAPSA promotes pupil personnel service programs in schools to meet the needs of children and to advocate for student success. NAPSA looks to achieve its goals by promoting professional development, mobilizing student program development, and speaking for student services programs. NAPSA members include professionals from every area of education and social services.

National Association of School Nurses
P.O. Box 1300
Scarborough, ME 04070-1300
(877) 627-6476
(207) 883-2117
(207) 883-2683 (FAX)
http://www.nasn.org

The National Association of School Nurses (NASN), founded in 1979, represents school nurses exclusively. The mission of NASN is to advance the health and educational success of all students by providing leadership and advocacy for the school nursing practice. In addition, NASN seeks to promote quality standards of practice, promote research to enhance the practice of the school nurse, and to influence health policy at the state and national level. Major focuses of NASN include the prevention of illness and disability, and the early detection and correction of health problems. NASN is also concerned with the management of children with special health care needs in the school setting and the support of children who may lack health care coverage or do not have access to health care services.

National Association of School Psychologists
4340 East West Highway, Suite 402
Bethesda, MD 20814
(301) 657-0270
(310) 657-0275
http://www.nasponline.org/index2.html

The National Association of School Psychologists (NASP) was founded to promote educationally and psychologically healthy environments for all children and youth by implementing effective, proven programs that address prevention, enhance independence, and promote learning. The mission is accomplished through research, training, advocacy, ongoing program evaluation, and caring service. NASP also provides resources and training for parents, educators, and graduate students.

National Association of Secondary School Principals
1904 Association Drive
Reston, VA 20191-1537
(703) 860-0200
http://www.nassp.org

The National Association of Secondary School Principals (NASSP) seeks to promote excellence in the leadership of the nation's secondary schools. NASSP's membership is approximately 40,000 middle school and high school principals, assistant principals, and aspiring principals from the United States and more than 60 other countries. By promoting high professional standards and focusing attention on the challenges faced by today's school leaders, NASSP works to improve the quality of education in the United States. NASSP looks to accomplish this goal by focusing special attention on the areas of administration, supervision, curriculum planning, and effective staff development. NASSP is also active in working to build public confidence in education, strengthen the role of the principal as instructional leader, and to publicize relevant issues and interests to the news media.

National Association of Social Workers
750 First Street NE, Suite 700
Washington, DC 20002-4241
(800) 638-8799
(202) 408-8600
(202) 638-8799 (FAX)
http://www.naswdc.org

The mission of the National Association of Social Workers (NASW) is the promotion, development, and protection of the practice of social work as a career. Through the support and advocacy of social workers, the NASW seeks to enhance the functioning and well-being of children, families, individuals, and communities. NASW also actively promotes professional development, consumer awareness, and public awareness of social work issues. In addition, NASW offers voluntary professional social work credentials for those who are practicing in the field.

National Association for Sport and Physical Education

1900 Association Drive
Reston, VA 20191
(800) 213-7193
(703) 476-8316 (FAX)
http://www.aahperd.org/naspe/template.cfm

The National Association for Sport and Physical Education (NASPE) is an organization comprising professionals concerned with the study of movement and physical activity. Through corporate and public partnerships, NASPE works to promote healthy behaviors and well-being for all people. However, the primary focus is on young people and actively supporting physical education in schools. Members include kindergarten through twelfth-grade educators, college and university faculty, and college athletic directors. NASPE actively advocates for quality physical education, quality sport programs, and overall fitness for children and adults.

National Association of State Boards of Education

277 S. Washington Street, Suite 100
Alexandria, VA 22314
(703) 684-4000
(703) 836-2313 (FAX)
http://www.nasbe.org

The National Association of State Boards of Education (NASBE)'s main objectives are to strengthen state leadership in educational policymaking, to help ensure that all students have equal access to a quality education, and to promote the continuation of public education in the United States. The role of the association is to assist and support state boards of education so that they can effectively lobby on behalf of public education. NASBE seeks to further its goals through the provision of services in the areas of training and technical assistance to the education community; sponsorship of conferences on policy issues; publishing research and resource materials; and communicating with Congress, legislative bodies, and school officials as well as with professionals in business and industry.

National Association of Student Assistance Professionals
4200 Wisconsin Avenue, NW, Suite 106–118
Washington, DC 20016
(800) 257-6310
(215) 257-6997 (FAX)
http://www.nasap.org

The National Association of Student Assistance Professionals (NASAP) is a nonprofit organization founded in 1987 by concerned professionals to address the issues of substance abuse, violence, and academic underachievement. The mission of NASAP is to advocate the highest standards of practice for student assistance professionals and continuing development of student assistance program services that promote student achievement and academic success; healthy, safe lifestyles; and a strength-based approach to working with youth. Student Assistance Programs (SAP) aim to provide a comprehensive model for the delivery of kindergarten through twelfth-grade prevention, intervention, and support services, which are designed to reduce student risk factors, promote protective factors, and increase asset development.

National Center for Children in Poverty
The Mailman School of Public Health of Columbia University
154 Haven Avenue
New York, NY 10032
(212) 304-7100
(212) 544-4200 (FAX)
http://cpmcnet.columbia.edu/dept/nccp/

The National Center for Children in Poverty (NCCP) was founded in 1989 at the Columbia School of Public Health. The organization seeks to identify and promote strategies that prevent child poverty in the United States and that improve the lives of low-income children and their families. NCCP has a particular focus on preventing or alleviating poverty among children under the age of six because of the serious risks poverty poses to health growth and development in this age-group. NCCP's social sciences research unit conducts original research and publishes reports that inform the nation and give policymakers insight into the dynamics of child poverty. NCCP's program and policy analysis unit identifies and evaluates promising approaches to preventing child poverty and improving the life chances of children in poverty.

National Center for Research on Education, Diversity, and Excellence
OERI/At-Risk Institute
University of California at Santa Cruz
1156 High Street
Santa Cruz, CA 95064
(831) 459-3500
(831) 459-3502 (FAX)
http://www.crede.ucsc.edu

The National Center for Research on Education, Diversity, and Excellence (CREDE) is a subdivision of the National Institute of the Education of At-Risk Students and is a federally funded research and development program. The mission of the Center is to address the needs of the nation's at-risk student population. The programs of CREDE can be categorized under these six headings: language and academic achievement; professional development; family, peers, school, and community; instruction in context; integrated school reforms; and assessment. The research of the CREDE focuses on the critical issues in the education of linguistic and cultural minority students as well as students who are at risk because of factors of race, poverty, and geographic location. The goal of this research is to discover and disseminate information on effective policies and practices that affect these students. To achieve this goal, the CREDE identifies four key strategies: instruction, training and development, community partnerships, and policy reform.

The National Center on Addiction and Substance Abuse
Columbia University
633 Third Avenue, 19th Floor
New York, NY 10017-6706
(212) 841-5200
(212) 956-8020 (FAX)
http://www.casacolumbia.org

The National Center on Addiction and Substance Abuse (CASA) has the mission of educating Americans on the costs, both in economic and social terms, of substance abuse and its impact on lives. CASA also analyzes which programs work in treatment and prevention, works toward the goal of removing the stigma surrounding abuse, and encourages individuals to take responsibility in combating abuse and addiction. In addition, CASA is focused on providing front-line workers with the tools they need to succeed in working with substance abuse. CASA's programs and research have focused on children at risk, ex-offender/ex-addicts, and most recently, substance-abusing women on welfare. CASA also conducts large-scale assessments of substance abuse treatment programs and attitudes of teenagers, parents, teachers, and principals toward substance abuse.

National Coalition for Parent Involvement in Education
3929 Old Lee Highway, Suite 91-A
Fairfax, VA 22030-2401
(703) 359-8973
(703) 359-0972 (FAX)
http://www.ncpie.org

The National Coalition for Parent Involvement in Education (NCPIE), founded in 1980, is dedicated to developing effective family-school partnerships in schools throughout North America. The goals of this organization are to help students do better in school and in life, to help empower teachers, to improve schools, to help improve teacher morale, and to help communities grow stronger. NCPIE works to attain their goals by serving as a visible representative and conducting activities that foster parent and family involvement, and by providing resources and legislative information that that can help member organizations promote parent and family involvement.

National Community Education Association
3929 Old Lee Highway, Suite 91-A
Fairfax, VA 22030-2401
(703) 359-8973
(703) 359-0972 (FAX)
http://www.ncea.com

The National Community Education Association (NCEA), founded in 1966, is a nonprofit organization whose mission is to provide leadership to professionals who build learning communities in response to community needs. NCEA works to achieve its mission by providing its members with national and regional training conferences and workshops, periodicals and publications, opportunities for peer support and networking, and information and referral services. The NCEA also acts as an advocate for community education by working with related organizations and promoting parent and community involvement in public education, by forming community partnerships, and by promoting and expanding life-long learning opportunities for all community residents.

National Education Association
1201 16th Street, NW
Washington, DC 20036
(202) 833-4000
http://www.nea.org

The National Education Association (NEA) is America's oldest and largest organization committed to advancing the cause of public education. Internationally, NEA connects educators from all over the world to discuss ways to make schools as effective as they can be. At the state level, NEA affiliates lobby legislators for the resources schools need, campaign for higher professional standards for the teaching profession, and file legal actions to protect academic freedom. At the national level, NEA works on projects such as restructuring how learning takes place and fighting congressional attempts to privatize public education.

National Federation of State High Schools Association
P.O. Box 690
Indianapolis, IN 46206
(317) 972-6900
(317) 822-5700 (FAX)
http://www.nfhs.org

The National Federation of State High Schools Association (NFHS) is the national service and administrative organization of athletics and fine arts programs in speech, debate, and music for our nation's high schools. The association's mission is to serve its members and its related professional groups by providing leadership and national coordination for the administration of interscholastic activities. The organization also seeks to enhance the educational experiences of high school students and reduce the risks of their participation in sports activities. The association publishes the playing rules for 16 sports and provides programs and services that state associations can use in working with high school students.

The National Institute on Out-of-School Time
106 Central Street
Wellesley College
Wellesley, MA 02481
(781) 283-2547
http://www.niost.org

The National Institute on Out-of-School Time (NIOST) is dedicated to helping children, youth, and families to have improved access to programs, activities, and other opportunities available during afterschool hours. NIOST believes that these experiences are essential to the healthy development of children and youth, who then can become effective and capable members of society. NIOST has brought national attention to the importance of afterschool time for children. In addition, NIOST has also worked to influence policy; increased standards and professional recognition; and lead community action aimed at improving the availability, quality, and viability of programs serving children and youth. To implement these services, NIOST focuses on research, evaluation and consultation, policy development and public awareness, and training and curriculum development.

National Mental Health Association
1021 Prince Street
Alexandria, VA 22314-2971
(703) 684-7722
(703) 684-5968
http://www.nmha.org

The National Mental Health Association (NMHA), established in 1909, is the nation's oldest and largest nonprofit organization that is dedicated to addressing all aspects of mental health and mental illness. NMHA's mission is to improve the mental health of all Americans through advocacy, education, research, and service. The association coordinates a number of programs to fulfill its mission, including a nationally recognized public awareness campaign, national and grassroots advocacy, the promotion and development of model community-based services for people with serious mental illness, and a safe schools initiative.

National Middle School Association
4151 Executive Parkway, Suite 300
Westerville, OH 43081

(800) 528-6672
http://www.nmsa.org

The National Middle School Association (NMSA) is concerned with meeting the developmental needs of the nation's young adolescents. NMSA's 28,000 members comprise teachers, principals, school personnel, professors, college students, parents, and community leaders. NMSA focuses on the social and emotional development of adolescents, but also tries to promote and encourage schools to strive for academic excellence. NMSA accomplishes these goals through information dissemination, conferences, journal publications, and book publishing.

National Network for Youth
1319 F Street, NW, Suite 401
Washington, DC 20004
(202) 783-7949
(202) 783-7955 (FAX)
http://www.nn4youth.org

The National Network for Youth (NNY), founded in 1975, is dedicated to ensuring that young people can be safe and lead healthy, productive lives. NNY has more than 700 members in its regional and state networks and works to inform public policy and to educate the public about the field of youth work. NNY focuses particularly on those who, because of life circumstances, disadvantage, past abuse, or community prejudice, have less opportunity to become contributing members of their communities. NNY serves as an advocate in Washington, D.C., for issues pertaining to youth and has developed Community Youth Development, which is a holistic, comprehensive approach for developing capable youth, strong families, and responsible communities. This program works to pair youths and adults together to help young people become actively involved in the community. NNY reports its guiding principles as valuing youth, empowering youth, strengthening families, and supporting diversity.

National Parent Teacher Association
330 N. Wabash Avenue, Suite 2100
Chicago, IL 60611-3690
(800) 307-4782
(312) 670-6783 (FAX)
http://www.pta.org

The National Parent Teacher Association (PTA) is the largest volunteer child advocacy organization in the United States. The National PTA comprises parents, educators, students, and concerned citizens in schools and communities. PTA seeks to inform public opinion and discussion on issues regarding youth in schools, and to affect public policy regarding schools. PTA works to support and speak on behalf of children and youth in the schools, in the community, and before government bodies and other organizations that make decisions affecting children. The PTA also works to assist parents in learning and developing the skills they need to raise children and to encourage parent and public involvement in the public schools of this nation.

The National Peer Helpers Association
P.O. Box 2684
Greenville, NC 27836-0684
(877) 314-7337
http://www.peerhelping.org

The National Peer Helpers Association (NPHA) supports a variety of activities that fall under the category of supportive services offered by peers to students. Peer helpers are young people, trained and supervised by professionals, who help fellow young people identify problems, seek professional help, or prevent problems from starting. A variety of programs—including mediation, drug and alcohol awareness, HIV/AIDS education, and guidance and emotional support—are all encouraged by NPHA. The NPHA reports that peer helpers provide people with opportunities for learning, guidance, and emotional support. These services can then translate into reduced drug and alcohol involvement, higher academic skills, reduced risk for HIV/AIDS and unwanted pregnancy, an increased understanding of differences, and an increased desire to serve others.

National School Boards Association
1680 Duke Street
Alexandria, VA 22314
(703) 838-6722
(703) 683-7590 (FAX)
http://www.nsba.org

The National School Boards Association (NSBA) seeks to foster equity in public education through the support of quality leadership in local school boards. The values espoused by NSBA include collaboration, comprehensive services, promoting safe and secure learning environments for our children, and learning across the lifespan. The proper use of public funds and the shaping of public policy are also at the forefront of goals for NSBA.

National School Safety Center
141 Duesenberg Drive, Suite 11
Westlake Village, CA 91362
(805) 373-9977
(805) 373-9277 (FAX)
http://www.nssc1.org

The goal of the National School Safety Center (NSSC) is to focus on solutions to problems that disrupt the educational process. There is an emphasis placed on addressing the problems of crime, violence, drugs, and on improving attendance, discipline, and achievement. NSSC advocates for the prevention of school crime and violence by providing information and resources and identifying strategies and promising programs that support safe schools. NSSC works with a network of law enforcement, legal, business, and civic leaders in this effort.

The National Urban League
120 Wall Street, 8th Floor
New York, NY 10005
(212) 558-5300
(212) 344-5332
http://www.nul.org

The National Urban League (NUL) is a nonprofit, community-based organization designed to assist African Americans in the achievement of social and economic equality. The NUL reflects a diverse body of community, government, and corporate leaders, and accomplishes its mission through advocacy, building bridges, and running programs and services. NUL strives to ensure that all youth are well educated as we enter the twenty-first century. The NUL also works to ensure economic self-sufficiency for adults and to eliminate racial barriers for inclusion into our society.

National Wellness Institute
P.O. Box 827
Stevens Point, WI 54481-0827

(715) 342-2969
(715) 342-2979 (FAX)
http://www.nationalwellness.org

The National Wellness Institute's (NWI) mission is to provide support and services for those professionals and organizations that promote optimal health in individuals and communities. NWI accomplishes this mission through education, information distribution, the development of wellness-related products and services, and the promotion of a culture of wellness in communities throughout the country. NWI focuses on the spiritual, emotional, social, intellectual, occupational, and physical aspects of health.

National Youth Development Information Center
1319 F Street NW, Suite 601
Washington, DC 20004
(877) NYDIC4U (toll free)
(202) 393-4517
http://www.nydic.org

The National Youth Development Information Center (NYDIC) is a project of the National Assembly, through its affinity group the National Collaboration for Youth. NYDIC provides practice-related information about youth development to national and local youth-serving organizations at little or no cost. One of the organization's primary goals is to provide community programs with the youth development information tools that they need to improve their services. Currently, NYDIC is concentrating in the following areas: research and evaluation of youth development programs, projects and programs demonstrating effective practices for working with youth, policies and regulations impacting youth, formulation and federal funding opportunities, and career development information.

President's Council for Physical Fitness and Sports
Ms. Sandra Perlmutter, Contact Person
Executive Director
Department W, Room 738-H
200 Independence Ave, SW
Washington, DC 20201-0004
(202) 690-9000
http://www.fitness.gov

The goal of the President's Council for Physical Fitness and Sports is to encourage all Americans to engage in activities for physical fitness as directed by executive order. One major mission of the President's Council is to develop and maintain physical fitness programs in schools and communities. Another goal is to develop programs consistent with the Healthy People 2000 initiative. The President's Council works in communities and uses outreach work to encourage physical fitness programs. The Council also works with private business and the health care community to promote fitness and reduce the health care costs associated with physical inactivity.

Public Education Network
P.O. Box 2121C
Berkeley, CA 94702-0212
http://www.publiceducation.org

The Public Education Network (PEN) is a national clearinghouse of research data and information on global inequities. The Network tracks data on education, health, employment, medical information, and disease. By providing this information, PEN hopes to help citizens vote, buy, and live more consciously. PEN's goal is to help others understand that the inequalities in the world today are due not to lack of resources, but to lack of understanding and political will.

School Social Work Association of America
P.O. Box 2072
Northlake, IL 60164
http://www.sswaa.org

The School Social Work Association of America (SSWAA) believes in promoting the professional development of school social workers to enhance the educational experience of all students and their families. School social workers are hired to enhance a school district's ability to meet its educational mission, especially where home, school, and community collaboration are keys to achieving that mission. The SSWAA's goals for the next two years are to ensure that SSWAA keeps pace with the changes in education and within the social work profession, and that the SSWAA continues to be responsive to its members.

The Society for Adolescent Medicine
1916 N.W. Copper Oaks Circle
Blue Springs, MO 64015
(816) 224-8010
http://www.adolescenthealth.org

The Society for Adolescent Medicine (SAM) is dedicated to improving the physical and psychosocial well-being of adolescents and young adults. SAM achieves its goals through promoting communication and collaboration among professionals of all disciplines involved in issues related to adolescent health. SAM also actively works to disseminate state-of-the-art research on adolescent health to professionals who work with young people across a wide range of disciplines. In addition, this organization seeks to increase the availability of health-related training to those service providers who work with adolescents and their families.

The Society for Nutrition Education
1001 Connecticut Avenue, NW, Suite 528
Washington, DC 20036-5528
(202) 452-8534
(202) 452-8536 (FAX)
http://www.sne.org

The Society for Nutrition Education (SNE) represents the needs of nutrition educators in the United States and worldwide. SNE is dedicated to promoting healthy and sustainable food choices and, to this end, provides important information via publications, education forums, and conferences. SNE also works to influence public policy regarding health and nutrition legislation, as well as to make public vital research findings concerning nutrition. SNE is divided into special interest divisions, which address issues from nutrition education for children to informing the public about realistic expectations for weight and eating habits.

Society for Public Health Education
750 First Street, NE
Suite 910
Washington, DC 20002-4242

(202) 408-9804
http://www.sophe.org

The Society for Public Health Education (SOPHE) is an international professional organization, founded in 1950 and made up of health education professionals and students. SOPHE's mission is to promote healthy behaviors, healthy communities, and healthy environments through its activities. The organization provides leadership to the profession of health education through a code of ethics, standards for profession preparation, research and practice, professional development, and public outreach.

Wellness Councils of America
9802 Nicholas Street, Suite 315
Omaha, NE 68114
(402) 872-3590
(402) 872-3594 (FAX)
http://www.health.gov

The Wellness Councils of America (WCA) is a national, nonprofit organization advocating for healthy lifestyles for all Americans. The organization acts as a clearinghouse for information regarding health and wellness and has established national standards as criteria in these areas. WCA works with corporations, community agencies, and health associations, and provides varied products and services.

FEDERAL AGENCIES

Division of Adolescent and School Health
Center for Disease Control
Mail-stop K-32
4770 Buford Highway, NE
Atlanta, GA 30341-3724
http://www.cdc.gov/nccdphp/dash

The Division of Adolescent and School Health (DASH) is a division of the Center for Disease Control's National Center for Chronic Disease Prevention. This division includes the office of the director, the research application branch, and the surveillance and evaluation research branch. DASH is committed to preventing serious health risk behaviors among children and youth. To address these complex issues, DASH implements four types of efforts: identifying and monitoring serious health problems; synthesizing and applying related research to improve school health programs and policies; assisting and supporting constituents in their efforts to implement programs; and evaluating the effectiveness of school health policies and programs. The Web site provides a wide range of statistics about teens and health-related risk factors.

United States Department of Education

400 Maryland Avenue, SW
Washington, DC 20202
(800) USA-LEARN
(202) 401-0689 (FAX)
http://www.ed.gov

The U.S. Department of Education (DOE) was established on May 4, 1980, by Congress with the Department of Education Organization Act. This Department seeks to strengthen the nation's commitment to assuring equal opportunities for education for every individual. To this end, the Department of Education supplements and complements the efforts of states, the local school systems, the private sector, public and private nonprofit educational research institutions, community-based organizations, parents, and students in an effort to improve the quality of education. The DOE also encourages the increased involvement of the public, parents, and students in national education programs and promotes improvements in the quality and usefulness of education through federally supported research, evaluation, and sharing of information. DOE is also dedicated to improving the coordination of federal education programs as well as the management of federal education activities. These efforts also help to increase the accountability of federal education programs to the President, the Congress, and the public.

FUNDING OPPORTUNITIES

Afterschool.gov

http://www.afterschool.gov

In 1997, the Domestic Cabinet Secretaries began an initiative to increase the federal government's support of afterschool programs for youth. This Web site is part of that initiative and its primary mission is to provide a comprehensive listing of federal resources that support children and youth during out-of-school hours. It is designed for anyone who is involved in planning afterschool activities or who is interested in helping children. The Web site provides information on running a program as well as provides links to community and national resources.

The Annie E. Casey Foundation
701 St. Paul Street
Baltimore, MD 21202
(410) 547-6600
(410) 547-6624 (FAX)
http://www.aecf.org

The Annie E. Casey Foundation, founded in 1948, has been working to create better futures for disadvantaged children and families in the United States. The mission of the foundation is to foster public policies, human service reforms, and community supports that more effectively meet the needs of today's children and youth. The foundation works with communities and state and local governments to provide grants to public and nonprofit organizations with the goal of strengthening support services, social networks, physical infrastructure, employment, self-determination, and economic vitality to distressed communities. In 1983 the foundation began to explore opportunities to expand its work to benefit children. Kids Count, a project of the Foundation, is a national and state-by-state effort to track the status of children in the United States.

Healthy Youth Funding Database
Centers for Disease Control
http://www2.cdc.gov/nccdphp/shpfp/index.asp

Formerly known as the Adolescent and School Health Funding Database, this resource contains information on federal, foundation, and state-specific funding sources for school health programs. The database is designed as a search engine that seeks out summaries of funding opportunities for the word or phrase entered. This database also has search features that allow you to look in a specific state or territory as well as narrow your search to current funding opportunities. The Healthy Youth Funding Database also has a drop-down menu that allows the user to select from a list of school health components.

International Youth Foundation
32 South Street, Suite 500
Baltimore, MD 21202 USA
(410) 347-1500

(410) 347-1188 (FAX)
http://www.iyfnet.org/

The International Youth Foundation (IYF) ranks among the world's largest public foundations. The IYF, which was established in 1990, is committed to improving various life conditions and opportunities for youth by identifying and supporting programs "that work." The IYF operates with the understanding that there are thousands of successful programs already serving young people, and the IYF seeks to strengthen the impact and broaden the reach of these programs. The IYF currently supports programs directed by hundreds of companies, foundations, and civil service organizations, touching the lives and future possibilities of more than 23 million young people. In addition to strengthening existing programs, the IYF focuses on raising public awareness of issues impacting children and youth, strengthening the organizational skills of program leaders, and promoting best practices for youth programs.

National Institute of Mental Health
NIMH Public Inquiries
6001 Executive Boulevard, Room 8184, MSC 9663
Bethesda, MD 20892-9663
(301) 443-4513
(301) 443-4279 (FAX)
http://www.nimh.nih.gov/grants/index.cfm

The National Institute of Mental Health (NIMH)'s Web site contains specific information on NIMH grants and contracts programs. The resources that are available include grant applications and review, program announcements, research training and career development, small business programs, program analyses of NIMH extramural research grants and applications, access to National Institute of Health (NIH) grants policy, and an NIH Guide to Grants and Contracts. The Web site also provides a link to the CRISP (Computer Retrieval of Information on Scientific Projects) database, a searchable database of federally funded biomedical research projects conducted at universities, hospitals, and other research institutions.

The Robert Wood Johnson Foundation
P.O. Box 2316
College Road East and Route 1
Princeton, NJ 08543-2316

(888) 631-9989

http://www.rwjf.org

The Robert Wood Johnson Foundation (RWJF), which was established in 1972, is the largest national foundation devoted to improving the health and health care of all Americans. The RWJF focuses on four areas of grantmaking: to ensure basic health care access for all Americans at a reasonable cost; to improve care for people with chronic health conditions; to promote healthy communities and lifestyles; and to reduce the negative personal, social, and economic impact of substance abuse. To accomplish its goals, the RWJF supports effective projects, training, education, and research provided by hospitals, schools, hospices, professional associations, research organizations, state and local government agencies, and community groups. Rather than paying for individual care, the RWJF concentrates its efforts on systemic interventions that promote the improved health of all Americans.

Notices of Funding Availability

http://ocd1.usda.gov/nofa.htm

Notices of Funding Availability (NOFAs) are announcements that appear in the Federal Register and invite applications for federal grant programs. These notices are printed each business day by the U.S. government. This Web site allows you to generate a customized listing of NOFAs. The Web site is essentially a search engine allowing access to the funding announcements and guidelines for federal grant programs.

Safe and Drug-Free Schools Program

(202) 260-3954

http://www.ed.gov/about/offices/list/osdfs/index.html

The Safe and Drug-Free Schools Program is the federal government's primary vehicle for reducing drug, alcohol, and tobacco use, and violence through education and prevention activities in our nation's schools. This program is designed to prevent violence in and around schools, and strengthen programs that prevent the illegal use of alcohol, tobacco, and drugs. The programs are designed to involve parents and are coordinated with related federal, state, and community efforts and resources. One of the major focuses of this initiative is the State Grants for Drug and Violence Prevention Programs. State Grants is a formula grant program that provides funds to state and local education agencies for a wide range of school- and community-based education and prevention activities. This Web site provides links to the applications and guidelines for applying for grants through this funding stream.

The Wallace Foundation
Two Park Avenue, 23rd Floor
New York, NY 10016
(212) 251-9700
(212) 679- 6990 (FAX)
http://www.wallacefunds.org

The DeWitt Wallace-Reader's Digest Fund was founded by DeWitt and Lila Wallace in the 1950s. The couple's success in the world of publishing enabled them to pursue a number of philanthropic endeavors. The DeWitt Wallace-Reader's Digest Fund is one such endeavor and its mission is the development of effective educational leaders to improve student learning and help provide high-quality informal learning opportunities for children and families in low-income communities. The Fund also has the goal of providing enriching community activities through the support of education, arts, and culture.

The William T. Grant Foundation
570 Lexington Avenue, 18th Floor
New York, NY 10022-6837
(212) 752-0071
(212) 752-1398 (FAX)
http://www.wtgrantfoundation.org/

The William T. Grant Foundation seeks to help develop communities that respect young people and enable them to reach their full potential. The Foundation pursues this goal by investing in research in three key areas: Youth Development; Systems Affecting Youth; and the Public's View of Youth. The William T. Grant Foundation supports research in many fields, including health, social, and behavioral sciences, marketing and communications disciplines, and fields traditionally involved with youth development. The Foundation is especially interested in interdisciplinary research and also supports postdoctoral, pretenure scholars from various disciplines.

6

Print and Non-Print Resources

This chapter is a compilation of prominent print and non-print resources on comprehensive school health services. The listing includes journal articles, books, periodicals, reports, on-line databases and Web sites, as well as video and audio materials. The chapter begins with a listing of print resources that represent some of the most innovative work in the area of comprehensive student health and service delivery in schools. The literature that exists in this area is vast and the listing provided is only a cross section of the larger body of literature written in this important area of study.

The second section of this chapter provides a list of non-print resources. The transformation in the way knowledge is passed on to the general public has now made the Internet the most expedient way to gain a wide base of knowledge on a specific subject matter or topic. Many organizations, funders, researchers, and policymakers use it as a means of communicating goals and achievements. Some of the resources address comprehensive student health services as a whole; most, however, focus on one or a few of the elements of a comprehensive approach. At the end of the chapter, we have included several resources on more specific issues in comprehensive student support services, for example, drug use, sexuality, and violence prevention.

LANDMARK JOURNAL ARTICLES

Adelman, Howard S. "Restructuring Education Support Services and Integrating Community Resources: Beyond the Full-Service School Model." *School Psychology Review* 25, no. 4 (1996): 431–45.

To comprehensively serve all of the students in our schools, we must first understand where the gaps are in programs designed to restructure education, community health, and social services. The author introduces measures to address the gaps in services and also to take the full-service model to the next step. Specifically, six clusters of programmatic enabling activity are detailed: classroom focused enabling, student and family assistance, crisis assistance and prevention, support for transitions, home involvement in schooling, and community outreach for involvement and support. The author also points out how these changes will affect the roles of professionals within the school, particularly the school psychologist.

Adelman, Howard S., and Linda Taylor. "Shaping the Future of Mental Health in Schools." *School Psychology and the 21st Century: Millennium Issue* 37, no. 1 (2000): 49–60.

For mental health issues and psychosocial concerns in the school to be adequately addressed, broad-based systemic reform in education needs to occur. This change in schools is redefining the roles of pupil service personnel. This paper reviews how schools currently attend to mental health needs and highlights new directions to build on emerging reform themes and to reframe the current reform models that are already in use. In addition, suggestions are made for pupil service personnel so that they can develop a proactive agenda for shaping the future of their field and the future of mental health in schools.

Birch, David A. "Identifying Sources of Social Support." *Journal of School Health* 68, no. 4 (1998): 159–161.

A variety of enrichment activities are presented to help young people become aware of the social support that is available to them within and around the school. Activities listed can also help students develop the necessary skills for obtaining the social support they desire. The benefits of this type of support are well documented and presented here. Students are introduced to different types of support, discussing social support, creating social support networks via the Web, and having discussion groups.

Birch, David A., and W. M. Kane. "A Comprehensive Approach to Health Promotion." *The Journal of Physical Education, Recreation, and Dance* 70 (1999): 57–60.

There are several areas of education that have been somewhat neglected in recent years, but are nonetheless critical for the overall health of students. A holistic approach is encouraged in this article, as physical education teachers are instructed to consider the needs of the whole child when developing a program for their school. A comprehensive health education program should focus on many aspects of health, including health services, food services, parent and community involvement, physical education, school environment, and psychological and counseling services. These services mirror the eight components as directed by the Centers for Disease Control and Prevention.

Carlson, Cindy, Deborah J. Tharinger, Patricia M. Bricklin, James C. Paavola, and Stephen T. Demers. "Health Care Reform and Psychological Practice in Schools." *Professional Psychology: Research and Practice* 27, no. 1 (1996): 14–23.

Schools have been identified as the ideal place for the placement of comprehensive and accessible health and social services programs targeting all of America's children. Although numerous programs have been initiated, the role of psychological services has been variable. This article focuses on the issue that psychological services are an essential ingredient in any comprehensive program and that, increasingly, the mental health needs of both students and staff are being recognized as critical components of the education system. Models of delivery for these services are given, and implications for those not currently working in schools are included.

Division of Adolescent and School Health. Centers for Disease Control and Prevention. "School Health Policies and Programs Study (SHPPS) 2000." *Journal of School Health* 77, no. 7 (2001).

This special issue of the Journal of School Health, underwritten by the Centers for Disease Control and Prevention, reports the findings of the second School Health Policies and Programs Study (SHPPS). Following its 1994 predecessor, this study examines all eight of the school health program components proposed by Diane Allensworth and Lloyd Kolbe in 1987. The study assesses these components at the state, district, and school levels. Like the 1994 study, this collection of articles examines the nation's current policy and program status for school-based health education, physical education and activity, health services, and food service. This issue broadens the scope of the original study by including assessments of school-based mental health and social services, school policy and environment, faculty and staff health promotion, and family and community involvement. The study was designed to provide valuable data to parents, school board members, school staff, community members, and policymakers to promote a deeper understanding of and improvements to current school health policies and programs. The study also compares the 2000 results with those found in 1994 to suggest possible school health trends.

Dryfoos, Joy G. "School-Based Social and Health Services for At-Risk Students." *Urban Education* 26, no. 1 (1991): 118–37.

To better serve students' educational needs, as well as their overall health, there has been an emergence of public schools as centers for social and health services. These services are especially critical for the at-risk population, which is identified and defined in this article. A variety of intervention programs are also outlined, with particular insight provided into their strengths and limitations. Dryfoos shares her vision of a comprehensive, centralized scheme in large public school districts to serve the needs of disadvantaged students and their families.

Dryfoos, Joy G. "School-Based Health Centers in the Context of Education Reform." *Journal of School Health* 68, no. 10 (1998): 404–8.

The rapid growth of school-based health centers nationwide seems to be occurring at the same time as school districts across the country are seeking to improve educational standards and achievement. Dryfoos argues that if the connection is not drawn between the provision of basic human services and the education reform movement, both may be heading for failure. Dryfoos also emphasizes the role played by the community-school model, where quality education can be integrated with effective mental health and social services in one-stop school centers. Dryfoos posits that in order to impact student learning, the needs of the whole child must be addressed. School-based health centers provide mental health and social services that attend to nonacademic barriers to learning so that both health and education are addressed in the schools, with the overall result being improved academic achievement.

Eber, Lucille. "Restructuring Schools Through the Wraparound Approach: The LADSE Experience." *Special Services in the Schools* 11, no. 1–2 (1996): 135–49.

The progressive development of a five-year, school-based systems change initiative for students with emotional and behavioral disabilities is described. The approach integrates mental health, education, and other family-oriented services into a more flexible system. From planning to implementation to evaluation, data is included in the context of the systems change process.

Epstein, Joyce L. "School/Family/Community Partnerships: Caring for the Children We Share." *Phi Delta Kappan* 76, no. 9 (1995): 701–12.

The main contention of the author is that the way schools care about children is directly reflected in the way they care about families. It is important to view families as partners in education and development, and to see the shared interests and responsibilities as opportunities to create better programs for students. Developing school, family, and community partnerships can improve school climate, provide family services and support, increase parent's skills and leadership, connect families with others in schools and in the community, and even help teachers with their work. Epstein's main theme is that partnerships should be developed primarily to help youngsters succeed in school and in life.

Franklin, Cynthia, and Calvin L. Streeter. "School Reform: Linking Public Schools with Human Services." *Social Work* 40, no. 6 (1995): 773–82.

A review of past and current school reform is presented in light of the effort to link public schools with human service agencies. Five alternative approaches to linking public schools to human services are discussed. They include informal relations, coordination, partnerships, collaboration, and integration. Suggestions are offered for planning, training, resources, and obtaining funding.

Greenberg, Mark T., Celene Domitrovich, and Brian Bumbarger. "The Prevention of Mental Disorders in School-Aged Children: Current State of the Field." *Prevention and Treatment* 4 (2001): n.p.

The goal of the article is to review and summarize the current state of knowledge on the effectiveness of preventive interventions intended to reduce the risk or effects of psychopathology in school-age children.

Critical issues and themes are identified and 34 prevention programs that actually reduce symptoms are analyzed. Elements of successful programs are examined and suggestions are given to improve the state of mental health care and program development for school-age children.

Hoagwood, Kimberly, and Holly D. Erwin. "Effectiveness of School-Based Mental Health Services for Children: A 10-Year Research Review." *Journal of Child and Family Studies* 6, no. 4 (1997): 435–51.

This article evaluates program reviews generated from the literature available from 1985 to 1995. After examining several school-based mental health service interventions, only three types were shown to have empirical effect on outcomes. The interventions were cognitive-behavioral, social-skills training, and teacher consultation. The authors suggest that future studies of school-based mental health should investigate the interventions with a wider range of disorders, broaden the range of outcomes, examine the combined effectiveness of these interventions, and evaluate the impact of these services when combined with home interventions.

Hoagwood, Kimberly, Peter S. Jensen, Theodore Petti, and Barbara J. Burns. "Outcomes of Mental Health Care for Children and Adolescents: A Comprehensive Conceptual Model." *Journal of the American Academy of Child Adolescent Psychiatry* 35, no. 8 (1996): 1055–63.

The authors suggest a dynamic and interactional model of outcomes to broaden the range of intended consequences of care. This is a response to the fact that, as managed care increases, the accountability for outcomes will increase as well. The model of outcomes suggested contains five domains: symptoms, functioning, consumer perspectives, environmental contexts, and systems. The model leaves room for the changeable interactions between a child's home and school environment. The authors suggest greater integration between research and practice, as attention to improved care is likely to require more evidence of its positive impact.

Jehl, Jeanne, and Michael Kirst. "Getting Ready to Provide School-Linked Services: What Schools Must Do." *Education and Urban Society* 25, no. 2 (1993): 153–65.

The primary contention of the authors is that school-linked services and education reform efforts are integrally related. Implementation of school-linked services requires new roles and responsibilities for all levels of school personnel. The planning process is described as including an initial feasibility study and community needs assessment, as well as the need to define the purpose and scope of the collaboration. Strategies for managing and directing funds and establishing financial linkages are also discussed. Another key to success is the involvement of parents at the school and increased efforts by the schools to reach out to families. Finally, any services model that is implemented requires increased accountability to measure whether the services meet defined goals.

Jensen, Peter S., Kimberly Hoagwood, and Edison J. Trickett. "Ivory Towers or Earthen Trenches? Community Collaboration to Foster 'Real World' Research." *Applied Developmental Science* 3, no. 4 (1999): 206–12.

The authors discuss the challenges of bringing research away from the university setting into the real world. They explore the implications of this move for children and adolescents who are at risk or in need of mental health services. The authors also outline the principles necessary for worthwhile and effective collaborations between university researchers and community agents.

Keys, Susan G., Fred Bemak, and Estes J. Lockhart. "Transforming School Counseling to Serve the Mental Health Needs of At-Risk Youth." *Journal of Counseling and Development* 76, no. 4 (1998): 381–88.

School counselors can play a critical role in helping schools respond to the ever-increasing number of students whose mental health needs place them at risk for school failure. The article points out several shortcomings of current guidance and counseling models as they relate to at-risk youth. A new model is proposed suggesting changes in the planning, organization, and implementation of the program, and a new way to look at the role and function of the school counselor. Potential barriers to change are also identified. The important issue of balancing school academic performance standards, while at the same time giving the proper time and planning to address mental health issues, is the larger theme.

Knitzer, Jane, Zina Steinberg, and Brahm Fleisch. "Schools, Children's Mental Health, and the Advocacy Challenge." *Journal of Clinical Child Psychiatry* 20, no. 1 (1991): 102–11.

A study describing some of the mental health services in schools and problems related to service delivery in schools is presented. The author describes ways in which schools and mental health agencies can enhance the school life of children and increase access to mental health services. The implications for advocacy are discussed as well as the ever-increasing role of schools in this process.

Levy, Janet E., and William Shepardson. "A Look at Current School-Linked Service Efforts." *The Future of Children* 2, no. 1 (1992): 44–55.

The authors contend there is no single correct model for school-linked services, but rather lessons from existing programs indicate that services must be shaped according to the needs of the particular community being served. Several school-linked programs are described in terms of goals, the population being served, where services are offered, and who is responsible for providing the services. It is fundamental that these services become a truly integrated system producing more positive outcomes for children. The authors identify a number of integrating elements that are key to starting the kind of reform needed to make school-linked services a lasting element of the educational systems nationwide.

Masten, Ann S., and J. Douglas Coatsworth. "The Development of Competence in Favorable and Unfavorable Environments: Lessons from Research on Successful Children." *American Psychologist* 53, no. 2 (1998): 205–20.

In this article, the authors explore the body of research on competence and resilience in children and adolescents to draw conclusions about policy and intervention. They discuss the bases of competence in early childhood and explore several domains of competence for older children, including conduct, peer relations, school, and work. The authors also highlight naturally occurring resilience in at-risk child populations, which they compare with deliberately enhanced competence in children receiving preventive interventions. They suggest that the same adaptive strategies protect development in both optimal and unfavorable environments.

McLloyd, Vonnie C. "Socioeconomic Disadvantages and Child Development." *American Psychologist* 53, no. 2 (1998): 185–204.

Research consistently demonstrates that children who face persistent conditions of poverty manage less well than children who experience transitory poverty, with children experiencing any poverty demonstrating poorer outcomes than children who never experience poverty. The author discusses the higher incidence of perinatal complications, limited access to resources that typically shield the effects of perinatal complications, elevated lead exposure, and less at-home cognitive stimulation, all of which contribute to diminished cognitive functioning in poor children. The author also notes that, when combined with decreased teacher expectations and diminished academic-readiness skills, these factors contribute to lower levels of school success for poor children. Research implications for practice and policy are included.

Resnicow, Ken, and Diane Allensworth. "Conducting a Comprehensive School Health Program." *Journal of School Health* 66, no. 2 (1996): 59–63.

The eight-component school health program model has been adopted widely in the United States and internationally since the late 1980s. It is taken for granted that these elements should be delivered in a coordinated, efficient manner. But it is less clear just how this should be done. Numerous issues about how this integration can be achieved have been raised and not addressed adequately. The article proposes the school health coordinator is an essential element in the eight-component model, and that the coordinator's responsibilities includes administration, integration of personnel and programs, evaluation, and direct intervention. By using a coordinator, the program elements can be reduced from eight to five.

Tyack, David. "Health and Social Services in Public Schools: Historical Perspectives." *The Future of Children* 2, no. 1 (1992): 19–31.

The article is one of the first to document the long history in the United States of providing noneducational services to children in a school setting. In urban areas, new forms of school-linked social work and social services were pioneered along with vocational guidance. The earliest efforts in schools were to help immigrant children who were struggling with poverty and the transition to a new country. Eventually services became more school-centered, for example, focusing on attendance. Today, the ultimate goal of providing noneducational services in schools is to help the students reach their potential. The author contends that today's approach to school services should focus on children at risk in urban schools, with the goal of meeting the health and social needs of underserved children.

Tyson, Harriet. "A Load off the Teachers' Backs: Coordinated School Health Programs." *Phi Delta Kappan* 80, no. 5 (1999): K1–K8.

The article discusses coordinated school health initiatives in light of recent educational reform efforts designed to raise academic achievement standards. The article points out that often these two movements are at odds with each other, particularly when children are poor, recent immigrants, unsupervised after school, lacking medical care, and exposed to risk in their neighborhoods. The article talks about the poor health of American children, the poor health of poor children, and the widespread lack of physical education programs still in existence. The coordinated school health initiative is introduced as a solution and is described in fair detail in light of the eight-component model for a coordinated program suggested by the Centers for Disease Control and Prevention.

Werthamer-Larsson, Lisa. "Methodological Issues in School-Based Services Research: Special Section: Mental Health Services Research with Children, Adolescents, and Their Families." *Journal of Clinical Child Psychology* 23, no. 2 (1994): 121–32.

This article reviews the predominant types of school-based care being provided today and the strengths and limitations of implementation of these services. The author suggests that school-based research can contribute to improving the system by investigating the impact of primary preventive and targeted preventive interventions, factors associated with early identification of mental health problems, the effectiveness of early intervention and treatment services, and the effectiveness of special education reforms, especially with regard to mental health. Strategies for building the next stage of school-based services are discussed.

BOOKS

Adler, Louise, and Sid Gardner, eds. *The Politics of Linking Schools and Social Services*. Washington: Falmer Press, 1993. ISBN 0–7507–0223–0.

The book includes chapters on a wide array of topics affecting the implementation of school-linked services. Included are chapters on legal, financial, interpersonal, interagency, and organizational issues. The book touches on some of the potential problems associated with school-linked services, including policy problems, funding problems, and invaluable services. The tendency is to link human service agencies and services to schools without integrating them with the school's existing programs, services, and staff members. There is a fundamental system and policy reform that must take place before services can be truly integrated and comprehensive in schools.

Allensworth, Diane D., Elaine Lawson, Lois Nicholson, and James Wyche. *Schools and Health: Our Nation's Investment.* Washington: National Academy Press, 1997. ISBN 0–3090–5435–4.

The authors have presented a readable and well-organized book on comprehensive school health programs for kindergarten through twelfth-grade students. Broad recommendations are given, with guidelines for local, state, and national planning. Elements of successful programs are listed, various models of comprehensive programs are shown, and steps to getting the community involved are included. Topics include the history of comprehensive student health programs, the state of services in mental health, physical health, and nutrition, as well as research findings and evaluations.

American Psychological Association. *Comprehensive and Coordinated Psychological Services for Children: A Call for Service Integration.* Washington: American Psychological Association, 1995 ERIC: E0392007.

The book is intended to present the needs of children and families, to identify the most obvious gaps in services, and to discuss how psychology as a profession can mobilize to address these gaps. Prominent indicators are highlighted to demonstrate that America's children and families are in crisis. A discussion of the needs of children is included, as well as a delineation of essential features of an integrated services system. Topics include an integrated perspective on child and family needs, elements of service integration, and the relevance to psychology. Social, demographic, and economic indicators are also included.

Anderson, Lorin W., and Sid F. Bourke. *Assessing Affective Characteristics in the Schools.* Mahwah: Erlbaum Associates, Inc., 2000. ISBN 0–8058–3198–3.

This book was written to help researchers design studies focusing on the affective characteristics of children in schools. The authors placed particular emphasis on using Likert scales and interpreting results to help students. Topics include reasoning for using affective assessment, obstacles one might face using these instruments, and choosing, implementing, and evaluating the right tool for a school.

Bibace, Roger, James J. Dillon, and Barbara Noel Dowds. *Partnerships in Research, Clinical, and Educational Settings.* Stamford, CN: Ablex Publishing, 1999. ISBN 1–56750–454–X.

The authors look at diverse aspects of partnerships, comparing them to traditional relationships among professionals and students, patients, and research participants. It is assumed that there are multiple definitions of partnerships, and there are many factors that will determine the professional identity of those in partnership. Whether one is a clinician, teacher, or researcher, the book is designed to help professionals realize their role in context with other professionals.

Burt, M.R., G. Resnick, and E.R. Novick. *Building Supportive Communities for At-Risk Adolescents: It Takes More than Services.* Washington: American Psychological Association, 1998. ISBN 1–5579–8466–2.

Many young people today live in environments or participate in behaviors that put them at risk for violence, substance abuse, pregnancy, or dropping out of school. Often these same youth suffer from a lack of support. Burt and colleagues explore the challenges and problems involved in developing and sustaining supportive communities for at-risk adolescents. The book focuses on a collection of case studies showing nine programs that serve youth and their families.

Cibulka, James G., and William J. Kritek. *Coordination among Schools, Families, and Communities: Prospects for Educational Reform.* New York: State University of New York Press, 1996. ISBN 0–7914–2858–3.

Information is provided on the diverse goals of the coordinated services movement, the problem of competing goals and agendas within it, and the political environment of educational reform in which the movement is emerging. The investigation is limited to the coordination of services for children and youth and among schools, families, and community organizations. Implications of field research, organizational and management issues, and evaluation models are also discussed as they relate to the health of children and school services.

Cohen, Jeffery J., and Marian C. Fish. *Handbook of School-Based Interventions: Resolving Student Problems and Promoting Healthy Educational Environments.* San Francisco: Jossey-Bass, 1993. ISBN 1–5554–2549–6.

This comprehensive handbook on school-based interventions discusses useful interventions that can be used for students from kindergarten through twelfth grade. The overall focus of the book is to promote a healthy and social school learning environment where all children will have a chance to succeed. Some of the topics presented include classroom management, cognitive and social competence, relationships with peers and adults, and health management. A perspective on the state of school-based interventions is also given as a foreword.

Comer, James P., Norris M. Haynes, Edward T. Joyner, and Michael Ben-Avie. *Rallying the Whole Village: The Comer Process for Reforming Education.* New York: Teachers College Press, 1996. ISBN 0–8077–3539–6.

The author presents specifics of his School Development Program (SDP), a holistic model approach to education. Topics include children's psychosocial development, group dynamics of effective school communities, increased student engagement and learning time, community health, government initiatives, and business-school partnerships. School-university partnerships are also discussed, as well as proper ways to evaluate the success of the program. It is a comprehensive plan that has shown proven effectiveness over time.

Corbett, Dick, Bruce Wilson, and Belinda Williams. *Effort and Excellence in Urban Classrooms: Expecting—and Getting—Success with All Students.* New York: NEA and Columbia Teachers College Press, 2002. ISBN 0–8077–4216–3.

Drawing directly from the experiences of teachers, students, and parents, this volume explores how educators have closed the achievement gap between low- and high-income students. Through their narration of successful journeys made by underserved students, the authors reveal how educators may assist low-income students to become academically competitive.

Cortese, Peter, and Kathleen Middleton. *The Comprehensive School Health Challenge (vols. I and II): Promoting Health Through Education.* Santa Cruz, CA: ETR Associates, 1994. ISBN 1–56071–344–5.

The authors have developed a resource for developing and implementing comprehensive health education programs for schools. The nation's top health and education specialists discuss how schools can play a vital role in shaping the health of today's young people. Topics addressed include guidelines for administrative planning; structuring a healthy school environment; integrating school counseling and health education programs; personal and social skills training; multicultural sensitivity; and involving students, families, and the community. Also addressed is the important issue of funding for school health programs.

Deroche, Edward, and Mary Williams. *Educating Hearts and Minds: A Comprehensive Education Framework.* Thousand Oaks: Corwin Press, 1998. ISBN 0–7619–7689–2.

This comprehensive guide provides a framework for organizing, designing, implementing, and maintaining a character education program that works for your school. Information is included on how to plan the content of your program, customize your program for your school's unique needs, and develop a teacher awareness program that helps to sustain teacher interest and participation. Also included is information on how to obtain the participation of the surrounding community.

Dryfoos, Joy G. *Full-Service Schools: A Revolution in Health and Social Services for Children, Youth, and Families.* San Francisco: Jossey-Bass, 1994. ISBN 1–55542–601–8.

Dryfoos defines a full-service school as one that combines education, physical health, mental health, and social and family services. Dryfoos looks at the inclusion of health clinics within schools and argues that far more services are needed and can fairly easily be incorporated with some practical planning. Dryfoos also looks at systems around the country that are effectively using full-service schools and suggests funding options. She also posits that community schools cannot work without the collaboration of community organizations, school professionals, and other citizens of a community. Everybody should work together to achieve a safe, caring, effective learning environment.

Dryfoos, Joy G. *Safe Passage: Making it Through Adolescence in a Risky Society.* New York: Oxford University Press, 1998. ISBN 0–1951–3785–X.

Dryfoos examines hundreds of successful programs and ideas that have worked in the real world. Dryfoos also looks at the trend toward full-service schools acting as centers for the community and serving as safe-havens for children and families. Programs that address drugs, sex, and violence are evaluated, and programs that are widely touted and respected, such as Drug Awareness Resistance Education, are also criticized for their failings. The good news is that there are many programs out there that are effective because of the participation of many members of the community.

Durlak, Joseph A. *Successful Prevention Programs for Children and Adolescents.* New York: Plenum Publishers, 1997. ISBN 0–3064–5645–1.

The author presents a wide variety of exemplary programs addressing behavioral and social problems, school failure, drug use, child abuse, physical health, and overall poor health. Focus is placed on programs that have been carefully conceptualized, implemented, and evaluated, and those that have shown measurable positive outcomes in the lives of children and adolescents. Durlak spends some time considering the validity of certain studies and outcomes and analyzes results. An appendix provides a valuable resource to prevention programs.

Elliot, Stephen N., and Frank M. Gresham. *Social Skills Intervention Guide: Practical Strategies for Social Skills Training.* Circle Pines, MN: American Guidance Service, 1991. ISBN 0–8867–1424–9.

This treatment manual ties intervention strategies directly to assessment. This manual can be used in tandem with the Social Skills Rating System (SSRS), or alone to teach prosocial skills in any setting. The manual includes information about selecting and grouping students, engaging parents in treatment, and setting treatment goals. Case studies and sample training lessons are also provided.

Epstein, Joyce L. *School, Family, and Community Partnerships: Preparing Educators and Improving Schools.* Boulder: Westview Press, 2001. ISBN 0–8133–8755–8.

Epstein's work is based on 20 years of intensive research on the growing field of school, family, and community partnerships. Epstein maintains that educators are not trained properly in how to deal with parents when problems occur and that it is now possible to give educators a solid knowledge base in partnerships. The concept of shared responsibility for raising a child is introduced, as is the idea that collaborative activities between home and school help promote student success and prevent problems. Epstein includes much research regarding the implementation of partnerships, as well as a framework for creating a partnership.

Eron, Leonard D., Jacquelyn H. Gentry, and Peggy Schlegel. *Reason to Hope: A Psychological Perspective on Violence and Youth.* Washington: American Psychological Association, 1994. ISBN 1–55798–272–4.

Examining the empirical, epidemiological, and clinical data on one of our most pressing social problems, the authors proceed with the conviction that violence is not inevitable. Youth violence is examined from developmental and sociological perspectives, including violence as experienced by minority groups such as gay and lesbian youth and youth with disabilities; the influence of societal factors such as the media and gangs; the most promising interventions and prevention programs; and the ways in which policy changes could make a difference. The basic thrust of the book is the hope and belief that violence among youth can be prevented.

Haggerty, Robert J., Lonnie R. Sherrod, Norman Garmezy, and Michael Rutter. *Stress, Risk, and Resilience in Children and Adolescents: Processes, Mechanisms, and Interventions.* New York: Cambridge University Press, 1996. ISBN 0–521–57662–8.

This volume covers physical and mental disorders, depression in youth, issues surrounding minority adolescence, and protective factors. Professional educators, social workers, clinical psychologists, and sociologists who wish to consider the problems of risk and stress, the phenomenon of resilience, and potential interventions will find this a valuable book. The main focus is on the processes and mechanisms that produce resilience in children and adolescents and how to develop interventions based on this information.

Haney, Regina, and Joseph O'Keefe. *Conversations in Excellence: Providing for the Diverse Needs of Youth and Their Families.* Washington: NCEA Press, 1998. ISBN 1–55833–211–1.

The book covers pedagogical approaches to meeting the diverse learning needs of students, changing models of collaboration nationwide, and theological perspectives on providing services to children. Standards for community-based educational collaborations are discussed, as is a health care perspective for providing services to meet the diverse needs of children and their families. Creating an effective and inclusive classroom for the twenty-first century is an important goal of the book.

Hawkins, J. David, David P. Farrington, and Richard F. Catalano. *Reducing Violence Through the Schools.* New York: Cambridge University Press, 1998. ISBN 0–5216–4418–6.

The book attempts to identify empirically grounded components fundamental to the prevention of violence in schools. The authors contend that schools should not be expected to confront the problems of youth violence on their own. School staff, parents, community residents, health and human service providers, law enforcement, and governmental agencies must unite to implement comprehensive strategies to reduce the risks of violence. There are key ways schools can contribute to the prevention of violence, such as ensuring that schools maintain an environment of opportunity and reward for academic achievement and prosocial behavior.

Illback, Robert J., Herbert Joseph, and Carolyn Cobb. *Integrated Services for Children and Families: Opportunities for Psychological Practice.* Washington: American Psychological Association, 1997. ISBN 1–5579–8431–X.

Promising new ways of meeting the complex needs of children and families are described, as are new ways of visioning the way the system works. Internationally recognized leaders and scholars are contributors to the book and case studies are recounted to display specific models of intervention. The book will be useful to a broad range of human service professionals: practitioners, trainers, educators, and administrators. The overall theme of the book is how to unite varied approaches of delivering services to children and families and to use resources in a more intelligent manner.

Kronick, Robert. *Human Services and the Full-Service School: The Need for Collaboration.* Springfield: Charles C. Thomas, 2000. ISBN 0–398–07063–6.

Kronick defines a full-service school as one in which the most basic needs of its children and their families are met. He discusses how these needs can be met, and emphasizes that they must be met for children to learn. Increased learning is the goal, and the hope is that full-service schools will also help the teaching process. Full service includes extending the hours the school operates, counseling and health services, and, in some cases, laundry facilities. The author encourages school districts to think outside the box and to address the needs families are raising. It is the school where prevention and intervention must take place. Kronick writes that it is no longer a question of whether the school will take on part of the responsibility for raising our children, but how well they will do it.

Lee, Courtland. *Counseling for Diversity: A Guide for School Counselors and Related Professionals.* Needham Heights: Allyn & Bacon, 1995. ISBN 0–2051–5321–6.

This book provides direction for developing, implementing, and evaluating essential components of counseling programs for culturally and ethnically diverse groups of students. The book is intended for use by elementary, middle, and secondary guidance counselors, but it can also be used effectively by other professionals in educational environments. Intervention strategies are offered, as well as specific techniques for counseling minority students in the United States The book is in the format of case studies, which helps give an authentic sense of the counseling process.

Lerner, Richard M. *America's Youth in Crisis: Challenges and Options for Programs and Policies.* Thousand Oaks, CA: Sage Publications, Inc., 1995. ISBN 0–8039–7068–4.

America's children are at risk for drug and alcohol abuse, unsafe sex, teen pregnancy, delinquency, and school failure. This book encourages academic researchers to respond to these problems by adapting their research endeavors to meet the needs of the community. Developmental contextualism—a framework for viewing child and adolescent development in relation to environmental context—is used to conceptualize the risk and resilience inherent in the development of children as well as to evaluate current policies and programs. Lerner highlights the importance of combining research with community outreach efforts to best serve our nation's youth.

Marx, Eva, Susan Frelick Wooley, and Daphne Northrop. *Health is Academic: A Guide to Coordinated School Health Programs.* New York: Teachers College Press, 1998. ISBN 0–8077–3713–5.

At the center of the school health movement is discussion on how to effectively link students, parents, and the many professionals in schools. This guide to coordinated school health programs discusses ways schools and communities can improve the school environment, as well as the health and educational status for students. Developed by the Education Development Center with assistance from the Center for Disease Control, the book draws from the experience of hundreds of school staff and administrators nationwide. The point is made that schools are perhaps in the best position in our society to make a difference in the health and well-being of children.

Melaville, Atelia, and Martin Blank. *Together We Can: A Guide for Crafting a Profamily System of Education and Human Services.* Washington, DC: Government Printing Office, 1996. ISBN 0–1604–1721–X.

Published as a joint effort between the U.S. Department of Education and the U.S. Department of Health and Human Services, this book is a guide for creating a system whereby human service agencies and education can work together. It reflects the work of researchers and frontline administrators working with programs that link human service agencies and schools. Landmarks and milestones in the process are shown through the telling of vignettes and case studies revealing the personal experiences of families and young people. The guide favors a holistic approach to treating the problems children and families face, and shows how early detection of problems, access to comprehensive services, preventive health care, and easier ability to secure federal and state funds can make a real difference in lives.

Millstein, Susan G., Anne C. Petersen, Elena Nightingale, and J.B. Richmond. *Promoting the Health of Adolescents: New Directions for the Twenty-First Century.* New York: Oxford University Press, 1997. ISBN 0–1950–9188–4.

Many habits are formed during adolescence that have a direct bearing on life-long health. The authors enter a discussion on how to encourage and promote good health-related behaviors among adolescents. This volume provides the most up-to-date and comprehensive review of the pertinent issues, including discussions on adolescent sexuality, substance abuse, and other health-related behaviors. The authors represent a wide variety of disciplines, and offer proven techniques and approaches to help youth and adults live longer and healthier lives. One of the focuses of the book is to help educators and administrators develop comprehensive health education programs in schools.

Mooney, J.F., and R. Tourse. *Collaborative Practice: School and Human Service Partnerships.* Westport, CN: Praeger Publishing, 1999. ISBN 0–2759–6307–1.

Schools alone can no longer meet the needs of young children and adolescents. Mooney and Tourse argue that schools are now required to institute large-scale, collaborative efforts among professionals. The authors propose a restructuring of schools to accomplish this task and to provide for necessary interprofessional collaboration. The disciplines of social work and education are the primary focus, but experts in psychology, counseling, law, and nursing are also contributors. The impact of socioeconomic forces on childhood development and family conditions are discussed and real-world solutions are given, particularly for problems faced by urban schools in addressing academic, social, and health needs of children.

National Research Council and Institute of Medicine. *Community Programs to Promote Youth Development.* Committee on Community-Level Programs for Youth. Jacqueline Eccles and Jennifer Appleton Gootman (eds.). Board on Children, Youth, and Families, Division of Behavioral and Social Sciences and Education. Washington, DC: National Academy Press, 2000. ISBN 0–309–07275–1.

Increasingly, experts in child development are realizing that after-school programs, scouting, community service, religious youth organizations, and other community-based organizations can have a profound effect on the lives of adolescents. In this book, the authors elucidate the essential factors contributing to adolescent well-being and optimal development. Using this developmental framework, the authors make policy, practice, and research recommendations designed to ensure development and promotion of sound, appropriate, successful youth programs. The book also explores adolescence as a transition to adulthood, and offers suggestions for program features that promote youths' successful progression into adulthood. The text offers help to those who work to benefit adolescents by including the following chapters: Promoting Adolescent Development, Personal and Social Assets that Promote Well-Being, Features of Positive Developmental Settings, The Landscape of Community Programs for Youth, Lessons from Experimental Evaluations, Generating New Information, Data and Technical Assistance Resources, Funding and Support for Programs, and Conclusions and Recommendations.

Power, Brenda. *Parent Power: Energizing Home-School Communication.* Portsmouth, NH: Heineman, 1999. ISBN 0–3250–0155–3.

Power has compiled 40 one-page sample essays, available in Spanish and English, to help educators improve parent-teacher relationships. The essays include parent newsletters and brochures, addressing topics such as reading at home, coping with conflict, and television and learning. The book also provides practical information about how parent involvement can be enhanced in chapters such as writing grants to support parent outreach programs, strategies for involving non-English speaking parents, and advice from teachers for communicating with parents. The book comes with computer software.

Rathvon, Natalie. *Effective School Interventions: Strategies for Enhancing Academic Achievement and Social Competence.* New York: Guilford Press, 1999. ISBN 1–5723–0409–X.

Rathvon presents a practical guide to more than 70 interventions that have been empirically shown to improve classroom learning, raise academic achievement, and improve student behavior and social competence. Each intervention is described in a standardized format, listing materials needed, its purpose, and step-by-step instructions for implementation. All of the interventions are designed to be easily implemented by classroom teachers. The author also demonstrates how combining several interventions together can form a comprehensive program.

Rutter, Michael. *Psychosocial Disturbances in Young People: Challenges for Prevention.* New York: Cambridge University Press, 1995. ISBN 0–5214–6187–1.

Since World War II, there has been a significant increase in many sorts of psychosocial problems in young people. This book charts the rise in crime, suicidal behavior, drug abuse, depression, and eating disorders.

Coincidentally, the overall physical health of most people has improved over the same time period. Several experts present their views of psychosocial disturbances, from depression to delinquency. The roles of individual factors, familial factors, and societal factors in the development of these disturbances are discussed, as well as risk and protective factors. The authors examine ways that problems may be prevented through schools and youth organizations.

Sammann, Patricia. *Active Youth: Ideas for Implementing CDC Physical Activity Promotion Guidelines.* Champaign, IL: Human Kinetics Publishing, 1998. ISBN 0–8801–1669–2.

In a brief volume, Sammann treats a subject of considerable importance: the physical inactivity of today's youth. She highlights the guidelines as outlined by the Center for Disease Control, and goes on to encourage physical activity that is enjoyable. Using case studies, Sammann is able to show how developmentally appropriate physical activity can lead to improved health among youth, and hopefully become an activity that spans a lifetime.

Schorr, Lisbeth. *Common Purpose: Strengthening Families and Neighborhoods to Rebuild America.* New York: Doubleday, 1997. ISBN 0–3854–7533–0.

Schorr argues for a reform of the underlying policies that govern welfare, education, and child protection in this 484-page text. Schorr outlines 22 pioneering programs that have been successful at achieving some level of reform, but that may not receive much public attention for various reasons. Among these programs are home visitation, school-community collaborations, and literacy programs. While not providing solutions, the book does present some interesting ideas and options for improving the lives of those that are disadvantaged and the neighborhoods in which they live.

Shirley, Dennis. *Community Organizing for Urban School Reform.* Austin: University of Texas Press, 1997. ISBN 0–292–77719–1.

Shirley describes how parents, teachers, clergy, business partners, social workers, and citizens are working to improve education in inner-city schools. Organizations such as the Industrial Areas Foundation are linking community organizations with schools in poor and working class neighborhoods throughout Texas. The main point of the book is to connect our institutions with our communities and link schools to the resources found there.

Walberg, Herbert J., Olga Reyes, and Roger P. Weissberg. *Children and Youth: Interdisciplinary Perspectives.* Thousand Oaks: Sage Publications, 1997. ISBN 0–7619–0907–9.

An interdisciplinary team of researchers examines the problematic circumstances of life for children living in the inner city and attempts to identify some solutions for enhancing the lives of those children. The book is structured into three parts: families, schools, and health. Topics that are covered include migration patterns, middle-class flight, coping resources, family coping skills, community-university partnerships, promoting academic success and healthy psychological development in urban schools, dangerous environments, and underfunding. Developing ways to implement successful collaborative programs is also discussed in order to better serve children and their families.

Weissberg, Roger P., Thomas P. Gullota, Robert L. Hampton, Bruce A. Ryan, and Gerald R. Adams. *Establishing Preventive Services: Healthy Children 2010.* Thousand Oaks, CA: Sage Publications, 1997. ISBN 0–7619–1089–1.

The youth of today face greater risks to their current and future health as evidenced by the involvement of younger and younger children in behavior risky to their health. This volume emphasizes developmentally and contextually appropriate prevention models and empirically based strategies to help strengthen the environments where children live. The book reviews ways to strengthen the family, child care, early childhood education, school-based health and mental health services, and community-based services. The importance of affecting policy change is discussed, as well as changing attitudes, hearts, and minds to consider the well-being of all children.

Wisconsin State Department of Social Services. *Wisconsin's Framework for Comprehensive School Health Programs: An Integrated Approach.* Madison: Wisconsin State Department of Health and Social Services, 1997 ERIC: ED415967.

This book outlines the multistrategy approach to addressing the entire range of youth risk behaviors and promote health, well-being, and positive development for students. The framework is a collection of empiri-cally supported strategies organized into these six components: healthy school environment; curriculum, instruction, and assessment; pupil ser-vices; student programs; adult programs; and family and community connections. The report is intended to inform educators and other expe-rienced education planners about the framework and how the program can help provide services to all children exposed to youth risk behaviors, health promotion, and youth development.

REFERENCE BOOKS

The Annie E. Casey Foundation. *Kids Count Data Book 2001: State Pro-files of Child Well-Being.* Baltimore: The Annie E. Casey Foundation, 2001. ISSN 1060–9814.

Kids Count is an annual project of the Annie E. Casey Foundation, and is a national and state-by-state effort to track the status of children in the United States. The purpose is to provide citizens, educators, and policy-makers with valid measures of child well-being in the United States. Another purpose is to promote local, state, and national discussions about the current state of the well-being of children and ways to improve it. This data book is the principal initiative for these purposes. The Foundation also goes into communities to provide an even more detailed community-by-community picture of the current state of children.

The DeWitt Wallace-Reader's Digest Fund. *Extended Service Schools Initiative National Directory.* New York: DeWitt Wallace-Reader's Digest Fund, 1999.

A brief directory of local, state, and national contacts for those inter-ested in the extended service initiatives. Contact names, addresses, and phone numbers are included, as well relevant e-mail addresses and Web sites where applicable. Adaptation sites are also listed under Beacons, Bridges to Success, Community Schools, and West Philadelphia Improve-ment Corporation (WEPIC). Contact information for the DeWitt Wallace-Reader's Digest Fund is listed at the end.

Dryfoos, Joy G. *Evaluation of Community Schools: Findings to Date.* Hastings-on-Hudson, NY: Coalition for Community Schools, 2001 ERIC: ED450204.

Data in this book is summarized from available evaluations of com-munity school initiatives. The first section provides a vision of community schools, discusses the essential nature and limits of existing research, and summarizes findings from 49 community initiatives. The next section offers research data on 49 different initiatives, with the hope that more programs will come forward with data from their initiatives. Dryfoos gives logical and coherent definitions of community schools and shares her vision of a community school.

National Center for Chronic Disease Prevention and Health Promotion. *Coordinated School Health Program: Infrastructure Development Process Evaluation Manual.* Washington: U.S. Department of Health and Human Services, 2001.

This manual addresses the development and institutionalization of coordinated school health programs at the state and local levels. Information is provided on the need for such programs, how an infrastructure for the programs can be created, as well as how to evaluate such a program. The manual also describes the elements needed for developing a program and indicators of progress for each element.

National Center for Education Statistics. *The Condition of Education 2000.* Washington: U.S. Department of Education, 2000. NCES 2000–2062.

A large reference and statistical source, this book addresses the mission of the National Center for Education Statistics to collect and publish information on the status and progress of education in the United States. The purpose of the book is to provide accurate information and data in order to promote and accelerate the improvement of American education. The book summarizes the health of education, shows trends, and monitors important new developments.

Spencer, Penny K. *The National Directory of Children, Youth, and Family Services.* Englewood, CO: Spencer, Penny K., 2001 ISBN 1–885461–10–0.

A national report published annually, this document includes social service providers, health care and mental health providers, and legal service agencies in both public and private sectors for major metropolitan areas and 3,300 counties. Information is also included on centers for runaway youth, child abuse projects and initiatives, and other national organizations concerned with family welfare. The names, contact information, and principal executives and staff persons are listed, as well as summaries of what services each agency provides.

JOURNALS

American Counseling Association, ed. *Journal of Counseling and Development*. Alexandria, VA: American Counseling Association.

As the official journal of the American Counseling Association, the *Journal of Counseling and Development* is published six times yearly and includes articles relevant to a broad range of professional interests. The *Journal of Counseling and Development* aims to serve professionals from the fields of counseling, psychology, school personnel, college student personnel, community agencies, and government agencies. Articles are encouraged that integrate published research or examine research that is relevant to practitioners, examine current professional issues, report new or innovative programs and novel techniques, or examine the American Counseling Association. Downloadable versions of the journal are available for American Counseling Association members, while the abstracts and tables of contents are available without a subscription.

American School Counselor Association, ed. *Professional School Counselor*. Alexandria, VA: American School Counselor Association.

The purpose of this journal is to disseminate the latest theory, practice, research, and techniques to assist school counseling professionals at all levels. An additional goal of the journal is to strengthen the professional bonds of school counselors everywhere and to maintain an awareness of the roles, problems, and progress of school counseling in various settings. Although most articles are research oriented, theoretical or philosophical analyses will also be considered. The journal is a publication of the American School Counselor Association.

American School Food Service Association, ed. *Journal of Child Nutrition and Management*. Alexandria, VA: American School Food Service Association.

The *Journal of Child Nutrition and Management* features current research and reviews on issues that significantly affect healthy child nutrition and quality school food service provision. Topics that are published in the journal include choices for school meals, child food preferences, nutritional quality of school lunches, low fat meals and desserts, and waste characteristics of large school cafeterias. Submitted manuscripts must be original, unpublished, and focused on areas related to food service, child nutrition, and the challenges that surround implementing effective child nutrition programs. The primary audience for the journal is food service professionals in schools, administrators, students, and researchers.

Association for Supervision and Curriculum Development, ed. *Educational Leadership*. Alexandria, VA: Association for Supervision and Curriculum Development.

This journal is intended foremost for leaders in elementary, middle, and secondary education but can also be informative for anyone interested in the subjects of curriculum, instruction, supervision, and leadership in schools. The publication represents a wide variety of viewpoints and topics, including education reform standards, learning differences, schools and the law, class size, professional development, and improving the quality of teachers. The full-color journal is published monthly from September through May, except for December/January, which is bimonthly.

Banks-Zakariya, Sally, ed. *The American School Board Journal*. Alexandria, VA: National School Boards Association.

The American School Board Journal, founded in 1891, contains several featured articles addressing important and frequently controversial issues that are pertinent to the more than 40,000 school administrators and school board members in the journal's readership. Examples include drug use and prevention, parent involvement, school leadership, student achievement, and student safety. Other features of *The American School Board Journal* include coverage of research, education news, school law, and recently published books. The journal also features an advisor column, where a problem is posed and suggestions for solutions are offered. The primary goal of the journal is to inform, but articles from a broad subject range are considered for publication.

Behrman, Richard E., ed. *The Future of Children*. Los Altos, CA: The David and Lucile Packard Foundation.

The purpose of the journal is to disseminate timely and accurate information regarding issues related to children's well-being, with an emphasis on providing quality analysis and evaluation. The journal seeks to translate existing knowledge into effective programs and policies. The target audience is a multidisciplinary group of national leaders, policymakers, practitioners, and business executives in the private sector. The content is not meant to duplicate technical research, but rather to complement, discuss, and examine the findings of research in the field.

Boyle, Patrick, ed. *Youth Today*. Washington, DC: American Youth Work Center.

Youth Today is a newspaper of youth work published 10 times a year by the American Youth Work Center in Washington. The publication is directed at administrators, managers, and providers of youth services. Many readers are professionals that work with at-risk youth and their families and other professionals in education. Programs aimed at youth health education are included in most issues, as well as child care issues, safety and school violence, and youth volunteering and peer mentoring. Information on organizations giving grants and funding to those that work with youth is also included.

Brown, B. Bradford, ed. *Journal of Research on Adolescence*. Ann Arbor, MI: Society for Research on Adolescence.

This journal is designed to advance knowledge about adolescence. It publishes original research with intensive measurement, longitudinal and comparative studies, demographic analyses, and laboratory experiments. Articles relevant to adolescent development are included, with cross-national and cross-cultural studies highlighted. Other topics include gender issues, racial diversity, and ethnic diversity.

Franklin, Cynthia G., ed. *Social Work in Education*. Washington, DC: National Association of Social Workers (NASW) Press.

Established in 1978, this journal publishes relevant information regarding professional issues for social workers employed in the education field. The journal defines education broadly to include early education and intervention; preschool, elementary, secondary, and postsecondary education; and adult education. In addition to school social workers, the journal seeks to address pupils, personnel, professionals, administrators, family agencies, health care and mental health agencies, the juvenile justice system, and anyone else concerned with education today. Articles on a variety of topics are welcomed, including innovative practice, interprofessional collaboration, research, program evaluations, and policy.

Good, Thomas L., ed. *The Elementary School Journal*. Chicago: The University of Chicago Press.

The Elementary School Journal was founded in 1900 and is designed to serve both the researcher and the practitioner in elementary and secondary educational settings. While exploring theoretical issues, the journal is also committed to addressing classroom problems and challenges. The journal also presents some of the latest research articles and findings that relate to child development, cognitive psychology, sociology, and anthropology. *The Elementary School Journal* publishes studies that contain data about school and classroom processes in elementary and middle schools that ideally combine educational theory with implications for teaching practice.

Guthrie, James W., ed. *Peabody Journal of Education.* Mahwah, NJ: Erlbaum Associates, Inc., and the Peabody College of Vanderbilt University.

The journal is a quarterly symposia on broad issues in education, human development, and public policy. The editors work with scholars to try to present integrated material on relevant topics. The editorial board also works to identify topics of interest, and guest editors and contributors for these topics. The submission of case studies is highly encouraged as they relate to the development of theory. Submissions for special editions are gladly accepted and the journal has considerable flexibility in its content.

Heppner, P. Paul, ed. *The Counseling Psychologist.* Washington, DC: The American Psychological Association.

The goal of *The Counseling Psychologist* is to publish scholarly work that is both relevant to counseling psychology and of the highest quality. This journal aims to present theme issues, especially in new or developing areas of practice, on topics of immediate concern to counseling psychologists. The topics covered are intended to both increase the knowledge base of counseling psychology as well as to inspire thoughtful debate. Each issue includes discussion on timely topics, including counseling HIV persons, counseling gay and lesbian clients, cross-cultural counseling, ethics, and racial identity. The journal seeks to report on issues across the lifespan and, therefore, accepts a wide range of submissions. Each issue of *The Counseling Psychologist* includes a Major Treatises section, which covers the current subjects in the field of counseling psychology and a Forums section, which gives the reader access to position papers. *The Counseling Psychologist* is widely abstracted and indexed across social science databases.

Johnson, Nancy, ed. *American Journal of Public Health.* Washington, DC: American Public Health Association.

The *American Journal of Public Health*, which was founded in 1911, publishes monthly and seeks to put forth authoritative articles in both broad and specific areas of public health. Areas of content may include the environment, maternal and child health, health promotion, epidemiology, administration, occupational health, education, and international health. Commentaries, editorials, and letters are also an integral part of the journal. All articles are originally researched and peer-reviewed. Each issue features a theme of current interest, with some recent examples including HIV/AIDS, Aging and Health, and Environmental and Occupational Health. The *American Journal of Public Health* is one of the most frequently cited journals in the field of public heath and has been covered by the nation's leading newspapers.

Lerner, Richard M., ed. *Applied Developmental Science.* Mahwah, NJ: Lawrence Erlbaum Associates, Inc.

The purpose of *Applied Developmental Science* is to disseminate descriptive and explanatory knowledge about human development to inform preventive and enhancing interventions that promote positive development across the lifespan. The multidisciplinary conceptual base of *Applied Developmental Science* reflects the view that human nature is a reciprocal process of person-environment interactions and stresses the importance of understanding normative and atypical processes within different developmental periods and across diverse cultural settings. The journal, which issued its first volume in 1997, is designed to serve a vast array of professionals, including developmental, clinical, school, counseling, aging, educational, and community psychologists; life course, family, and demographic sociologists; health professionals; family and consumer scientists; human evolution and ecological biologists; and practitioners in child and youth governmental and nongovernmental organizations.

Litt, I.F., ed. *Journal of Adolescent Health.* New York: Society for Adolescent Medicine.

The *Journal of Adolescent Health* is a multidisciplinary, scientific publication dealing with the biochemistry, endocrinology, physiology, psychology, and sociology of adolescence and with the acute, chronic, or preventive health of adolescents. Original research articles, brief reviews, letters, scholarly case reports, and scientific reports are considered for publication. Some sample topics include adolescent sexuality, adolescent medicine, and guidelines for effective school health education. The journal is published by the Society for Adolescent Medicine and does not accept submissions that contain any data that has been previously published elsewhere.

Lomotey, Kofi, ed. *Urban Education.* Thousand Oaks, CA: Sage Publications.

Urban Education is a refereed journal covering topics of interest in inner-city schools. The journal is published five times a year, starting in 1964, with funding from the University of Buffalo foundation. The journal is now housed at Medgar Evers College, which is part of the City University of New York. Many of the articles discuss issues relevant to urban schools and the difficulties and everyday problems associated with teaching and learning in those environments.

Ollendick, Thomas H., ed. *Journal of Clinical Child and Adolescent Psychology.* Mahwah, NJ: Erlbaum Associates, Inc., and the American Psychological Association.

The *Journal of Clinical Child and Adolescent Psychology* is focused on research and commentary from child advocates across professional fields. Topics in clinical child psychology are investigated, including theory, assessment, intervention, program development, and training. Social, physical, and other developmental influences on children are part of each issue's editorial focus, as well as original research, reviews, and articles from respected professionals in the field. Colleagues in all branches of the American Psychological Association are encouraged to submit articles and research.

Phi Delta Kappa International, ed. *Phi Delta Kappan.* Bloomington, IN: Phi Delta Kappa International.

Phi Delta Kappan is a professional print journal for education that addresses policy issues for educators at all levels; from those who teach preschool to those who educate adults. The journal serves as an advocate for research-based school reform and provides a debate forum for controversial issues. The journal comes out monthly September through June and has been published since 1915. *Phi Delta Kappan* addresses a variety of topics, ranging from articles of interest to administrators, to articles that address subjects that are relevant to teachers and counselors, as well as school nurses and food service providers. *Phi Delta Kappan* presents a combination of theories and practice-oriented research that is designed to span the entire field of education. This journal is available worldwide; it is footnoted and an author index is available in the June issue.

Pigg, R. Morgan Jr., ed. *Journal of School Health.* Kent, OH: American School Health Association.

The *Journal of School Health* is published 10 times a year by the American School Health Association and has been published since 1930. Major themes regarding school health issues today are addressed through regular columns and special issues. Topics that may be covered include healthy school learning environments, school nursing and other primary health care services, school nutrition, physical education in schools, health and wellness education, and counseling and other psychological services in schools. The journal advocates a coordinated approach to health in schools by bringing together students, teachers, families, communities, and other education professionals.

Pressley, Michael, ed. *Journal of Educational Psychology.* Washington, DC: American Psychological Association.

The purpose of the *Journal of Educational Psychology* is to publish original, primarily psychological research relating to education at every level. The journal also publishes commentaries or editorials pertaining to issues affecting policy and practice in education, or commentaries on turning research into educational practice. Topics include scholarship and learning, cognition, development, special populations, and individual differences in both teachers and learners. The journal is published quarterly by the American Psychological Association.

Pro-Ed, Inc., ed. *Journal of Emotional and Behavioral Problems.* Austin: Pro-Ed, Inc.

The journal is published quarterly and attempts to bring practical solutions to problems that children are facing of an emotional or behavioral nature. The journal seeks research-oriented articles and validated strategies for approaching problems children may be having at school, at home, or in the community. Emotional and behavioral problems are reframed as opportunities for growth in the areas of prosocial behavior and values. Topics may include rage and aggression, teaching resilience and responsibility, and education on sexuality.

Rinsky, Robert, ed. *Public Health Reports*. Boston: The Oxford University Press and the Association of Schools of Public Health.

Published for more than a century, *Public Health Reports* addresses important issues, such as tobacco use, teenage violence, immunization, drug abuse, and control of infectious diseases. The publication presents essays, findings, and commentaries in an easy-to-read format. Each issue contains editorials, letters, news and notes, original research reports, and international news and features.

Sheridan, Susan M., ed. *School Psychology Review*. Lincoln, NE: NASP Press.

This journal is published quarterly by the National Association of School Psychologists. The primary purpose of the journal is to evaluate the impact of the delivery of psychological services in schools. Scholarly and research-oriented material is published covering issues from academic research and training to practice. Reviews of theoretical and applied topics are welcomed, as well as original research. Some sample topics include multiculturalism in schools; the treatment of gay, lesbian, and bisexual students; assessment and treatment of students with depression; and promoting school success with students with chronic medical conditions. In addition, sections of two or three issues per year are devoted to a miniseries, which covers themes that are of major interest to school psychology practitioners. The Editorial Advisory Board chooses the specific themes to be discussed in the special issues.

Thomas, Lori G., ed. *The School Community Journal*. Lincoln, IL: Academic Development Institute.

The School Community Journal, started in 1990, is intended to give a voice to the growing field of school, family, and community partnerships around the country. It serves as an outlet for exploratory and intensive research, formative and summative program evaluations, and discussion of important topics. The target audience includes professionals in the fields of sociology, psychology, and education. The main goal of the journal is to stimulate further growth of the field as research, policy, and programs continue to expand.

Winne, Philip H., ed. *Educational Psychologist*. Mahwah, NJ: Erlbaum Associates, Inc. and the American Psychological Association.

The publication includes scholarly essays, reviews, theoretical and conceptual pieces, and critiques contributing to the understanding of issues and research of a broad range of topics related to educational psychology. From teaching methods to historical perspectives on the impact of textbook content, the journal seeks to provide insight into new educational concepts as well as accepted practices. The journal does not publish articles that primarily focus on the results and methods of an empirical study. The *Educational Psychologist* is published for educational psychologists, researchers, teachers, administrators, and policymakers.

CURRICULA

Cooperative Discipline
American Guidance Service
4201 Woodland Road
Circle Pines, MN 55014-1796
(800) 328-2560
(800) 471-8457 (FAX)

"Cooperative Discipline" is a curriculum focused on discipline in the classroom. It is designed to help the teacher to cooperate with his or her class by establishing a climate in the classroom conducive to learning and discussion. Harmful situations can be diffused and problem-solving strategies can be encouraged with disruptive children. In the process, the curriculum is also designed to help students increase their own self-concept and realize their own involvement in situations. The program can be adapted to fit each school according to its needs.

Get Real Health Series Curriculum
Comprehensive Health Education Foundation
22419 Pacific Highway South
Seattle, WA 98198
(800) 323-2433
http://www.chef.org

The "Get Real" series is based on the latest research regarding health-related risk behavior of youth and adolescents. There are three programs: Get Real about AIDS, Get Real about Tobacco, and Get Real about Violence. The curriculum provides accurate information, and emphasizes real-world concerns appropriate to each particular age-group. Vulnerability to violence, abstinence, alternatives to tobacco, and social skills training are just some of the topics covered by the series.

Growing, Growing Strong: A Whole Health Curriculum for Young Children

Redleaf Press
450 North Syndicate, Suite 5
St. Paul, MN 55104-4125
(800) 423-8309
e-mail: jhendricks@wwisp.com

The authors of this health curriculum for young children seek to make children's growing experience interesting and successful by teaching children about their bodies and their health. The curriculum is interactive and so can be an enjoyable way for young people to learn. The important themes are integrated through dozens of topics and hundreds of activities. The curriculum is also able to be customized to fit the particular health education goals for a group of children ages three to eight.

Growing Healthy

National Center for Health Education
72 Spring Street, Suite 208
New York, NY 10012
(212) 334-9470
(212) 334-9845
http://www.nche.org

"Growing Healthy" is a comprehensive school health education program addressing the needs of students in kindergarten through sixth grade. Lessons are sequential and are planned with engaging and varied activities considering the physical, social, and emotional aspects to health. On each grade level, lessons are organized around a single health theme with strong consideration given to gender and cultural equity. The program is aimed at health education coordinators, teachers, and parents of school-age children.

Health Skills for Life: A Comprehensive School Health Program for K-12

Health Skills for Life

Dr. Jim Terhune
8055 Rosebery Court
Sacramento, CA 95829
(888) 283-6902
http://www.healthskills.com

The curriculum is a comprehensive health education program that promotes a healthy school, home, and community environment. Ten major content areas are covered, as well as the teaching of various skills, such as decision making, comparing, problem solving, coping, evaluating, planning, and refusing. Parents, school staff, community agencies, and local businesses are strongly encouraged to become involved to help kids achieve a high level of wellness. Content areas include fitness, dental health, disease prevention, nutrition, alcohol and drugs, mental health, and human sexuality.

Open Circle
Reach Out to Schools
Social Competency Program
Stone Center
106 Central Street
Wellesley, MA 02481-8203
(617) 283-3277
(617) 283-3646 (FAX)

"Open Circle" is a social competency program geared toward grades kindergarten through fifth. The goal of the program is to build on the ideas and concepts learned each year in order to develop social skills throughout the school-age years. Lessons are taught in three areas: creating a cooperative classroom environment, solving interpersonal problems, and building positive relationships. Teachers are offered suggestions for each lesson and are trained on how to implement the instruction in their own classroom.

PATHS (Promoting Alternative Thinking Strategies)
PATHS Training, LLC
Carol A. Kusche, Ph.D.
927 10th Avenue East
Seattle, WA 98102
(206) 323-6688

"PATHS" is a social and emotional competency curriculum designed to be used with grades kindergarten through fifth. The broad goal is to improve social and emotional competency as well as decrease problem behaviors and affect. The focus is on three areas: emotional literacy, positive peer relations, and problem solving. One hundred thirty-one lessons are included, as well as materials to be used for each lesson, such as posters, pictures, and so on. The program is to be implemented by classroom teachers with the hope that children will generalize the skills learned in the classroom into their life outside school.

School Health Index for Physical Activity and Healthy Eating: A Self-Assessment and Planning Guide
National Center for Chronic Disease Prevention and Health
    Promotion
U.S. Department of Health and Human Services
200 Independence Avenue, SW
Washington, DC 20201
(202) 619-0257
http://www.cdc.gov

"The School Health Index" is a tool that can enable schools to look at the strengths and weaknesses of their physical activity and nutrition programs, develop a plan for improving student health, and successfully involve parents, teachers, students, and the community. The index is available at no cost and can be completed in five hours. Often the suggested improvements can be done with existing staff and resources. The index has been praised for its ease of use and the practicality of the solutions it offers.

Steps to Respect: A Bullying Prevention Program
Committee for Children: Leaders in Social-Emotional Learning
568 First Avenue South, Suite 600
Seattle, WA 98104-2804
(800) 634-4449
(206) 438-676 (FAX)

"Steps to Respect" is a search-based, schoolwide program aimed at fostering healthy student relationships and decreasing bullying behavior. The program comes with lessons for students in grades three through five and four through six. To curb bullying, language arts and social-emotional learning are combined into the literature lessons. This program contains a staff-training manual (complete with video) to prepare teachers and staff to implement the program.

REPORTS

Allen, Marylee, and Jamila Larson. 1998. "Healing the Whole Family: A Look at Family Care Programs." Washington, DC: Children's Defense Fund. ISBN 1–881985–20–2.

This report focuses on family care programs that treat or serve families struggling with substance abuse, homelessness, domestic violence, and teen parenting. All of the programs included provide comprehensive, individualized services to both the parent and child, as well as other services to strengthen the family. The report is intended as a resource for child and family advocates, staff of public and private child and family service agencies, substance abuse treatment programs, as well as legislators and other policymakers committed to finding better ways to keep children and families together.

American Bar Association Steering Committee on the Unmet Needs of Children. 2001. "America's Children: Still at Risk." Chicago, IL: American Bar Association. ISBN 1–57073–939–0.

The Steering Committee on the Unmet Legal Needs of Children was created in 1993 to implement the recommendations put forth in "America's Children at Risk"—the report of its predecessor, the American Bar Association's presidential Working Group on Children and Families. Acknowledging the unresolved legal issues still facing children, this report focuses on topics not addressed in the original "Children at Risk" report, including rural and Native America, immigration, technology, children of violence, and the developmental transition through adolescence into adulthood. The report also provides descriptions of programs designed to benefit children that can be replicated by lawyers and the organized bar, and makes recommendations about the main areas of concern for children's legal rights, including improvement in the quantity and quality of representation of children; more holistic and interprofessional collaboration to address children's unmet legal needs; increased child advocacy by lawyers at the policy level; and heightened efforts to address children's legal needs in innovative ways.

Bachman, J.G., L.D. Johnston, and P.M. O'Malley. 2001. "Monitoring the Future: Questionnaire Responses from the Nation's High School Seniors, 2000." Ann Arbor, MI: Institute for Social Research. ISBN 0–160509–20–3.

"Monitoring the Future," first published in 1975, is an ongoing study of the behaviors, attitudes, and values of American secondary school students, college students, and young adults. Each year, the Institute for Social Research collects data on approximately 50,000 eighth-, tenth-, and twelfth-grade students (twelfth graders since 1975, and eighth and tenth graders since 1991). "Monitoring the Future" endeavors to examine changes in young people's opinions toward many issues, including government and politics; alcohol and other drug use; gender roles; and protection of the environment. These data are useful to policymakers at all levels of government for monitoring progress toward National Health and National Education Goals. Study results are also used by the Office of National Drug Control Policy to monitor trends in substance use and abuse among adolescents and young adults.

Blank, Helen, Karen Schulman, and Danielle Ewen. 1999. "Key Facts: Essential Information About Child Care, Early Education, and School-Age Care." Washington, DC: Children's Defense Fund. ISBN 1–881985–23–7.

The Children's Defense Fund issues this report, which includes a series of fact sheets concerning child care, early education, and school-age care. Also included is information on major child care, early education, and school-age policies and programs. The format can be easily adapted to various individual and organizational needs. When put together, the information here makes a compelling case for investing in efforts to help children and families overcome the complex choices of child care, which they face each day, so they can receive the quality assistance they need. An appendix of tables at the end provides vital statistics regarding child care and school-age care across the United States.

Brown, Wanda, and Lynn DeLapp. 1995. "Stopping the Violence: Creating Safe Passages for Youth." Sacramento: California State Legislature Assembly Office of Research.

The report documents the incidence of youth violence in California, including youth homicide rates, student-to-student assaults, and knife and gun possession. The report points out that, while plenty of resources have gone into creating penalties for the perpetrators of violence, very little has been done in the way of prevention. Key factors to youth violence are mentioned, including being victimized or abused at home, witnessing domestic violence, living in unsafe neighborhoods, engaging in substance abuse, easy access to guns, television violence, and dealing with poverty and unemployment in their home or community. Focus groups from law enforcement, juvenile justice, community youth programs, and education have made proposals for prevention programs. The programs are primarily designed to develop integrated services in schools, encourage schools to implement decision-making and values curricula, and make schools safer.

Cahill, Michele. 1996. "Toward Collaboration: Youth Development, Youth Programs, and School Reform." Washington, DC: Center for Youth Development and Policy Research.

This report reviews the growth of school-community collaborations over the past decade, and discusses the ways in which they are enriching our knowledge about education and youth development. The purpose of the report is to encourage discussion about the real contributions of school-community collaborations, and to understand how youth development is a relevant framework for education reform. Understanding that not all collaborations are the same, the report documents where similarities and differences exist and ways to unify youth development efforts.

Children's Defense Fund. 2001. "2001 Children in the States." Washington, DC: Children's Defense Fund.

The Children's Defense Fund Annual Report on children in the United States includes timely and accurate data that can be useful in making decisions for the best interest of children and families. The need for data is increasing, as state and local governments, as well as businesses, take on more responsibility for the design and implementation of programs affecting children. This resource provides key state data so comparisons can be made from state to state, and the information is presented in a consistent and concise format. States are also ranked from best to worst in a number of categories, including infant mortality, education spending, child support collections, and children in poverty.

Children's Defense Fund. 2001. "The State of America's Children Yearbook 2001." Washington, DC: Children's Defense Fund. ISBN 1–881985–24–5.

The Children's Defense Fund publishes this yearly report, which is designed to give a detailed update of the state of children in America by providing relevant data in many areas. These areas include family income, child health, child care, education, children and families in crisis, juvenile justice and youth development, and appendix tables on national trends with children and state statistics on health and education. The format is easy to read and tables and statistics are straightforward and referenced.

Collaborative for Integrated School Services. 1999. "Full-Service Schools: New Practices and Policies for Children, Youth, and Families." Cambridge, MA: Harvard University Graduate School of Education.

A report on the Conference on Full-Service Schools from March of 1999, where U.S. Secretary of Education Richard W. Riley challenged educators and community policymakers to envision schools as "centers of community." The purpose of the report is to document the contents of the conference, which covered topics from changing basic assumptions, changing roles, changing school-community relationships, cultural competence, institutional change, outcomes and benchmarks, collaboration, and relationships with funders.

The David and Lucile Packard Foundation. 1999. "The Future of Children: When School is Out." Los Altos, CA: The David and Lucile Packard Foundation. ISSN 1054–8289.

This volume in the "Future of Children" series is to examine America's schoolchildren during afterschool time. A series of articles on afterschool initiatives are included covering developmental issues, parenting issues, cultural issues, afterschool child care, youth development, and the role of the school in addressing afterschool hours. The larger purpose of the journal is to disseminate timely information about major issues related to children's well-being, with special emphasis on objective analysis and evaluation. This volume was produced because of the growing awareness of the risks and potential that afterschool hours introduce.

Davis, William E. 1996. "Collaborating with Teachers, Parents, and Others to Help Youth at Risk." Toronto, Ontario: Annual Meeting of the American Psychological Association.

The report recognizes the exponential growth of school-based and community-based collaboration efforts to improve the quality of the overall human services delivery system for at-risk youth and their families. The responsibilities of psychologists in formulating, implementing, and evaluating these models are discussed in the report. Obstacles to effective collaboration are identified, and specific strategies are examined whereby school psychologists can overcome common obstacles to effective collaboration and can participate more effectively in promoting the well-being of all youth and their families.

Eber, Lucille, and Karen Rolf. 1997. "Education's Role in the System of Care: Student/Family Outcomes." Tampa, FL: Annual Research Conference: A System of Care for Children's Mental Health.

This report highlights a three-year evaluation of an Illinois program designed to provide community-based services for youth with emotional and behavioral disabilities. Application of the wraparound process was used at all sites and then studied. The findings concluded that poverty was a high risk factor for families, many families reported not having enough money to meet basic needs, placement of child in school was restricted based on emotional/behavioral functioning, and teachers and clinicians agreed with each other more frequently than they did with the parents.

Educational Leadership. 2000. "Healthy Bodies, Minds, and Buildings." Alexandria, VA: Association for Supervision and Curriculum Development. ISSN 0013–1784.

In this special issue of the periodical *Educational Leadership*, the subject of school health is addressed. Several leading experts in the field contributed articles to this edition, and the articles reflect the growing trend toward full-service schools and collaboration among professionals. Topics covered include the relationship between school health and school reform, different ways to shape a full-service school, profiles of schools that are functioning at full service, coordinated health programs, and the role of research in developing comprehensive health programs in schools.

George Washington University. 1997. "The Picture of Health: State and Community Leaders on School Based Health Care." Washington, DC: George Washington University.

Information and opinions are presented in this report advocating for school-based health centers. Each section starts with a brief introduction followed by quotes from leaders in the field. The overwhelming theme of the report is that school-based health centers are part of the solution in decreasing childhood and adolescent health problems. Topics include the need for more health care for children, how families and communities can play a vital role in the push for more health care, the role of states in funding health care initiatives, and the role of health care providers in the delivery of service. The coordination of efforts is also discussed as multidisciplinary teams are responsible for not only providing medical and mental health services, but also for coordinating care with primary care physicians and other health professionals.

Harrell, Adele. 1996. "Intervening with High Risk Youth: Preliminary Findings from the Children At-Risk Program." Washington, DC: U.S. Department of Justice and National Institute of Justice.

The report examines a drug and delinquency prevention program that targets high-risk adolescents, ages 11 to 13, who live in high-risk neighborhoods. The program highlights integrated delivery of comprehensive services tailored to the community. The program features case management of individual families, with each family being assessed for their particular needs. An outcome evaluation is being conducted by the Urban Institute to assess whether the program affects school performance, family functioning, delinquent behavior, and substance abuse. Education is also a large component of the program. Youths from four cities are studied: Austin, Bridgeport, Memphis, and Seattle.

Horsch, Karen. 1998. "Evaluating School-Linked Services: Considerations and Best Practices." Cambridge: Harvard Family Research Project.

Nine evaluators of school-linked services programs were asked to identify considerations and best practices related to evaluating outcomes, sustainability, and collaboration. The report attempts to give information on determining how school-linked services programs work, what sort of impact they have, and the potential for expansion. Recognizing that the traditional boundaries between education and social services are giving way to more integrated approaches, the report seeks to address concerns related to the fragmentation and duplication of services so often seen in school-linked services.

Journal of School Health. May 2000. "Achieving Coordinated Mental Health Programs in Schools." Kent, OH: American School Health Association. ISSN 0022–4391.

This special edition of the *Journal of School Health* specifically addresses the delivery of mental health services to children in schools. Several leading researchers in the field of mental health contribute to this edition. Some of the topics addressed include promoting mental health in schools in the midst of education reform, social and emotional learning as a framework for mental health, effective school-based mental health interventions, implementing mental health services in a large urban school district, and overcoming challenges in outcome evaluations of school mental health programs.

Kober, Nancy. 1994. "Caring Schools, Caring Communities: An Urban Blueprint for Comprehensive School Health and Safety." Washington, DC: Council of the Great City Schools.

The report is based on a National Invitational Symposium on Urban School Reform, Health and Safety. The report summarizes the key themes from the symposium addressing the health and safety of America's children. Problems such as childhood HIV infection, epidemic gun violence, alcohol and drug abuse, adolescent pregnancy, and lack of primary health care in urban schools are all discussed. The point is made that, too often, programs that seek to service these issues are administered separately and distinct from each other, and that there is a great need to see all safety and health issues as being interconnected. Addressing these issues effectively calls for integrated, comprehensive reform strategies, developed jointly with schools and communities.

Lawson, Hal, and Katherine Briar-Lawson. 1997. "Connecting the Dots: Progress Toward the Integration of School Reform, School-Linked Services, Parent Involvement and Community Schools." Oxford, OH: The Danforth Foundation and the Institute for Educational Renewal at Miami University.

This report documents the outcomes of research on school reform, school-linked services, community school programs, and parent involvement in 36 states. Results showed that services were often added to a school program without any consideration of school reform. A model composed of 10 strategies is presented as an attempt to enhance the learning process for students, particularly those with disabilities.

Learning First Alliance. 2001. "Every Child Learning: Safe and Supportive Schools." Washington, DC: Author. Available online at http://www.learningfirst.org.

The Learning First Alliance is a permanent partnership of 12 of the foremost education associations in the United States established to promote the philosophy that schools must become safe and supportive learning communities. In this report, members of the Learning First Alliance present research findings to conclude that the four core elements—safe, supportive, learning, and community—are fundamental to establishing schools as institutions of learning. The Alliance makes recommendations about how schools under varied economic circumstances can weave the four core elements into daily school life to achieve and maintain optimal safety and learning through deliberate systemic and collaborative efforts.

Melaville, Atelia, and Martin Blank. 1998. "Learning Together: The Developing Field of School-Community Initiatives." Flint, MI: Mott Foundation.

This is a resource book prepared by the Institute for Educational Leadership and the National Center for Community Education in partnership with the Center for Youth Development and Policy Research and Chapin Hall Center for Children at the University of Chicago. The report maps out the growing number of school-community initiatives that have started in recent years across the country. The authors maintain that this expansion reflects the call for improved educational quality and outcomes, the demand for more effective and efficient health and social service delivery to meet the comprehensive needs of children, and expanded efforts to strengthen the human, social, and economic underpinnings of neighborhoods and communities.

Merseth, Katherine K., Lisbeth B. Schorr, and Richard F. Elmore. 1999. "Schools, Community-Based Interventions and Children's Learning and Development: What's the Connect?" Washington, DC: Council of Chief State School Officers.

The report briefly outlines the consensus opinion that seems to exist regarding the problems facing America's children and the desired outcomes. The major perspectives that are seen in evidence are identified, as well as those the authors believe are the most likely to result in improved outcomes for children. A call to all those involved in working with children is issued to design and implement strategies concerning ways to enhance children's learning and well-being, that reflect a complete understanding of existing empirical data. The authors' views are offered to stimulate further conversation about the implementation of effective action plans and priorities. The authors hope to bring all the seemingly disparate voices on this issue together to speak in harmony when it comes to the nation's hopes for its children.

National Center for Chronic Disease Control and Health Promotion. 1999. "Youth Risk Behavior Surveillance: United States 1999." Atlanta, GA: U.S. Department of Health and Human Services.

An annual broad and comprehensive survey covering priority health-risk behaviors that can contribute to the leading causes of mortality and morbidity among youth and young adults in the United States. The survey system monitors behaviors such as tobacco use, alcohol and drug use, sexual behaviors that lead to unwanted pregnancy and sexually transmitted diseases, unhealthy dietary behaviors, and physical inactivity. The survey operates locally at the school-based level, as well as at the state and territorial levels. The statistics included here are often used to develop comprehensive health education programs in schools.

National Center for Chronic Disease Control and Health Promotion. 2000. "Promoting Better Health for Young People Through Physical Activity and Sports: A Report to the President from the Secretary of Health and Human Services and the Secretary of Education." Washington, DC: U.S. Department of Health and Human Services and the U.S. Department of Education.

The report acknowledges that our nation's youth are increasingly inactive, unfit, and overweight. The level of inactivity threatens to reverse the long progress in reducing deaths from cardiovascular disease. Also, this could have a devastating effect on our national health care budget. The report outlines 10 strategies to help promote health and reduce obesity through lifelong participation in enjoyable and safe physical activity and sports. A bibliography and appendices are also included.

Pittman, Karen J., and Michele Cahill. 1992. "Pushing the Boundaries of Education: The Implication of a Youth Development Approach to Education Policies, Structures and Collaborations." Washington, DC: Center for Youth Development and Policy Research.

The report recognizes the changes that have occurred in recent years in school structure, school finance, and school administration are due to many driving forces. One of the forces driving change is a growing national concern about youth issues and problems and the fact that many young people are not making successful transitions to adulthood. As the boundaries have continued to grow, the implication for educators, policymakers, and community members is clear: collaboration is a necessity, not an additive.

Sherman, Arloc. 1997. "Poverty Matters: The Cost of Child Poverty in America." Washington, DC: Children's Defense Fund.

This brief report looks at the impact of childhood poverty in America. The text is broken into chapters to include topics such as the odds against poor children, economic costs of children's poverty, and how to end child poverty. Also included are sections dedicated to poverty and schools, child care, health care, and hunger. The book provides compelling evidence to show the substantial costs of poverty to our nation's well-being.

U.S. Department of Education. 1995. "School-Linked Comprehensive Services for Children and Families: What We Know and What We Need to Know." Washington, DC: U.S. Department of Education.

Descriptions of 22 exemplary school-linked comprehensive programs are included in this report, outlining the collaborators, the project goals, project participants, services provided, and evaluations. The report is divided into groups, including early childhood, elementary, adolescent, and year-in-transition school-linked programs. Other groups in the report focus on interprofessional development and evaluation. Major themes included committed leadership, cultural sensitivity, participant-driven systems, interprofessional development, and flexibility in policies.

U.S. Department of Education. 1996. "Putting the Pieces Together: Effective Communities for Children and Families. A Report of the Working Group on Comprehensive Services." Washington, DC: U.S. Department of Education.

This major report suggests ways to build communities through effective partnerships and services that are coordinated across disciplines. The report discusses how federal, state, and local government agencies can improve learning outcomes for preschool and school-aged children. The first part of the report discusses issues regarding at-risk youth, and the proper allocation of resources to address the problems of these youth. The second part discusses ways in which the government can make it easier to implement comprehensive health services in schools and communities. The key theme is how to achieve better results for children and their families.

U.S. Department of Health and Human Services. 1993. "School-Based Clinics that Work." Rockville, MD: U.S. Department of Health and Human Services.

This document describes a set of successful school-based clinics that provide primary health care for underserved populations and clearly identifies factors contributing to their success. A case study was developed for each site based on the following criteria: geographic characteristics, characteristics of the student population, history and mission, management, space and facilities, outreach efforts, services offered, costs and funding, impact of services offered, and ongoing concerns and problems. An important factor was the presence of measurable impact as a demonstrated measure of success.

U.S. Department of Health and Human Services. 2000. "Report of the Surgeon General's Conference on Children's Mental Health: A National Action Agenda." Available on-line at http://www.surgeon general.gov/cmh/childreport.htm.

Children's mental health needs are not being met in the United States. This national agenda is a call to action to prevent mental health problems and treat mental illness in youth. The report introduces an outline for addressing children's mental health needs in the United States as well as the needs of their families. The purpose of the conference was to begin a dialogue about issues of prevention, identification, recognition, and referral of children with mental health needs to appropriate, evidence-based treatments or services.

Veale, James R., Raymond E. Morley, and Cynthia L. Erickson. 2002. "Practical Evaluation for Collaborative Services: Goals, Processes, Tools and Reporting Systems for School-Based Programs." Des Moines, IA: State of Iowa Department of Education.

This report documents the effort to evaluate outcomes from school-based collaborative service programs. The report serves as an introduction for those who will step into the ring of collaborative services in the future and for those currently involved in collaborative services who want to address accountability through assessment and evaluation. In particular, this report documents a program in Iowa for youth and families serving 27 school districts. The importance of this type of report is to document real results for use in policymaking and fundraising at the national, state, and local levels.

Waggoner, Jan E. 1995. "Adolescents in Crisis: Implementing Carnegie Recommendations in Middle Level Teacher Education by Collaborating with Community Service Agencies." Detroit, MI: Annual Meeting of the Association of Teacher Educators.

According to the Carnegie Council on Adolescent Development, young people are more at risk for self-destructive behaviors than ever before, and, in particular, middle schools are failing to meet the needs of students. Illinois has created a middle school endorsement to elementary and secondary teacher certification and has developed a model for integrating health, education, and social services into middle level education. The goal is to embed these issues within the curriculum for regular education. These areas include self-esteem, peer relationships, gangs and violence, nutrition, sexual activity, alcohol and drugs, and communicable diseases. Representatives from the community and agencies will be on hand to teach units.

DATABASES

American School Health Association
On-line Database
P.O. Box 708
Kent, OH 44240
(330) 678-1601
http://www.ashaweb.org

The American School Health Association works with the many professionals in schools who are committed to developing coordinated school health programs to protect and improve the well-being of children and youth. This site offers resources for teachers, nurses, and other school professionals to develop health curriculum. Along with school health programs, the Association supports the integration of counseling, psychological and social services, physical education programs, and outside agencies into the school to better serve the youth and school personnel.

CDC: Adolescent and School Health Program Funding Database

National Center for Chronic Disease Prevention and Health Promotion
Adolescent and School Health
http://www.cdc.gov/nccdphp/dash/cshpdef.htm

This database provides information on Coordinated School Health Programs, strategies for implementation of programs, and key elements of a comprehensive health education program. The site also provides information on adolescent and school health in general, with research, guidelines, funding, and many other health-related resources.

CHID Online (The Combined Health Information Database)

CHID Technical Coordinator
7830 Old Georgetown Road
Bethesda, MD 20814
http://chid.nih.gov/

This database is produced by health-related agencies of the federal government and provides health education resources and informational program descriptions. This database covers 16 topics from AIDS to weight control.

Education-Social Sciences Database

Trade Wave Corporation
3636 Executive Center Drive, Suite. 100
Austin, TX 78731
http://www.einet.net/galaxy/Social-Sciences/Education.html

The Education-Social Sciences Database, which is part of Galaxy, The Professional's Guide to a World of Information, contains a plethora of information and resources involving academic institutions. Covered topics include adult education, curriculum and instruction, guidance and counseling, and higher education resources. Other topics include history and philosophy, kindergarten through twelfth-grade education, measurement and evaluation, and special education—including periodicals, reference collections, instructors, and institutions.

Kids Count Data Online 2000

Annie E. Casey Foundation
701 St. Paul Street
Baltimore, MD 21202
(410) 547-6600
(410) 547-6624 (FAX)
http://www.aecf.org/kidscount/kc2000/index.htm

This on-line database offers graphs, maps, ranked lists, and state-by-state profiles generated from information gather by the annual KIDS COUNT assessment. The assessment is conducted to evaluate the status of America's children and to assess trends in their well-being. Visitors can view national indicators as well as individual state rankings.

The National Longitudinal Study of Adolescent Health

Carolina Population Center
University of North Carolina at Chapel Hill
CB# 8120, University Square
123 West Franklin Street
Chapel Hill, NC 27516-2524
(919) 966-2157
(919) 966-6638 (FAX)
E-mail: cpcweb@unc.edu
http://www.cpc.unc.edu/projects/addhealth/

The Web site includes public-use dataset and restricted-use dataset. Tens of thousands of interviews and questionnaires have been completed in a nationally representative sample of adolescents who were attending grades seven through twelve. The surveys were completed in 1994–95, 1996, and 2000. The word health is used to cover physical, mental, emotional, and reproductive health.

Suicide Information and Education Center

On-line database
1615 10th Avenue, SW, Suite 201
Calgary, AB, Canada T3C 0J7
(403) 245-3900
(403) 245-0299 (FAX)
http://www.siec.ca

This database was designed to provide information to persons who are suicidal or know someone who is. For the school counselor, this database provides information on Suicide Prevention Training Programs (SPTP), which give caregiver training in suicide intervention, awareness, bereavement, crisis management, and related topics. This site provides a plethora of useful information regarding suicide and suicidal behavior.

WORLD WIDE WEB SITES

American School Counselor Association

801 North Fairfax Street, Suite 310
Alexandria, VA 22314
(703) 683-2722
http://www.schoolcounselor.org

The American School Counselor Association (ASCA), a subdivision of the American Counseling Association (ACA), is the national organization that represents the profession of school counseling. ASCA focuses on providing professional development, enhancing school counseling programs, and researching effective school counseling practices. The mission of ASCA is to promote excellence in professional school counseling and the development of all students. This Web site offers links with information about ASCA membership, professional development for school counselors, featured books, as well as information about ACA publications, parent tips, and information about careers in school counseling.

Annie E. Casey Foundation

701 St. Paul Street
Baltimore, MD 21202
(410) 547-6600
(410) 547-6624 (FAX)
http://www.aecf.org/

The Annie E. Casey Foundation provides research data and analysis on issues affecting children and families. Information regarding this research, as well as support services, grantmaking, evaluation, and advocacy, can be found on this Web site.

CDC: A Coordinated School Health Program

National Center for Chronic Disease Prevention and Health Promotion
Division of Adolescent and School Health
http://www.cdc.gov/nccdphp/dash/cshpdef.htm

This Web site highlights the "CDC Eight-Component Model of School Health Programs." The eight key components include health education, physical education, health services, nutrition services, health promotion for staff, counseling and psychological services, healthy school environment, and parent-community involvement.

Center for Adolescent and Family Studies

ADOL@indiana.edu (Feedback)
http://www.iub.edu/~cafs/

This site features the Center for Adolescent and Family Studies, based at the School of Education at Indiana University. This center focuses on meeting social and emotional growth and development needs of adolescents through the provision of support to adults working with youth. Its Web site includes links to information on other programs, and various counselor resources, including Links to Suicide Prevention, Internet Resources for Special Children, Planned Parenthood, Psych-Web, School Mental Health Project, and YouthInfo, which includes statistical profiles of American teens, recent reports and publications, speeches by federal officials, and other federal agencies.

Center for Community Change

1000 Wisconsin Avenue, NW
Washington, DC 20007
(202) 342-0576
(202) 333-5462 (FAX)
http://www.communitychange.org/

The Center for Community Change has been helping people attain the skills necessary to improve their communities for nearly 30 years. The Center is committed to reducing poverty and rebuilding low-income housing. Providing assistance to grassroots organizations, connecting people to resources, and improving and involving community-based organizations is an important aspect of building strong community-based organizations. The site includes links for jobs and economic development, housing and community development, changing policies, and building organizations.

Center for Community Partnerships—UPENN

University of Pennsylvania
3451 Walnut
Philadelphia, PA 19104
(215) 898-5000
http://pobox.upenn.edu/~bowman/center.html

This Web page provides a summary of some of the University of Pennsylvania's (UPENN) engagements with the West Philadelphia Public Schools. This summary largely focuses on UPENN's academically-based community service courses, especially their work with the West Philadelphia Improvement Corps (WEPIC) and its attempts to develop university-assisted community schools. Other projects described include the University-Community Outreach Program, Keeping Teens Healthy, Penn-Merck Science Collaborative, the Adolescent Care Network, the West Philadelphia Tutoring Project, Say Yes To Education, and UPENN's cooperation with the Philadelphia Education Fund.

Center for Mental Health in Schools

Department of Psychology
P.O. Box 951563
Los Angeles, CA 90095-1563
(310) 825-3634
(310) 206-8716 (FAX)
http://smhp.psych.ucla.edu

The Center was founded in 1995 in response to an initiative promoting mental health in schools. The Center addresses mental health by focusing on barriers to learning and development. The Center creates programs that work in an integrated system.

Centers for Disease Control and Prevention

1600 Clifton Road
Atlanta, GA 30333

(404) 639-3311
http://www.cdc.gov

The Centers for Disease Control and Prevention (CDC) has designed a model of school health that uses eight components in a comprehensive plan for delivering nonacademic services (student support or student health). This site provides links to information about the CDC; announcements about events; topics, reports, and publications; data and statistics regarding health and laboratory issues; information about grant and cooperative agreement funding opportunities; health topics/information; current health news; other related sites; publications/software/products and subscriptions to receive them; training and employment information; health information in relation to travel; and a visitor survey to provide feedback about the CDC Web site. This Web site also contains links to highlighted resources, such as CDC En Espanol.

Charles Stewart Mott Foundation

1200 Mott Foundation Building
Flint, MI 48502-1753
(810) 238-5651
(810) 766-1753 (FAX)
http://www.mott.org

The Mott Foundation attempts to build strong communities through collaboration. The foundation also attempts to enhance the capacity of individuals, families, or institutions at the local levels and beyond. Its mission is to support efforts that promote a just, equitable, and sustainable society. The Mott Foundation supports many programs, such as the 21st Century Schools.

Children's Aid Society

105 East 22nd Street
New York, NY 10010
(212) 949-4800
http://www.childrensaidsociety.org

The Children's Aid Society (CAS) is one of the oldest social welfare agencies in the country, providing health, education, recreation, and emergency services to children and families in New York City. CAS emphasizes prevention and early intervention, targeting the needs of the whole child. The site provides links to many documents related to CAS.

Children's Defense Fund

25 E Street, NW
Washington, DC 20001
(202) 628-8787
http://www.childrensdefense.org

The Children's Defense Fund (CDF) began in 1973 and is a private nonprofit organization supported by foundations, corporation grants, and individual donations. The CDF provides a voice for America's children, specifically those that are poor, minority, or disabled. The CDF attempts to ensure that all children have a healthy start, head start, fair start, safe start, and moral start. The site contains information on these aspects, as well as information on programs designed to meet the needs of children.

Children's Safety Network

Education Development Center, Inc.
55 Chapel Street
Newton, MA 02458-1060
(617) 969-7101 ext. 2207
(617) 244-3436 (FAX)
http://www.childrenssafetynetwork.org/about.asp

The Children's Safety Network (CSN) National Injury and Violence Prevention Resource Center is located in Newton, Massachusetts, and is funded by the Maternal and Child Health Bureau of the U.S. Department of Health and Human Services. Their Web site provides resources and information to agencies and organizations seeking to reduce violence and child and adolescent injuries. This Web site also contains lists of publications and resources that address the issue of improving the safety of children.

Citizen Schools

308 Congress Street, 5th Floor
Boston, MA 02210
(617) 695-2300
http://www.citizenschools.org/

Citizen Schools, a nonprofit corporation, was founded in 1995 and has a mission of educating children and building strong communities. Citizen Schools comprises a network of 11 Boston afterschool and summer programs that have engaged approximately 1,500 students (ages 9 to 14) and 1,200 community volunteers in a series of learning apprenticeships. These apprenticeships challenge both children and adults to gain skills and understanding while creating products that add value to the community. The Web site provides information on the history and background of Citizen Schools, the organization's plans for growth, important partnerships within the Boston area, and volunteer and job opportunities.

Coalition for Community Schools

c/o Institute for Educational Leadership
1001 Connecticut Avenue, NW, Suite 310
Washington, DC 20036
(202) 822-8405
(202) 872-4050 (FAX)
http://www.communityschools.org

The Coalition for Community Schools brings together local, state, and national organizations that are committed to creating and sustaining community schools. The Coalition aims toward improving education and helping students learn and develop by offering a range of supports and opportunities to children, youth, families, and communities.

Collaborative for Academic, Social, and Emotional Learning (CASEL)

University of Illinois at Chicago
Department of Psychology (M/C 285)
1007 W. Harrison Street
Chicago, IL 60607-7137
(312) 413-1008
http://www.casel.org

CASEL is a collaborative of educators, scientists, human service providers, policymakers, and citizens working together to improve social and emotional learning in education. CASEL emphasizes that social skills and emotional development are critical components of teaching, learning, and community life. This site provides information on research initiatives, practice initiatives, and many relevant publications.

Comprehensive School Reform Program

U.S. Department of Education
Washington, DC 20202
(202) 205-4292
http://www.ed.gov/programs/compreform/index.html

The Comprehensive School Reform (CSR) Program strives to increase student achievement by helping public schools implement successful, comprehensive school reforms with an emphasis on basic academics and parental involvement. These comprehensive school reforms are based on reliable research and effective practices. The CSR Program supports ongoing efforts at the local level to connect challenging academic standards with school improvement. This Web site describes CSR, explains what is current or new with CSR, discusses legislation and funding, provides a state application and guidance, and lists resources and related sites.

Connect for Kids

950 18th St., NW
Washington, DC 20006
(202) 638-5771
http://www.connectforkids.org

Connect for Kids is a virtual encyclopedia of information for adults who want to make their communities better places for children. The organization utilizes an award winning Web site, e-mail newsletters, radio, and television ads to help people become more active citizens in such activities as volunteering and voting. Connect for Kids is under the auspices of The Benton Foundation.

Cross City Campaign for Urban School Reform

407 South Dearborn Street, Suite 1500
Chicago, IL 60605
(312) 322-4880
(312) 322-4885 (FAX)
http://www.crosscity.org

The Cross City Campaign is a network of school reform leaders consisting of parents, educators, researchers, community members, and funders. The Cross City Campaign attempts to improve quality and equity within urban public schools. The Campaign accomplish these goals by strengthening the roles of parents and community members in the reform movement as well as improving policies regarding teaching, learning, and school administration. This Web site provides information on programs within urban public schools, as well as research within this area.

CTOnline

American Counseling Association
5999 Stevenson Avenue
Alexandria, VA 22304-3300
http:www.counseling.org/ctonline

CTOnline is the Web version of "Counseling Today," a monthly newspaper published by the American Counseling Association (ACA). In addition to current articles featured in the newspaper, CTOnline offers viewers links to the ACA homepage, a classified section, the editor's page, a subscription page, and a link to the "Counseling Today" archives.

Department of Education Publications and Products

U.S. Department of Education
400 Maryland Avenue, SW
Washington, DC 20202-0498
(800) USA-LEARN
http://www.ed.gov/pubs/index.html

The U.S. Department of Education publishes an extensive amount of information for teachers, administrators, policymakers, researchers, parents, students, and others who have an interest and a stake education. This Web site provides easy access for the public to link to journals, newsletters, guidelines, and statistical information, as well as their ED Publications. On-Line Ordering System. This site can be of great assistance to counselors, administrators, teachers, and communities who are involved in the education of young people in the United States.

Development Training Institute

2510 St. Paul Street
Baltimore, MD 21218
(410) 338-2512
(410) 338-2751 (FAX)
http://www.dtinational.org

The Development Training Institute (DTI) was founded in 1981 and is considered to be the nation's leading trainer of community development leaders. DTI follows a comprehensive community building approach to community development.

Educational Resources Information Center Clearinghouse on Counseling and Student Services (ERIC/CASS)

201 Ferguson Building
University of North Carolina at Greensboro
Greensboro, NC 27402
(800) 414-9769
(910) 334-4114
(910) 334-4116 (FAX)
http://www.ericcass.uncg.edu

The Web site for the Educational Resource Information Center Clearinghouse on Counseling and Student Services provides information on such topics as school counseling, social work, psychology, mental health, counseling, marriage and family counseling, career counseling, and student development. This Web site contains ordering and pricing information of materials catalogued or published by the Clearinghouse and posts contact information.

The Education Trust

1725 K
Street, NW, Suite 200
Washington, DC 20006
(202) 293-1217
(202) 293-2605 (FAX)
http://www.edtrust.org

This Web site highlights the work of The Education Trust, a special project established in 1990 by the American Association for Higher Education, which aims to encourage colleges and universities to support kindergarten through twelfth-grade reform efforts. The Education Trust has since grown into an independent nonprofit organization with the mission of making schools and colleges work for all youth. This Web site offers links to education reform news and data, reports and publications relevant to education reform, and links to upcoming events.

Focus on Children II: Comprehensive Reform Plan

26 Court Street, 4th Floor
Boston, MA 02108
(617) 635-9014
(617) 635-9689 (FAX)
http://www.boston.k12.ma.us/teach/foc.asp

This site offers a description of the Boston Public Schools comprehensive reform plan, "Focus on Children II: 2001–2006." The links included in this site are about the Boston Public Schools, School Committee, Superintendent, Schools, Family Resources, Teaching and Learning, Administration, and Employment.

Gay, Lesbian, and Straight Education Network (GLSEN)

GLSEN National Office
121 West 27th Street, Suite 804
New York, NY 10001
(212) 727-0135
(212) 727-0254 (FAX)
http://www.glsen.org

Through its growing network of 85 chapters in 35 states, GLSEN strives to ensure that each member of every school community is valued and respected, regardless of sexual orientation or gender identity. GLSEN went national in 1994 and has since become one of the nation's leading voices for equality and safety in the educational system. This Web site provides information on conferences, trainings, and local workshops that serve to end discrimination and educate educators. The GLSEN Web site provides information on various topics such as legal matters, fundraising, reaching the public, running an effective meeting, new Title 9 guidelines, an annotated bibliography of children's books with gay and lesbian characters, as well as information about how to get involved with the organization.

Girls Inc. Home Page

National Headquarters
120 Wall Street, 3rd Floor
New York, NY 10005
(212) 509-2000

(212) 509-8708 (FAX)
http://www.girlsinc.org

Girls Incorporated is a national youth organization dedicated to helping every girl become strong, smart, and bold. For more than 50 years, Girls Incorporated has provided vital educational programs to millions of American girls. Today, innovative programs help girls confront subtle societal messages about their value and potential, and aim to prepare them to lead successful, independent, and complete lives. Their Web site provides information about advocacy, research, conferences, math and science education, pregnancy prevention, media literacy, adolescent health, substance abuse prevention, and sports participation.

Hampshire Educational Collaborative (HEC)

30 Industrial Drive
East Northhampton, MA 01060
(413) 586-4900
(413) 586-4727
(413) 586-0180 (FAX)
http://www.collaborative.org

The Hampshire Educational Collaborative (HEC) is a nonprofit, multiservice agency linking education, schools, families, and communities to opportunities and resources that advance student learning. HEC offers a wide range of programs and services providing opportunities to educators for professional advancement and growth.

Learning First Alliance

1001 Connecticut Avenue, NW, Suite 335
Washington, DC 20036
(202) 296-5220
(202) 296-3246 (FAX)
http://www.learningfirst.org

The Learning First Alliance is a partnership of 12 educational associations working to improve student learning in public schools. The alliance carries three main goals: to ensure high academic expectations are held for all students, to ensure that schools are a safe and supportive place of learning, and to engage parents and community members in helping students achieve academic success.

Michigan Model Health Curriculum

139 Combined Services Building
Central Michigan University
Mt. Pleasant, MI 48859
(800) 214-8961
(989) 774-3943 (FAX)
http://www.emc.cmich.edu/mm/default.htm

Established in 1985, the Michigan Model for Comprehensive School Health Education is the fastest growing school health education program in the country. Currently, the program is being implemented in 90 percent of Michigan's public schools, along with more than 200 private and charter schools. The Michigan Model was established as a cooperative effort of seven state agencies that agreed to collaborate in providing an efficient delivery model for key disease prevention and health promotion messages. The Michigan Model curriculum facilitates interdisciplinary learning through lessons that integrate health education into academic curricula. This Web site contains a brief description and history of the Michigan Model for Comprehensive School Health Education, as well as information about the benefits of the program for teachers and schools. The Web site includes links to each grade level for a more in-depth look at the Michigan Model Health Curriculum.

Montgomery County Public Schools

850 Hungerford Drive
Rockville, MD 20850
(301) 279-3391
http://www.mcps.k12.md.us/departments/oscs

The Office of Student and Community Services provides a program of student services within a model that fosters equal opportunity for academic success for all students. The Montgomery County Public Schools offer many different kinds of services such as career coordinators/scholarship database, psychological and guidance services, pupil personnel workers, school health services, home and hospital teaching, alternative programs, and student service learning. Included in the site are videos and documents related to the theme at the school, "Our Call to Action: Raising the Bar and Closing the Gap, Because All Children Matter." This site also has a link to related resources for children and families.

National Coalition for Parent Involvement in Education (NCPIE)

3929 Old Lee Highway, Suite 91-A
Fairfax, VA 22030-2401
(703) 359-8973
(703) 359-0972 (FAX)
http://www.ncpie.org

The National Coalition for Parent Involvement in Education is committed to establishing partnerships between families and schools. The NCPIE recognizes that family involvement in education enhances student success. The Coalition works to promote these family school partnerships.

National Conference of State Legislatures: Funding School Health Programs

444 North Capitol Street, NW, Suite 515
Washington, DC 20001
(202) 624-5400
(202) 737-1069 (FAX)
http://www.ncsl.org/programs/health/pp/schlfund.htm

The Nation Conference of State Legislatures (NCSL) site provides comprehensive information about coordinated school health programs, as well as information on funding opportunities. The two divisions of funding are the "Block Grant Database" and the "State Revenue Database." The site also provides access to many NCSL reports and access to state legislative sites dealing with school health programs.

National Governors Association

Center for Best Practices
Hall of States
444 North Capitol Street
Washington, DC 20001-1512

(202) 624-5300
http://www.nga.org/center

The Center for Best Practices is a nonprofit corporation managed by a board of four governors who report to the National Governors Association's Executive Committee. The board makes recommendations about priorities, provides direction on projects, and approves the Center's annual budget. The Center for Best Practices aims to help governors develop and execute creative solutions to policy challenges in their states. This Web site provides information about the Center's projects and events, and offers a link to "Front and Center," a weekly newsletter published by the Center. The Web site also highlights states' best practices, federal policies affecting states, and links to relevant research.

National Institute of Mental Health

6001 Executive Boulevard
Room 8184, MSC 9663
Bethesda, MD 20892-9663
(301) 443-4513
(301) 443-4279 (FAX)
http://www.nimh.nih.gov

The National Institute of Mental Health (NIMH) is a division of the National Institute of Health (NIH) designed to address issues of public mental health. This Web site provides resources for the general public, mental health practitioners, and mental health researchers. The site also includes information about clinical research studies, sources of funding, and upcoming conferences and workshops in the field.

National Institute on Out-of-School Time: Center for Research on Women

Part of The Wellesley Centers for Women
Wellesley College, 106 Central Street
Wellesley, MA 02481
(781) 283-2547
http://www.niost.org

The National Institute on Out-of-School Time (NIOST) ensures that children, youth, and families have access to high-quality programs and opportunities during nonschool hours. This Institute bridges the worlds of research, policy, and practice. This site describes current projects and publications and provides links to other out-of-school time Web sites.

The National School Safety Center Home Page

141 Duesenberg Drive, Suite 11
Westlake Village, CA 91362
(805) 373-9979
(805) 373-9277 (FAX)
http://www.nsscl.org/home.htm

This Web site is designed to train educators and other youth-serving professionals in school crime prevention and safe school planning. An advocate for prevention of school crime and violence, the National School Safety Center provides information and describes programs dedicated to supporting safe schools throughout the world.

Office of Psychological Services, Baltimore County Public Schools

9610 Pulaski Park Drive, Suite 219
Baltimore, MD 21220
http://www.schoolpsychology.net

This Web site provides information on many topics of interest to professionals working in comprehensive school counseling programs. Designed to be useful for psychologists, parents, and educators, the components of the site include learning disabilities, assessments/evaluation, violence, and a host of other issues pertinent to the field of school counseling. Additionally, the site provides links to brochures, pamphlets, reference lists, and journals that may be useful to school counselors.

Peer Resources

1052 Davie Street
Victoria, B.C., Canada V85 4E3
(250) 595-3503
http://www.peer.ca/profile.html

This nonprofit educational corporation has existed since 1975. The mission of Peer Resources is to provide high-quality training, superior educational resources, and practical consultation to individuals seeking to establish peer helping or mentoring programs. This Web site provides examples of peer work, links to services and programs, and lists of workshops that may prove helpful to those interested in peer relationships. This site also describes research that has been conducted on mentoring programs.

School Counseling in North Carolina

North Carolina Department of Public Instruction
301 N. Wilmington Street
Raleigh, NC 27601-2825
(919) 715-1643
http://www.ncpublicschools.org/alternative/counseling/index.html

This Web site gives an introduction to comprehensive school counseling programs. The introduction describes the aim of a comprehensive school counseling program; the importance of collaboration with teachers, parents, and community agencies; and the necessity of addressing the needs of the school community. The Web site contains information about school counseling programs in North Carolina, as well as the purpose of these programs. Links to counseling sites and other related sites are also included.

School Development Program

55 College Street
New Haven, CT 06510
(203) 737-1020
(203) 727-1023 (FAX)
http://info.med.yale.edu/comer/

The School Development Program, developed by James Comer, is a systemic school reform strategy currently being implemented in more than 62 school districts and 18 in Washington, D.C. The Comer Process is a comprehensive educational reform strategy based on the principles of child, adolescent, and adult development. It mobilizes teachers, administrators, parents, and other concerned adults to support students' personal, social, and academic growth. It also helps them make better programmatic and curriculum decisions based on students' needs and on developmental principles.

School-Linked Comprehensive Services for Children and Families Home Page

School-Based Youth Services Program
Gail Reynolds, Director
1125 Livingston Street
New Brunswick, NJ 08901
(908) 745-5301
(908) 745-5496 (FAX)
http://www.ed.gov/pubs/Compre/app1n.html

This site outlines some of the various school-linked comprehensive services for children and families. The School-Based Youth Services Program in New Jersey is one model that has been integrated into the community. This site explains the goals of the project, the collaborators, what services are provided, how success is evaluated, and whom to contact for further information.

Seattle Public Schools

815 4th Avenue, N
Seattle, WA 98109
(206) 298-7010
http://www.seattleschools.org

This Web site contains information about the Seattle Public Schools. The site provides links to the Seattle Public Schools' educational standards, enrollment, schools, leadership, learning resources, services/departments, employment, general information, and a site map. The link to the different schools within the Seattle Public School system provides detailed information about each school, its philosophy, the services provided, the population of students, the student-teacher ratio, and other related information. This link within the site also addresses academic offerings and other services, community involvement, and facility and atmosphere. Through these links and the provided information, site visitors can get an overview of the different schools and services provided to the students and parents.

Student Support Services Project

310 Blount Street, Suite 215
Tallahassee, FL 32301

(850) 922-3727
(850) 921-4755
http://sss.usf.edu

The Student Support Services Project is a joint venture between the University of South Florida and the Bureau of Instructional Support and Community Services, Florida Department of Education. The project provides training and technical assistance to Florida school districts and state agencies. The site contains information on professional development, student services professions, legislative information, and links to other resources.

UCLA School Mental Health Project

Center for Mental Health in Schools
Department of Psychology
P.O. Box 951563
Los Angeles, CA 90095-1563
(310) 825-3634
http://smhp.psych.ucla.edu

The Center is one of two national training and technical assistance centers focused on mental health in schools. The Center addresses barriers to learning and promoting a healthy development in a school-based setting. This Web site contains information on the status of mental health in schools, trends in the field, continuing education and training, and links to other mental health resources.

ON-LINE SERVICES

Community Update, Electronic Newsletter

Community Update
400 Maryland Avenue, SW, Room 5E217
Washington, DC 20202
(202) 205-067 (FAX)
http://mirror.eschina.bnu.edu.cn/Mirror/ed.gov/bcol01.ed.gov/CFAP
    PS/OIIA/communityupdate/page1.html

"Community Update" is a newsletter geared to parents, educators, and other citizens involved in the betterment of schools across the country. It covers best practices and model programs from around the United

States. "Community Update" conveys current, important updates from the Secretary of Education. The newspaper is easy to read and provides links to past issues and educational programming.

Education Week on the Web

6935 Arlington Road, Suite 100
Bethesda, MD 20814
(301) 280-3100
http://www.edweek.org

Editorial Projects in Education Inc. publishes "Education Week" on the Web. This is a nonprofit, tax-exempt organization based in Washington, D.C. The primary mission is to help raise the level of awareness and understanding among professionals and the public about important issues in American education. "EdWeek" covers local, state, and national news and issues from preschool through the twelfth grade. "EdWeek" also provides special reports on issues ranging from technology to textbooks, as well as books of special interest to educators.

Homophobia 201: Advanced Anti-Homophobia Training: On-line Workshop

Type: On-line workshop
Length: Approximately 60 minutes
Cost: None
Source: GLSEN
National Office
121 West 27th Street, Suite 804
New York, NY 10001
(212) 727-0135
http://www.glsen.org/binary-data/GLSEN_ARTICLES/pdf_file/249.
   pdf

This workshop was developed because, once convinced that they needed to care about homophobia, most educators wanted training on how to respond to actual incidents that might arise. In developing this workshop, the creators pulled a set of such incidents from GLSEN membership and developed brief case studies from them. These case studies are used as the basis of role-plays that give participants the opportunity to think on their feet about how to respond appropriately to any situation that might arise. The goal is to help participants feel like they can handle unexpected situations and move past the fight-or-flight response that some may have when issues concerning gay populations arise.

PAVNET Online: Partnerships Against Violence Network Home Page

http://pavnet.org/

PAVNET Online is a library of information concerning violence and at-risk youth. The data are represented from seven different federal agencies. The library provides clear and comprehensive access to information for state and local communities. There are more than 600 descriptions of prominent programs that have prevention and intervention bases. The cause and effect of violence are explained and acknowledged. The program topics are community violence, youth violence, family violence, substance abuse, and victims.

MATERIALS AND VIDEOTAPES

Materials

Academic Net

Academic Systems Corp.
444 Castro Street, Suite 1200
Mountain View, CA 94041
(800) 694-6850
http://www.academic.com

This organization provides instructional software and comprehensive services to educators, students, and parents. Along with information about their products, this site is an on-line information and communication resource for educators interested in technology-mediated instruction and learning.

Can We Talk? Training Kit

Type: Training Kit/Prevention Program. Planning and Training
          Manual, Family Activity Book, and Video
Date: 1999
Cost: $75.00

Source: National Education Association Professional Library
P.O. Box 2035
Annapolis Junction, MD 20701
(800) 229-4200
http://home.nea.org/books/

"Can We Talk?" is a community partnership program designed to help parents and educators talk with children about healthy relationships and sexuality, including the prevention of pregnancy, HIV/STDs, drug abuse, and violence. "Can We Talk?" parent workshops enhance family discussions about self-esteem, puberty and sexuality, mixed messages, and peer pressure.

Children of Divorce

Type: Activity books and cards
Date: 1991
Cost: $63.95 Instructors Kit, $4.95 Parent's Book, $7.95 Kid's
          Book
Source: American Guidance Service
4201 Woodland Road
Circle Pines, MN 55014-1796
(800) 328-2560
(800) 471-8457 (FAX)

This is a support program that helps children to adjust to divorce. The program is designed with two specific goals: (1) to promote academic, social, and emotional growth; and (2) to promote self-esteem. The program provides students with a supportive group environment in which they can strengthen their communication skills, learn about feelings, and practice problem solving and anger management. The program is intended for use with groups of five to eight children in grades three through six.

Department of Education: Partner's Idea Book: Answering a Call to Action

Type: Disk
Date: 1998
Cost: $0.00
Source: U.S. Department of Education
400 Maryland Avenue, SW
Washington, DC 20202

(800) USA-LEARN
(800) 437-0833 (TTY)
(202) 401-0689 (FAX)
http://www.ed.gov/pubs/edpubs.html

This disk contains information to help organizations and their local members get more involved in education through the Partnership for Family Involvement in Education. It provides basic information about nationwide initiatives that give organizations new opportunities to get involved and examples of what local partners are doing. This disk is a useful resource for those involved with development of comprehensive student service programs and those who are interested in strengthening the family involvement in schools.

Emotional Quotient in School Counseling. Promoting Emotional Intelligence: The Key to Student Success

Type: Kit (information guide, overheads, and three presentations)
Date: 1996
Cost: $24.95
Source: Innerchoice Publishing
P.O. Box 2476
Spring Valley, CA 91979
(619) 698-2437

This kit contains an informational guide, a group of overhead masters, and three presentations. Together, these materials provide the information needed to present training sessions on emotional intelligence to teaching staff, parents, and students.

Magna Systems Developmental Video Programs

95 West County Line Road
Barrington, IL 60010
(800) 203-7060
(815) 459-4280 (FAX)

The Magna Systems video programs were designed by professionals to effectively communicate knowledge and understanding of early childhood, childhood, early adulthood, and middle adulthood. The program provides educational techniques and curriculum that are helpful in understanding a child at different stages of development. The Magna

System covers many comprehensive topics, such as the learning environment, curriculum, teacher/student interaction, diversity and communication, violence prevention, and parenting.

Partners for Learning: Preparing Teachers to Involve Families

Type: Transparencies
Length: 17 pages
Date: 1998
Cost: $0.00
Source: U.S. Department of Education
ED Publications
P.O. Box 1398
Jessup, MD 20795-1398
(877) 4ED-PUBS
http://www.ed.gov/about/ordering.jsp

These transparencies contain presentation materials to assist teachers in enhancing family involvement in schools. The kit includes speakers' notes and overheads, a video clip from a teleconference hosted by former Vice President Al Gore and former U.S. Secretary of Education Richard W. Riley, as well as a publication of examples of effective practice.

Partnership for Family Involvement in Education: Presentation Materials

Type: CD-ROM
Date: 1998
Cost: $0.00
Source: U.S. Department of Education
400 Maryland Avenue, SW
Washington, DC 20202
(800) USA-LEARN
(800) 437-0833 (TTY)
(202) 401-0689 (FAX)
http://www.ed.gov/pubs/edpubs.html

This CD-ROM outlines the Partnership for Family Involvement in Education (PFIE). It contains speaker's notes and overheads that address each of the four sectors of the PFIE family—school groups, community organizations, religious groups, and employers. The CD-ROM also outlines the research-based rationale and activities that can support family involvement in education at the local level. The information provided is helpful for those interested in gaining support for the development of a comprehensive program or for those seeking to implement school components designed to increase involvement of community and family.

Tackling Gay Issues in School: A Comprehensive Resource Module

Type: Three-part module (including print and Internet
          resources)
Length: 208 pages
Date: 1999
Cost: $24.00
Source: GLSEN Connecticut
Tackling Gay Issues in School
179 A Louisiana Avenue
Bridgeport, CT 06610
http://www.glsen.org/templates/index.html

This training program is intended for school use and includes three modules. The first module, Rationale (for the inclusion of lesbian, gay, bisexual, and transgender (LGBT) issues in school), includes National Statutes and Policies on LGBT Youth, the Facts on LGBT Students and Schools, What Does Homosexuality Have to do with Education?, and How Homophobia Hurts Everyone. The second module, Recommended Curriculum and Staff Development Activities, includes Getting the Facts: Homosexuality and Homophobia in Our Culture (teacher-friendly lesson plans adapted from the Community Health Project and the Office of Lesbian and Gay Health Concerns in New York City), The Connection Between Homophobia and Other Forms of Oppression, and When Someone Close to You Comes Out: For Parents and For Friends. The second module also includes annotated bibliographies, books, periodicals, curricula, and other resources for LGBT youth and people who work with them. The third module, Recommended Extracurricular Activities and Resources, includes Recommendations and Strategies from the Safe Schools Coalition of Washington, How to Start a Gay/Straight Alliance (GSA), and local and national organizations that focus on LGBT youth. The third module also includes transgender resources, Internet resources, Web sites, and listserves. The three-component module is available in English and Spanish.

Youth Risk Behavior Survey

Type: CD-ROM
Date: 1997
Cost: $0.00
Source: Division of Adolescent and School Health (DASH)
National Center for Chronic Disease Prevention and Health Promotion
Centers for Disease Control and Prevention
4770 Buford Highway, NE
Mail Stop K-33
Attn: Youth97
Atlanta, GA 30341-3717
(770) 488-3257
(770) 488-3112 (FAX)
E-mail: ccdinfo@cdc.gov

Youth97 is an easy-to-use CD-ROM that provides access to five years of Youth Risk Behavior Survey data. This CD-ROM allows examination of youth risk behaviors in six risk categories—injuries, tobacco use, alcohol and other drug use, sexual behaviors, dietary behaviors, and physical activity. The CD-ROM includes comparisons of national, state, and local data; examines trends over time; and allows viewers to access videos on how state and local agencies are using these data. New features include state and local data by race/ethnicity and results reported as tables and graphs. Individuals may order up to 20 CD-ROMs by e-mail or call for larger orders.

Videotapes

Comprehensive School Reform Demonstration

Type: Videocassette (five types)
Length: Varying (14 to 130 minutes)
Date: 1999
Cost: None, may borrow
Source: Northwest Regional Educational Laboratory
101 SW Main, Suite 500
Portland, OR 97204
(800) 547-6330

These five different videos of varying lengths are available for schools to borrow for a three-week period. The first is a 14-minute tape describing the Comprehensive School Reform Demonstration. The second is a two-hour model presentation with brief interviews with model representatives. A third video is a two-volume set of interviews with developers of the models, which addresses frequently asked questions. The fourth tape is a 30-minute presentation by the superintendent of the Clover Park School District in Washington State. The superintendent outlines his district's experience implementing research-based models in 13 Title I schools. Lastly, a 38-minute presentation providing detailed information on keys to selecting and implementing comprehensive school reform models is included.

Dealing with Anger: Givin' it, Takin' it, Workin' it out.

Type: Three videocassettes with teacher's guide
Length: 25 minutes
Date: 1991
Cost: Unknown
Source: Research Press
2612 North Mattis Avenue
Campaign, IL 61821

This is a violence prevention program developed specifically to help at-risk African American youth reach their potential and reduce their chances for becoming victims of violence. The videos may be used as a basis for small groups to develop skills in conflict resolution.

Discipline: Appropriate Guidance of Young Children

Type: Film
Length: 28 minutes
Date: 1988
Cost: $39.00
Source: National Association for the Education of Young
            Children
1509 16th Street, NW
Washington, DC 20019
(800) 424-2460
http://www.naeyc.org/

This film illustrates how positive guidance of young children toward healthy social and emotional development is the foundation of a good early childhood program. The film also explores how teachers can incorporate self-discipline in early childhood curricula.

Hablando en Serio

Type: Videocassette with discussion guide
Length: 30 minutes
Date: 1992
Cost: Unknown
Source: U.S. Department of Education
400 Maryland Avenue, SW
Washington, DC 20202

The Hablando en Serio video is a 30-minute documentary in Spanish that profiles three Hispanic teenagers from inner-city neighborhoods who have chosen not to use drugs or alcohol. Their real-life experiences demonstrate the value of setting goals, developing talents, and staying in school. The target group of students is ninth through twelfth grades.

High-Risk Youth/At the Crossroads

Type: Videocassette
Length: 22 minutes
Cost: $50.00
Source: National School Safety Center
141 Duesenberg Drive, Suite 11
Westlake Village, CA 91362
(805) 373-9979
(805) 373-9277 (FAX)

This video addresses drug abuse prevention by focusing on the specific behavioral, social, and economic problems that contribute to youths' vulnerability for abusing drugs. This video takes a risk-focused approach to drug abuse prevention by going beyond the Just Say No campaign. This documentary focuses on several high-risk youths and examines the characteristics that have contributed to their placement in this category.

Intensive Early Intervention and Beyond: A School-Based Inclusion Program: Breaking the Barriers III

Type: Videocassette
Length: 22 minutes
Date: 1999
Cost: $195.00

Source: Research Press
Department 22W
P.O. Box 9177
Champaign, IL 61826
(800) 519-2707
(217) 352-1221 (FAX)
http://www.researchpress.com/

This video discusses and illustrates the successful application of a school-based inclusion program between the Millville School District and the Groden Center, both in Illinois. The video provides a brief overview of the Groden/Millville model, an early intervention program for children with pervasive developmental disorders. Components of this model include applied behavior analysis, early academics, communication, and stress management. The video follows two children with autism who have shown personal, social, and academic improvement since the program was implemented.

Moving Towards Diversity: A Model for Community Change

Type: Videocassette
Length: 33 minutes
Date: 1996
Cost: $50.00
Source: Education Development Center, Inc.
P.O. Box 1020
Sewickley, PA 15146-1020
(800) 793-5076
(412) 741-0609 (FAX)
http://www.edc.org/

This video is a guide for creating communities that involve all members and emphasize active roles for everyone. The video stresses the importance of empowerment and shared responsibility in community activities and discusses the problems that arise when community members practice exclusion.

National Symposium on School Design: Schools as Centers of Community: Special Teleconference

Type: Videocassette (special teleconference)
Length: 60 minutes

Date: October 5, 1998
Cost: $0.00
Source: U.S. Department of Education
400 Maryland Avenue, SW
Washington, DC 20202
(800) USA-LEARN
(800) 437-0833 (TTY)
(202) 401-0689 (FAX)
http://www.ed.gov/pubs/edpubs.html

This is a video recording of a national symposium focusing on how redesigning schools can help student and community members learn at new levels. The participants in the symposium include parents, teachers, principals, policymakers, business and community leaders, and architects. This video is intended to assist schools in both major renovations and minor revisions to the layout of the current school building to optimize student learning.

Overcoming Student Support Services Confusion

Type: Audiovisual/Videocassette
Length: 120 minutes
Date: 1996
Cost: $0.00
Source: National Council of Educational Opportunity Associations
1025 Vermont Avenue, NW
Suite 900
Washington, DC 20005
(202) 347-7430
202-347-0787 (FAX)

This video discusses support systems for underserved, handicapped, and other marginalized student populations. Panelists also discuss academic problems that eligible students encounter in various institutions. The video elements are gathered from a live satellite teleconference broadcast on October 16, 1996, with permission from participants.

Recovering Bodies: Overcoming Eating Disorders

Type: Videocassette
Length: 34 minutes
Date: 1997

Cost: $125.00–$175.00
Source: Katherine Sender
Media Education Foundation
60 Masonic Street
Northampton, MA 01060

This video presents stories and testimonies of seven college students and the wide range of pressures that contributed to the development of their eating disorders. The film focuses not only on the problem but on the hope that counselors can provide comprehensive services for recovery and prevention. This video also provides basic information about the psychological and physical symptoms of eating disorders.

Safe Schools Now

Type: Nine videocassettes plus discussion guide
Length: Varies
Date: 2000/2001
Cost: $19.95 each/$153.00 for the set
Source: National Education Association
1201 16th Street, NW
Washington, DC 20036
(202) 833-4000

These research-based videos look at the many aspects needed to establish a nurturing and consistent school climate. The series includes (1) Reasons for Hope; (2) Building a Safe and Responsive School Climate; (3) Early Signals of Distress; (4) Forging Community Alliances; (5) Safer Schools: Helping Students Resist Drugs; (6) Violence-Related Stress: A Guide for School Staff; (7) Can't We All Just Get Along? Dealing with Hate and Bias in School; (8) Building Skills to Manage Student Anger; and (9) Mind over Media: Helping Kids Get the Message. The videos can be purchased separately or as a set.

Safe Schools, Safe Students: What Parents Need to Know: Teleconference

Type: Videocassette (teleconference)
Date: August12, 1998
Cost: $0.00
Source: U.S. Department of Education
400 Maryland Avenue, SW

Washington, DC 20202
(800) USA-LEARN
(800) 437-0833 (TTY)
(202) 401-0689 (FAX)
http://www.ed.gov/pubs/edpubs.html

Hosted by former U.S. Secretary of Education, Richard W. Riley, this is a video of a discussion about school safety. The video was designed to help parents and educators across the United States. Former Attorney General Janet Reno, former National PTA President Ginny Markell, local educators, community leaders, law enforcement officials, and mental health professionals join Riley. This publication stresses the importance of the involvement of families, students, school officials, community health organizations, service organizations, and faith communities in the development and implementation of school safety plans. This video aims to help counselors and other professionals plan comprehensive programs by providing national support for school-community partnerships.

School Crisis: Under Control

Type: Videocassette
Length: 25 minutes
Cost: $75.00
Source: National School Safety Center
141 Duesenberg Drive, Suite 11
Westlake Village, CA 91362
(805) 373-9979
(805) 373-9277 (FAX)

This video combines news footage of school crises with recommendations from school officials who have firsthand experience with these tragedies. The video offers educators and administrators advice on school violence prevention, management, and resolution. This documentary covers topics such as staff responsibilities, media management, quality communication systems, and grief counseling.

School Stories: Take a Front Row Seat in America's Classrooms

Type: Videocassette
Length: 30 minutes

Date: 1997
Cost: $20.95
Source: National Education Association Professional
          Library
P.O. Box 2035
Annapolis Junction, MD 20701
(800) 229-4200

This 30-minute video features one of the nation's most talented principals, Steve Scroggs, in his new school. The video includes material on how Scroggs engages his students, stretches his staff, and involves parents. The recording also provides an interview with Scroggs, detailing his thoughts on the importance of building a strong sense of community and overcoming the roadblocks along the way.

Set Straight on Bullies

Type: Videocassette
Length: 18 minutes
Cost: $75.00
Source: National School Safety Center
141 Duesenberg Drive, Suite 11
Westlake Village, CA 91362
(805) 373-9979
(805) 373-9277 (FAX)

Created to help school administrators educate faculty, parents, and students about the severity of bullying, this video seeks to raise awareness about bullying. This video is designed to trigger discussion among its viewers and lead to strategic planning of how to combat this problem and create bullying prevention plans. By telling the story of a victim of bullying, the aim is to reveal that bullying affects everyone: the victim, the bully, other students, parents, and educators.

Student Health and Well-Being

Type: Videocassette
Length: 22 minutes
Date: 1993
Cost: $9.95
Source: National Education Association Professional
          Library

P.O. Box 2035
Annapolis Junction, MD 20701
(800) 229-4200

This video addresses how schools can provide full-scale health care services and teach students healthy decision-making skills. The video also recommends strategies for integrating comprehensive health and wellness services into traditional school systems.

Students at the Center: A National Teleconference on School Reform

Type: Videocassette
Length: 90 minutes
Date: 1998
Cost: $23.00
Source: U.S. Department of Education
   P.O. Box 371954
   Pittsburgh, PA 15250-7954
   http://www.edpubs.org

This video provides information for teams that are working to improve schools and for staff supporting school reform efforts. The video focuses on educational improvement, school-community relations, family involvement with schools, and school restructuring, all of which would be useful in a comprehensive student support services program.

Teen-Adult Conflict: Working It Out

Type: Videocassette and a guide
Length: 28 minutes (videocassette) 44 pages (guide)
Date: 1998
Cost: Unknown
Source: Sunburst Communications

This tape offers useful techniques for those trying to help students develop the skills necessary for effective communication with parents, teachers, and employers.

**The Comprehensive School Counseling Program: An
   Interview with Norman Gysbers**

Type: Videocassette
Length: 50 minutes
Date: 1992
Cost: Unknown
Source: ERIC Counseling and Personnel Services Clearinghouse
201 Ferguson Building
Greensboro, NC 27402
(800) 414-9769
(910) 334-4116 (FAX)

This video was taped live at the National American Copy Editors Society (ACES) Conference in San Antonio. The recording provides a description of the comprehensive school-counseling model for kindergarten through twelfth-grade counseling programs. The video also provides arguments supporting the program concept's superiority over traditional services provided in schools and why the comprehensive model is successful.

Index

About the Authors

MARY E. WALSH is Professor in the Department of Counseling, Developmental, and Educational Psychology, Lynch School of Education, Boston College, and Director of the Center for Child, Family, and Community Partnerships. She is the author of numerous books and articles.

JENNIFER A. MURPHY is a doctoral student in counseling psychology at Boston College.